PASTOR,
CHURCH
&
LAW

SUPPLEMENT

Richard R. Hammar

GOSPEL PUBLISHING HOUSE
SPRINGFIELD, MISSOURI

02–0582

This publication is designed to provide accurate and authoritative information in regard to the subject matter covered. It is sold with the understanding that the publisher is not engaged in rendering legal, accounting, or other professional service. If legal advice or other expert assistance is required, the services of a competent professional person should be sought. *From a Declaration of Principles jointly adopted by a Committee of the American Bar Association and a Committee of Publishers and Associations.*

ISBN 0-88243-582-5
Library of Congress Catalog Card No. 85-82192

Printed in the United States of America

EXPLANATORY NOTE

I had three reasons for writing this supplement to *Pastor, Church & Law*. First, I wanted to update materials in the text that have been rendered obsolete or inaccurate by subsequent changes in the law. For example, the Tax Reform Act, signed into law by President Reagan in July 1984, affected the minister's housing allowance exclusion, IRS audits of churches, the liability of churches for social security taxes, and substantiation of certain charitable contributions. All of these subjects have been updated in this supplement. In addition, recent decisions by the United States Supreme Court have altered the construction and application of the First Amendment's nonestablishment and free exercise of religion clauses. These changes also have been fully detailed.

Second, this supplement is designed to present the most recent judicial decisions, statutes, and administrative pronouncements pertaining to those materials in the original text that have not been affected by change.

Third, this supplement contains a significant amount of new material not directly addressed in the original text. Some of the new subjects include home education, the Equal Access Act, exemption of members of certain religious faiths from social security coverage, the practice of psychology by ministers, and judicial review of church determinations.

Changes and additions are arranged by chapter and keyed to sections and pages of the original text.

Church law continues to be a rapidly expanding and evolving area of our jurisprudence. This supplement will ensure that the objective of the original text—providing seminary students, clergymen, attorneys, and accountants with a comprehensive yet readable analysis of the major laws affecting churches and clergymen—will be perpetuated.

Springfield, Missouri
August 1985

RICHARD R. HAMMAR

CONTENTS

1

DEFINITIONS AND STATUS

§ A. Definitions

p. 20. *Add at the end of line 6 of text:*

The Immigration and Naturalization Act confers preferential "special immigrant" status upon alien "ministers" who have been engaged continuously in the ministry for two years immediately preceding their application for admission to the United States and whose services are needed by a domestic religious denomination.[14a]

[14a]8 U.S.C. § 1101(a)(27)(c).

p. 20. *Add as second sentence to the first complete paragraph:*

The Tax Court has held that when the phrase "minister of the gospel" stands without legislative or administrative explanation or definition it must be given its "ordinary conventional meaning."[15a]

[15a]Lawrence v. Commissioner, 50 T.C. 494 (1968).

p. 21. *Add after first incomplete paragraph:*

An individual who was ordained by the Universal Life Church after mailing in a fee and subscribing to the church's sole dogma of "believing that which is right as one defines it for himself" was held not to be qualified to perform marriages under a statute that authorized "ordained ministers of any religious denomination" to perform marriage ceremonies.[20a] The court noted that the Universal Life Church encouraged all who subscribed to its one tenet to become ordained ministers, and that the church had over one million ordained ministers

7

divided among 9,000 churches. In concluding that such persons were not "ministers" qualified to perform marriages, the court held: "The minister . . . is the head of a religious congregation, society or order. He is set apart as the leader. He is the person elected or selected in accordance with the ritual, bylaws or discipline of the order."[20b]

A New York court has ruled that Universal Life Church "ministers" are not authorized to perform marriages since they do not satisfy the definition of the term *minister* as set forth in section 2 of the state religious corporations law, which includes any "duly authorized pastor, rector, priest, rabbi, and a person having authority from, or in accordance with, the rules and regulations of the governing ecclesiastical body of the denomination or order, if any, to which the church belongs, or otherwise from the church or synagogue to preside over and direct the spiritual affairs of the church or synagogue."[20c]

A federal appeals court, in deciding whether a theological seminary was exempt from the reporting requirements of Title VII of the Civil Rights Act of 1964, rejected the seminary's contention that all of its faculty, administrators, and support staff were "ministers."[20d] The court found that the seminary's faculty members were ministers since (1) no course taught at the seminary had a strictly secular purpose, (2) faculty members were chosen largely on the basis of personal religious commitment rather than church allegiance or academic abilities, (3) most faculty members were ordained ministers, and (4) faculty members were expected to teach by example as well as by other means.[20e] However, it concluded that members of the seminary's support staff were not "ministers," even though they all claimed to be "called" to the seminary's maintenance departments and some were ordained, since "these support personnel are not engaged in activities traditionally considered ecclesiastical or religious."[20f] Finally, those administrative staff members who "equated to or supervised faculty" were considered to be ministers, but those whose function related exclusively to non-academic departments were not.

[20a]Cramer v. Commonwealth, 202 S.E.2d 911 (Va. 1974).

[20b]*Id.* at 915.

[20c]Ravenal v. Ravenal, 338 N.Y.S.2d 324 (1972).

[20d]E.E.O.C. v. Southwestern Baptist Theological Seminary, 651 F.2d 277 (5th Cir. 1981).

[20e]*But cf.* E.E.O.C. v. Mississippi College, 626 F.2d 477 (5th Cir. 1980), wherein faculty members of a college owned and operated by the Mississippi Baptist Convention were held not to be "ministers" since they did not attend to "the religious needs of the faithful" or "instruct students in the whole of religious doctrine," even though they were expected to serve as exemplars of the Christian faith.

[20f]*Id.* at 284. As to the maintenance workers who were ordained ministers, the court observed that "ordination was not a requirement for the position" and "these workers' ordination is not an integral part of their total vocation."

§ B. Status—Employee or Self-Employed

p. 21, note 20. *Add:*

But see People v. Tuchinsky, 419 N.Y.S.2d 843 (1979) (Jewish cantor held not to be a "minister").

p. 23. *Add after the second complete paragraph:*

The IRS definition of *employee* is misleading in stating that the right to discharge is "an important factor indicating that the person possessing that right is an employer," since it is indisputable that companies and individuals who hire self-employed persons ordinarily have the authority to discharge them. For example, if a homeowner retains a self-employed plumber, carpenter, or gardener to perform work around his home he ordinarily has the authority to discharge the worker, and such authority certainly does not transform the worker into an "employee" of the homeowner.

p. 25. *Add after the first complete paragraph:*

Ministers who report their church compensation as self-employment earnings may also fund an IRA with such earnings to the extent that annual contributions do not exceed the lesser of (1) the annual contribution ceiling for an IRA (currently $2,000, or $2,250 for a "spousal IRA") or (2) the minister's net earnings from self-employment reduced by any Keogh plan contributions for the year.[33a]

[33a]I.R.C. § 219(f)(1).

§ C. Status—Ordained, Commissioned, or Licensed

p. 29, note 52. *Add:*

See also E.E.O.C. v. Southwestern Baptist Theological Seminary, 651 F.2d 277, 284 (5th Cir. 1981) ("one need not be ordained to be a minister").

p. 30, note 59. *Add:*

See also Magee v. United States, 392 F.2d 187 (1st Cir. 1968) (Jehovah's Witness who considered himself a minister held not to be a minister for draft purposes, since he was employed full time in secular work, performed ministry on an irregular and limited basis, and was not a minister by reason of formal education or ordination); United States v. Willard, 312 F.2d 605 (6th Cir. 1963) (similar facts); E.E.O.C. v. Southwestern Baptist Theological Seminary, 651 F.2d 277 (5th Cir. 1981) (seminary employees who were considered "ministers" by the seminary were not deemed ministers for purposes of determining the applicability of the reporting requirements imposed by Title VII of the Civil Rights Act of 1964).

p. 30. *Add after the third complete paragraph:*

Similarly, the Tax Court has held that an unordained minister of education in a Southern Baptist church did not qualify for a housing allowance exclusion since he was not an "ordained, commissioned, or licensed minister of a church."[61] The minister was a seminary graduate and had been commissioned by a local church as a minister of education. His principal duties included the administration of the church's Sunday school, youth program, visitation program, and men's and women's organizations. In addition, he visited the sick, provided spiritual counseling, and assisted in worship services. Despite such duties, the court concluded that the minister was not an "ordained, commissioned, or licensed minister" and thus was not eligible for the housing allowance exclusion. In reaching its decision, the court emphasized that "it is more important to note the religious rites and ceremonies which [the minister] did not perform" than those which he did perform. The court found it determinative that the Southern Baptist Convention had two "ordinances"—baptism and communion—and that the minister had never assisted with either.

Unfortunately, the Tax Court's faulty reasoning led to the wrong result in the Southern Baptist case. As was noted in a dissenting opinion, the income tax regulations require that a housing allowance be "provided as remuneration for services which are ordinarily the duties of a minister of the gospel." The regulations define such services as (1) the administration of sacerdotal (i.e., religious) functions, (2) the conduct of religious worship, and (3) church administration. The dissenting judge correctly observed:

> I firmly believe that this record contains sufficient proof that the [minister] spent his full time . . . performing for the congregation services of all three types. He ministered to the sick. He conducted funeral services. He made the pulpit announcements and the opening prayer at the Sunday morning service and, on occasion, he preached and led the congregation in worship. He often conducted the Wednesday night worship service. . . . He had under his supervision and direction the administration of the educational service organizations of the [church]. [He] was trained for the ministry . . . and he functioned as one of the religious leaders of his church in a real sense.[62]

Finally, some cases suggest that persons who are the functional equivalents of "ordained, commissioned, or licensed ministers" may be treated as belonging to that classification.[63]

[61]Lawrence v. Commissioner, 50 T.C. 494 (1968).

[62]*Id.* at 501.

[63]*See, e.g.,* Ballinger v. Commissioner, 728 F.2d 1287 (10th Cir. 1984); Silverman v. Commissioner, 57 T.C. 727 (1972).

2

THE PASTOR–CHURCH RELATIONSHIP

§ A. Initiating the Relationship

p. 31. *Add after the first complete paragraph:*

For example, one court has held that "a church may be hierarchical in terms of internal administration and discipline, and yet congregational as far as control and use of its property is concerned."[3a]

   [3a]Antioch Temple v. Parekh, 122 N.E.2d 1337, 1342 (Mass. 1981).

p. 31. *Add before each usage of the word "bylaws" on the second line of the second paragraph:*

constitution or

p. 33. *Add after line 4 of text:*

The United States Supreme Court has ruled that "[f]reedom to select the clergy, where no improper methods of choice are proven, we think, must now be said to have federal constitutional protection as a part of the free exercise of religion against state interference."[8a] This principle has been applied in several cases. For example, it has been held that the civil courts have no jurisdiction to resolve a case alleging that an interim minister was improperly appointed, since "[t]he appointment of a minister is a purely ecclesiastical matter which should not be subject to review by a civil or secular court."[8b] There will be instances, however, where the appointment or election of a minister will be contested on the basis of allegations not involving religious discipline, faith, rule, custom, or law. For example, a minister may have been elected at a meeting which was not properly called. There would appear to be no legitimate basis, constitutional or otherwise, for a civil court to refrain from resolving such a dispute. The Supreme Court has observed that the civil courts need not stay their hand in every case involving a church dispute, since "not every civil court decision jeopardizes values protected by the First Amendment."[8c]

[8a]Kedroff v. St. Nicholas Cathedral, 344 U.S. 94, 116 (1952).

[8b]Wilkerson v. Battiste, 393 So.2d 195, 197 (La. App. 1980).

[8c]Presbyterian Church in the United States v. Mary Elizabeth Blue Hull Memorial Presbyterian Church, 393 U.S. 440, 449 (1969).

§ B. The Contract

p. 33. *Add after the second complete paragraph:*

Often, a contract of employment will be implied between a church and its minister though no written agreement was signed. As one court has observed, "[t]he absence of a written contract is completely immaterial; the conduct of the parties clearly indicates an agreement to retain [the] pastor until his dismissal by the church."[10a]

[10a]Vincent v. Raglin, 318 N.W.2d 629 (Mich. 1982).

p. 34. *Add after the first complete paragraph:*

The contract of a minister who accepts the call of a hierarchical church includes all the canons and applicable rules set forth in the organizational documents of the parent hierarchical body.[13a]

[13a]Olston v. Hallock, 201 N.W.2d 35 (Wis. 1972).

p. 37. *Add after the indented quotation:*

Remedies other than breach of contract occasionally are available. One minister, who was physically ejected from his church by armed security guards hired by church trustees, was awarded injunctive relief prohibiting the trustees from interfering with his ministerial duties, and also received an award of monetary damages against the trustees and the security guards.[24a]

[24a]Vincent v. Raglin, 318 N.W.2d 629 (Mich. App. 1982) (the trustees did not have authority to terminate the minister's services).

§ C. Compensation

p. 39. *Add after the last complete paragraph:*

Similarly, the Tax Court has denied a charitable contribution deduction to a minister for that portion of his church salary that he voluntarily canceled, since the claimed contribution represented the cash equivalent of nondeductible services.[33a]

[33a]Winston v. Commissioner, 48 T.C.M. 55 (1984).

p. 40, note 38. *Add:*

See Charles M. Grace, B.T.A. Memo Op., Dkt. 100759 (1941).

p. 40. *Add after the last complete paragraph:*

Ministers should scrupulously avoid any diversion of church funds to their own personal benefit in excess of their agreed upon compensation. Ministers should also avoid "commingling" their own funds with church assets. Diversion of church funds by a minister to his own benefit and in excess of his salary has resulted in (1) a charge of embezzlement and fraudulent conversion;[40a] (2) a tax fraud conviction for failure to report interest earned on an alleged "church account" that was used essentially for a minister's personal benefit;[40b] (3) the placing of a church in receivership by order of a state attorney general to prevent further diversion of church funds.[40c]

[40a]Commonwealth v. Nichols, 213 A.2d 105 (Pa. 1965).
[40b]United States v. Moon, 718 F.2d 1210 (2nd Cir. 1983).
[40c]Worldwide Church of God, Inc. v. California, 623 F.2d 613 (9th Cir. 1980). *See generally* chapter 4, § I, *infra*; Comment, 73 J. CRIM. L. & CRIMINOL. 1204 (1982); Note, 53 S. CAL. L. REV. 1277 (1980); Note, 6 WEST. ST. L. REV. 269 (1979).

§ D. Termination

p. 41. *Add after the first complete paragraph:*

The law or practice of a church ordinarily is set forth in the church's constitution, bylaws, or charter. But if none of these documents addresses the subject of termination of ministers, then the established custom of the church will control.[45a] Of course, a church's established custom, if any, must be proven by competent evidence.

[45a]Covington v. Bowers, 442 So.2d 1068 (Fla. App. 1983).

p. 41. *Delete line 6 of the second complete paragraph and substitute the following:*

could have been legally transacted";[47] where the vote was taken after the minister had properly dismissed the meeting;[47a] or where the congregation had not been

[47a]Brooks v. January, 321 N.W.2d 823 (Mich. App. 1982).

p. 41. *Add after the second complete paragraph:*

Similarly, if a church's bylaws vest authority to remove a minister in the general membership, then the board of directors has no such authority.[48a]

[48a]Reddick v. Jones, 304 S.E.2d 389 (Ga. 1983).

p. 41, note 44. *Add:*

Antioch Temple, Inc. v. Parekh, 422 N.E.2d 1337 (Mass. App. 1981).

p. 41, note 48. *Add:*

Brooks v. January, 321 N.W.2d 823 (Mich. App. 1982).

p. 42. *Delete the first line of the second complete paragraph and substitute the following:*

Where a church has no constitutional or bylaw provision dealing with dismissal of ministers,

p. 42, note 52. *Add:*

See also Covington v. Bowers, 442 So.2d 1068 (Fla. App. 1983) (church custom dictates appropriate procedure for removal of minister if a church has no applicable constitution or bylaw provision).

p. 43. *Add after the indented paragraph in the text:*

In a subsequent ruling, the Court held that civil courts are compelled to defer to the rulings of hierarchical church tribunals only in cases involving "religious doctrine or polity."[57a]

[57a]Jones v. Wolf, 443 U.S. 595 (1979).

p. 43, note 54. *Delete the first two lines and substitute the following:*

[54]Providence Baptist Church v. Superior Court, 251 P.2d 10 (Cal. 1952); LeBlanc v. Davis, 432 So.2d 239 (La. App. 1983) ("Nor are ecclesiastical matters at issue when the court is required to determine whether church members conducted an election according to the procedures set forth in the church's charter."). Waters v. Hargest, 593 S.W.2d 364 (Tex. 1979). *Contra* Simpson v. Wells Lamont Corp., 494

p. 43, note 55. *Add:*

Accord LeBlanc v. Davis, 432 So.2d 239 (La. App. 1983).

p. 44. *Add after the first complete paragraph:*

The subject of judicial intervention in church disputes is considered fully in another chapter.[60]

[60]*See* chapter 11, § J, *infra.*

3

AUTHORITY, RIGHTS, AND PRIVILEGES

§ C. Property Matters

p. 45. *Add as first paragraph under § C:*

A minister can engage in property transactions on behalf of his church only if authorized to do so. Authority may be expressly granted in the church's constitution or bylaws, but more frequently a church's board of directors or congregational membership votes to authorize the minister to represent the church in a specific transaction.[2a]

[2a]Brooks v. January, 321 N.W.2d 823 (Mich. App. 1982).

p. 46, note 5. *Add:*

Diocese of Buffalo v. McCarthy, 458 N.Y.S.2d 764 (1983).

§ D. Performance of Marriage Ceremonies

p. 46. *Add at the end of the first complete paragraph under § D:*

It is the state, and not a minister or religious organization, that will ordinarily decide whether a minister is in fact "ordained" or "licensed" and therefore qualified to perform marriages. To illustrate, ministers receiving ordination credentials through the mail-order Universal Life Church have been denied the right to perform marriage ceremonies under state laws permitting "ordained ministers" or "ministers" to conduct such ceremonies.[10a] The courts obviously are faced with a difficult task when they attempt to deny legal privileges to some ministers on the basis of principles that do not involve a judgment on the legitimacy of religious belief. The difficulty of such a task is reflected in the unsatisfactory attempts by the courts to explain the distinction between ministers who are eligible for certain legal privileges and those who are not.

[10a]Ravenal v. Ravenal, 338 N.Y.S.2d 324 (1972); Cramer v. Commonwealth, 202 S.E.2d 911 (Va. 1974).

p. 47. Add as the last paragraph to § D:

It has been held that a state's right to regulate marriage and divorce is the same whether a marriage is performed in a church by a minister or in a civil ceremony by a judge. Thus, a state's divorce law can be applied to a Christian marriage performed in a church by a minister though one of the spouses maintains that the state's divorce law conflicts with his or her religious beliefs.[13a]

[13a]Trickey v. Trickey, 642 S.W.2d 47 (Tex. App. 1982).

§ E. Exemption From Military Duty

p. 50. Add at the end of line 2 of text:

One court, in upholding the constitutionality of the military chaplaincy program, relied on the following considerations: (1) civil courts ordinarily must defer to congressional determinations, such as the establishment of the chaplaincy program, in military affairs; (2) the same Congress that drafted the First Amendment authorized a paid chaplain for the Army; (3) the chaplaincy program did not pose a "real threat to the establishment clause" and therefore did not constitute an impermissible establishment of religion; (4) a "voluntary chaplaincy" consisting of civilian clergymen paid and appointed by the respective sects and denominations might not adequately protect the constitutional right of soldiers to freely exercise their religion.[30a]

[30a]*Id.*

p. 50, note 30. Delete note 30 and substitute the following:

[30]Katcoff v. Marsh, 582 F. Supp. 463 (E.D.N.Y. 1984), *aff'd,* 755 F.2d 223 (2nd Cir. 1985). *See also* Elliott v. White, 23 F.2d 997 (D.C. Cir. 1928).

§ G. Confidential Communications

p. 52. Add at the end of the last complete paragraph:

In a case involving a challenge to the will of an elderly decedent, a minister who testified concerning the speech, hearing, and sight of the decedent was held not to have "waived" the privilege since he only testified concerning personal "observations." He therefore was permitted to claim the privilege with respect to confidential communications he had conducted with the decedent.[49a] And a minister who assumed the custody of a two-month-old child was permitted to testify concerning the child's condition and the conduct of the child's parents, since such testimony related only to observations and not to communications arising out of spiritual counseling.[49b]

[49a]Snyder v. Poplett, 424 N.E.2d 396 (Ill. App. 1981).

[49b]Jones v. Department of Human Resources, 310 S.E.2d 753 (Ga. App. 1983).

p. 52, note 46. *Add:*

For an excellent treatment of the history of the privilege, written by two clergymen who advocate a broad privilege, see W. TIEMANN AND J. BUSH, THE RIGHT TO SILENCE: PRIVILEGED CLERGY COMMUNICATIONS AND THE LAW (1983).

p. 53. *Add at the end of the first complete paragraph:*

Similarly, statements made to a minister will not be privileged if the person making the statements intends that the minister disclose them to a third party.[50a]

[50a]Bottoson v. State, 443 So.2d 962 (Fla. 1983) (murder suspect handed written confession to two ministers intending that it be relayed to the prosecutor's office); Naum v. State, 630 P.2d 785 (Okla. App. 1981).

p. 53, note 50. *Add:*

Perry v. State, 655 S.W.2d 380 (Ark. 1983) (statements made by a murder suspect to his minister and a church elder were not privileged).

p. 53, note 56. *Add:*

Masquat v. Maguire, 638 P.2d 1105 (Okla. 1981) (privilege did not apply since nun was consulted in her capacity as a hospital administrator and "not in her capacity as a 'clergyman' ").

p. 54. *Delete the second complete paragraph and note 62.*

p. 54. *Add at the end of the second complete paragraph under § 4:*

However, statements made by a murder suspect to a minister were held not to be privileged when the suspect was not a church member, he had entered the minister's home to conceal himself from the police, he did not seek spiritual counseling and did not request that their conversation be kept confidential, and the minister did not believe that the conversation was confidential. The court reasoned that the facts did not establish the confidential nature of the statements or that the minister was acting in his professional capacity as a spiritual adviser.[63a]

[63a]Lucy v. State, 443 So.2d 1335 (Ala. App. 1983).

p. 54, note 63. *Add:*

See also People v. Police, 651 P.2d 430 (Colo. App. 1982); Fahlfeder v. Commonwealth, 470 A.2d 430 (Pa. 1984) (minister consulted in his capacity as a parole rehabilitation counselor and not a spiritual adviser).

p. 54, note 64. *Add:*

United States v. Gordon, 655 F.2d 478 (2nd Cir. 1981) (conversation pertaining to business relationships not privileged).

p. 56. *Add at the end of the first complete paragraph:*

In 1982, the Supreme Court ruled that "when we are presented with a state law granting a denominational preference, our precedents demand that we treat such a law as suspect" and that it be invalidated unless it (1) is justified by a compelling governmental interest, and (2) is closely fitted to further that interest.[69a] This standard could not be satisfied by a state law recognizing the privileged status of confidential communications only in the context of a few religious organizations.

[69a]Larson v. Valente, 102 S. Ct. 1673, 1684-85 (1982).

p. 56. *Delete the last sentence of the second complete paragraph.*

p. 57. *Insert the following material after the second sentence under subsection b:*

One court has observed that the presence of the minister, as a third party, "did not destroy the confidential nature of the admissions the husband made during marriage counseling. . . . On the contrary, the very purpose of marriage counseling—to attempt reconciliation of the parties in a troubled marriage—reinforces the confidential nature of communications made during those sessions."[72a]

[72a]Spencer v. Spencer, 301 S.E.2d 411 (N.C. App. 1983).

p. 58. *Add after the first complete paragraph:*

e. *Federal Courts*

In 1972, the United States Supreme Court adopted a set of rules of evidence for use in federal courts.[75a] Congress later suspended implementation of these rules pending a thorough review. In 1975, Congress enacted into law a revised version of the Federal Rules of Evidence, incorporating several changes in the rules originally proposed by the Supreme Court. One of the most significant congressional modifications pertained to privileged communications. The Supreme Court had proposed nine specific privileges for use in the federal courts, including the clergyman-parishioner, attorney-client, husband-wife, and psychotherapist-patient privileges. Congress, however, deleted all of the Supreme Court's specific rules of privilege and replaced them with a single principle:

> [T]he privilege of a witness . . . shall be governed by the principles of the common law as they may be interpreted by the courts of the United States in the light of reason and experience. However, in civil actions and proceedings, with respect to an element of a claim or defense as to which State law supplies the rule of decision, the privilege of a witness . . . shall be determined in accordance with State law.[75b]

[75a]56 F.R.D. 184 (1972).
[75b]FED. R. EVID. 501.

p. 58. *Add after the first complete paragraph:*

f. *Constitutionality*

Often, a communication made to a minister will fail one or more of the requirements of a valid privilege, yet the minister or the person making the communication will argue that the First Amendment's free exercise of religion clause prohibits compelled disclosure of the communication. To illustrate, in one case a Catholic nun who was not eligible for the privilege argued that the First Amendment protected her from being compelled to testify regarding communications made to her by a murder suspect. The court, in rejecting the nun's claim, observed that "this case calls for a balancing of interests—that of the state in enforcing the power of the grand jury to inquire into the commission of a crime, and that of [the nun] who claims that she responds to a call of conscience. In the particular circumstances of this case the latter must give way to the former."[75c] Another court, in rejecting a priest's claim that requiring a bishop to produce unprivileged records relating to the priest violated the First Amendment, observed: (1) production of documents pertaining to the priest would not interfere with the bishop's "right to believe as he chooses and to engage in the religious observances of his faith," (2) no impermissible entanglement between church and state would result, (3) information in the possession of a church "has always been subject to civil process," and (4) there would be no need for the clergyman-parishioner privilege if the First Amendment's free exercise of religion clause protected information in the possession of a church from civil process.[75d]

[75c]In re Murtha, 279 A.2d 889, 894 (N.J. 1971).
[75d]Pagano v. Hadley, 100 F.R.D. 758 (D. Dela. 1984).

p. 58. *Change § I to § J and insert the following new § I:*

§ I. Immigration of Alien Ministers

Federal immigration law gives preferential treatment to certain classes of aliens. Under certain conditions, ministers are entitled to "special immigrant" status and therefore may be admitted to the United States without the numerical limitations that ordinarily apply to immigrants. To be entitled to this special immigrant status, a minister must establish that (1) for at least two years immediately preceding the time of application for admission to the United States, he was engaged continuously in carrying on the vocation of a minister; (2) he seeks to enter the United States solely for the purpose of carrying on the vocation of a minister; and (3) his services are needed by a religious denomination having a bona fide organization in the United States.[78a] The minister's spouse and dependent children also receive special immigrant status.

These requirements are strictly construed. In one case, a Turkish clergyman of the outlawed Bektashi faith sought special immigrant status as a "minister." His application was denied by the Immigration and Naturalization Service on the ground that the applicant had not functioned as a minister for two years immediately preceding the time of his application for admission to the United States, despite the applicant's claim that he had been unable to function as a minister because the Turkish government had outlawed his sect.[78b]

The Immigration and Naturalization Service has held that the term *minister* as used in the Immigration and Naturalization Act means a person duly authorized by a recognized religious denomination having a bona fide organization in the United States to conduct religious worship and to perform other duties usually performed by a regularly ordained clergyman of that denomination. Therefore, the Service has held that an ordained "minister of music" was not a "minister" since her education was primarily in music and not theology; she never officiated at weddings or funerals, and never performed preaching or visitation functions, although she allegedly had the authority to do so; and she did not have two continuous years of ministry experience immediately preceding the filing of her application for admission to the United States.[78c]

[78a]8 U.S.C. § 1101(a)(27)(c).

[78b]First Albanian Teqe Bektashiane in America v. Sahli, 231 F. Supp. 516 (E.D. Mich. 1964).

[78c]Re Rhee, I & N Interim Decision No. 2682 (1982).

LIABILITIES, LIMITATIONS, AND RESTRICTIONS

§ B. Defamation

p. 65. *Add after the first incomplete paragraph:*

Not every derogatory statement will constitute defamation. For example, one court held that it was not defamatory for a religious official to tell a minister that she should have consulted with her religious superiors before choosing a particular minister as her co-pastor since the denomination had "been after [him] for a long time." The court found these remarks to be "wholly lacking in defamatory content" and "not capable of a defamatory meaning."[11a] Other statements that have been held not to be defamatory are the following: newspaper articles describing ex-members' criticisms of a church;[11b] derogatory statements contained in a letter to a minister when the person who sent the letter had no reason to believe that the minister would share it with others;[11c] and a newspaper article referring to a minister as the "former pastor" of a church.[11d]

[11a]Joiner v. Weeks, 383 So.2d 101, 103 (La. 1980).

[11b]Missouri Church of Scientology v. Adams, 543 S.W.2d 776 (Mo. 1976) (court refused to decide whether a church "can maintain an action for libel on the basis of statements as to its tenets and practices in the light of the First Amendment to the United States Constitution").

[11c]Bretz v. Mayer, 203 N.E.2d 665 (Ohio 1963) (defamation requires that the defamatory statements be published or publicly disseminated).

[11d]Nichols v. Item Publishers, 113 N.Y.S.2d 701 (1952).

p. 66. *Add at the end of the first complete paragraph:*

Malice also must be proven when allegedly defamatory statements relate to a matter of public interest. In one case, a minister who sued a weekly news magazine for publishing an allegedly defamatory article on religious diploma mill racketeering was denied recovery on the grounds that religious racketeering is a matter of public interest and the minister had failed to prove that the magazine published the statements maliciously.[15a] The requirement of proving malice in cases involving public figures on matters of public interest is known as the "New York Times standard."[15b]

[15a]Spern v. Time, Inc., 324 F. Supp. 1201 (W.D. Pa. 1971) (the court noted that "the requisite malice has been found only in cases in which the plaintiff proves with 'convincing clarity' that the complained-of article was published with actual malice or with reckless disregard of whether it was false or not").

[15b]New York Times Co. v. Sullivan, 376 U.S. 254 (1964).

p. 66. *Add after note 21 in the text:*

ineptness in administrative ability;[21a]

[21a]Lathan v. Journal Company, 140 N.W.2d 417 (Wis. 1966).

p. 66. *Add at the end of the final paragraph:*

Ministers also may be barred from recovering monetary damages for alleged defamation if one of the elements of defamation is absent. For example, a statement, no matter how derogatory, cannot be defamatory if it does not injure the reputation of a minister.

p. 66. *Add note 24a at the end of the final paragraph:*

[24a]*See, e.g.,* Washington v. New York News, Inc., 322 N.Y.S.2d 896 (1971) (gossip column article stating that a minister had attended a nightclub performance at which one of his choir members was performing was a matter of public interest and was not made with malice, therefore minister's claim of defamation was denied).

p. 67. *Add at the end of subsection c:*

Similarly, if a minister agrees to submit an issue to binding arbitration, he cannot later assert that the arbiter's decision is defamatory. For example, in one case the qualifications of an individual engaged in the business of testing garments for *shatnes* (a mixture of wool and linen in one garment prohibited by Mosaic law) were questioned by another person engaged in the same business. Both parties agreed to submit the question of qualifications to a tribunal of three rabbis. The tribunal ultimately decided that the person whose qualifications had been questioned was in fact not qualified to test for shatnes. The disqualified party refused to honor this ruling, which caused the complaining party to publish circulars informing the public of the decision of the rabbis. The disqualified party charged that the circulars were defamatory, but a court disagreed on the ground that the parties had voluntarily agreed to be bound by the decision of the rabbis which was "in the nature of a common law award in arbitration [that] acts as a bar to relitigating essentially the same issue."[24b]

[24b]Berman v. Shatnes Laboratory, 350 N.Y.S.2d 703 (1973).

p. 67. *Add at the end of the last paragraph:*

To illustrate, disparaging statements made by several church members concerning their minister during a church disciplinary proceeding were held not to be defamatory since they were entitled to a "qualified privilege" and hence could be defamatory only if made with malice.[24c]

[24c]Joiner v. Weeks, 383 So.2d 101 (La. App. 1980).

p. 68. *Add after note 28 in the text:*

an article in a publication produced by a religious denomination describing difficulties in missions work in an area under the control of a particular minister;[28a]

[28a]Herndon v. Melton, 195 S.E.2d 531 (N.C. 1958).

§ C. Undue Influence

p. 69. *Add after note 34 in the text:*

Similarly, gifts to an Episcopal rector and his church were invalidated on the basis of undue influence since the donor was a seventy-six-year-old woman suffering from arteriosclerosis, senility, and severe loss of memory.[34a]

[34a]Tallahassee Bank and Trust Co. v. Brooks, 200 So.2d 251 (Fla. App. 1967). *See also* Hensley v. Stevens, 481 P.2d 694 (Mont. 1971) (gift to minister held to be product of undue influence and fraud since minister induced gift by falsely representing that he would reconvey a portion of the property to the donor's husband but never did).

p. 70. *Add after first incomplete paragraph:*

Similarly, a gift of property by an eighty-two-year-old single woman to a Catholic church to assure the saying of masses for deceased members of her family was upheld despite the claims of her nearest relatives that such was not her real intention and that she had been unduly influenced by the church without her family's knowledge or consent. In upholding the validity of the gift, the court noted the following factors: (1) the donor's desire to make provision for the saying of masses for her family preceded the date of the gift; (2) the donor's will, which had been executed prior to the gift to the church, left nothing to surviving family members; (3) the donor did not conceal the gift; (4) there was no evidence that the donor was in a weakened condition of mind or body at the time of the gift; and (5) she reaffirmed the gift in subsequent letters, one of which was written five years after the day of the gift.[35a]

[35a]Guill v. Wolpert, 218 N.W.2d 224 (Neb. 1974).

§ D. Invasion of Privacy

p. 73. *Add at the end of the first complete paragraph:*

The Freedom of Information Act requires that each federal agency promptly make available to any person upon request any identifiable record, subject to various exceptions.[46a] The Act also mandates the publication of certain categories of agency information in the Federal Register, and requires that various other kinds of records be made available for public inspection and copying. The purpose of the Act is to promote public access to the information in the possession of federal agencies. Several states have enacted similar laws applying to state agencies. None of these laws applies to churches or other nonprofit religious organizations.

[46a]5 U.S.C. § 552(a)(3).

§ E. Clergyman Malpractice

p. 74. *Add at the end of the first incomplete paragraph:*

A state appeals court subsequently reversed the trial court's determination, in effect remanding the case back to the trial court.[49a] The appeals court concluded that the church and its minister "either followed a policy of counseling suicidal persons that, if one was unable to overcome one's sins, suicide was an acceptable and even desirable alternative to living, or recklessly caused . . . extreme emotional distress through their counseling methods if those persons did not measure up to the pastor's religious ideals."[49b] The court based its conclusion primarily upon the following excerpt of a tape recording of one of the church's pastors entitled "Principles of Biblical Counseling": "[S]uicide is one of the ways that the Lord takes home a disobedient believer.

We read that in the Bible. . . . [S]uicide for a believer is the Lord saying, 'Okay, come on home. Can't use you any more on earth. If you're not going to deal with those things in your life, come on home.' "

The court rejected the contention that a minister or church should be immune from liability for counseling simply because the counseling has a spiritual aspect: "[W]hile [a minister's] religious beliefs are absolutely protected by the First Amendment, the free exercise clause of the First Amendment does not license intentional infliction of emotional distress in the name of religion and cannot shield defendants from liability for wrongful death for suicide caused by such conduct."[49c]

The state appeals court's decision was condemned in a lengthy and well-reasoned dissenting opinion authored by one of the court's three justices. The dissenting justice emphasized the following considerations: (1) if a duty cannot be imposed upon a psychiatrist to prevent the suicide of a patient being treated on an out-patient basis, such a duty should not be imposed upon ministers; (2) ministers should not be discouraged from seeking to help persons overcome suicidal tendencies through spiritual guidance; (3) there was no proof that the suicide victim had ever heard the tape recording which allegedly discussed suicide as an acceptable alternative; (4) the suicide victim never lost the ability to refrain from suicide if he so desired, and thus his suicide was an "independent intervening force" that absolved the church and its ministers from any culpability; (5) the victim's parents were aware of his suicidal tendencies, and yet failed to have him committed to a psychological hospital; and (6) church members encouraged the victim to seek professional psychological help. In 1985, the trial court again ruled in favor of the church and its ministers.

In another case, a church member sued a minister for malpractice after learning that his wife had been carrying on an adulterous relationship with the minister for nearly two years. The suit was dismissed because it was based largely on the concept of "alienation of affections" which previously had been abolished as a matter of state law.[49d]

[49a]Nally v. Grace Community Church of the Valley, 204 Cal. Rptr. 303 (1984).
[49b]*Id.* at 306.
[49c]*Id.* at 308-09.
[49d]Lund v. Caple, 675 P.2d 226 (Wash. 1984).

p. 80. *Delete all five paragraphs under § H and substitute the following:*

All fifty states have enacted child abuse reporting statutes in an effort to protect abused children and prevent future abuse. Most statutes contain the following provisions: (1) a definition of child abuse, (2) a list of persons who are under a legal duty to report, (3) elimination of the privilege against disclosing confidential communications, (4) immunity of the reporter from legal reprisal, and (5) penalties for failure to report.

Child abuse is defined by most statutes to include physical abuse, emotional abuse, neglect, and sexual molestation. A *child* ordinarily is defined as any person under the age of eighteen years. A typical statute defines *child abuse* as "any physical injury, sexual abuse, or emotional abuse inflicted upon a child other than by accidental means by those responsible for his care, custody, and control, except that discipline, including spanking, administered in a reasonable manner shall not be construed to be abuse."[62]

Many states exempt from the definition of child abuse a parent's refusal, based on religious convictions, to consent to the administration of medical treatment to his or her child.[63] Such exemptions ordinarily provide, however, that they are not to be construed so as to prevent a court from ordering medical treatment when a child's health requires it.

All fifty states enumerate categories of persons who are under a legal duty to report abuse. In most states, such "reporters" must report both actual and reasonably likely or imminent cases of child abuse. The designated categories of reporters generally include physicians, dentists, hospital employees, nurses, coroners, school employees, nursery school workers, law enforcement officers, and licensed psychologists. Most states add "any other person with responsibility for the care of children." Several states permit but do not require persons to make a report who have reasonable cause to believe that a child may be abused. A small minority of states impose a legal duty to report on *any* person having reasonable cause to believe that child abuse has occurred. A minister may not come within one of the designated reporter categories in some states. However, a minister sometimes will fall within the category of "any other person with responsibility for the care of children." And ministers will be required to report child abuse in those few states that impose a legal duty to report on *any* person with knowledge of actual or suspected cases of child abuse.

The privilege against disclosing confidential communications is waived by most child abuse reporting statutes. One statute provides: "The privileged quality of the communication between any professional person required to report and his patient or client shall not constitute grounds for failure to report."[64] This means that ministers who ordinarily cannot be compelled to disclose communications made to them in confidence in the course of professional services cannot justify a failure to report child abuse on the basis of the clergyman-parishioner relationship. Unfortunately, the elimination of the privilege in the context of child abuse reporting disregards the therapeutic purpose of the privilege. Many child abusers will be discouraged from seeking spiritual counsel if the privilege does not assure the confidentiality of their communications. This will only compound the problem. If, on the other hand, the privilege were preserved, many child abusers would seek out ministers for spiritual counseling, and the underlying causes of such behavior could be isolated and in many cases corrected. A few states, recognizing that the elimination of the privilege in the context of child abuse reporting may have been counterproductive, are considering reinstatement of the privilege.

Similarly, every state grants legal immunity to reporters of child abuse. This means that a reporter cannot be sued simply for reporting child abuse.[65] However, several states require that the report be based on "reasonable cause to believe" that abuse has occurred or is imminent. Persons who knowingly transmit false reports are criminally liable in some states.[66]

The purpose of extending legal immunity to reporters obviously is to encourage child abuse reporting. However, several recent studies indicate that numerous false reports have also been encouraged.[67] Such studies have raised serious legal questions concerning the propriety of legal immunity. One expert has observed that the large number of false reports "invite the intolerable situation of falsely accusing large numbers of parents of abuse."[68]

Persons who are legally required to report generally make their report by notifying a designated state agency by telephone and confirming the telephone call with a written report within a prescribed period of time. Most states have toll-free numbers that receive initial reports of child abuse.

While persons who are legally required to report child abuse are subject to criminal prosecution for failure to do so, instances of actual criminal prosecution are rare.

[62]MO. REV. STAT. § 210.110.

[63]ILL. REV. STAT. CH. 23, § 2054.

[64]*Id.*

[65]*See, e.g.,* Nelson v. Freeman, 537 F. Supp. 602 (W.D. Mo. 1982); People v. McKean, 418 N.E.2d 1130 (Ill. App. 1981).

[66]ILL. REV. STAT. CH. 23, § 2054.

[67]*See, e.g.,* A. SUSSMAN & S. COHEN, REPORTING CHILD ABUSE AND NEGLECT: GUIDELINES FOR LEGISLATION (1975) (56% of all reports are valid).

[68]R. Light, *Abused and Neglected Children in America: A Study of Alternative Policies,* 43 HARVARD EDUCATIONAL REVIEW 556, 569 (1973).

p. 80. *After § H add the following new sections:*

§ I. Diversion of Church Funds

Church income ordinarily consists of designated and undesignated contributions, interest on bank accounts, gain on investments, and rent from church-owned property. Some churches have income from the rendition of services, such as the operation of child care facilities or private schools. Church income, from whatever source, is held by the church in trust for the church's religious and charitable purposes. Such a trust may be express, such as when a donor contributes funds for a specified purpose, or implied, such as when funds are contributed without designation as to their use or are church rents, interest income, service income, or gains. [69]

The principle that church funds and assets are held in trust for the religious and charitable uses of the church is codified in the Internal Revenue Code, which conditions the exemption of churches from federal income taxation on several factors, including the following: (1) none of a church's net earnings inures to the benefit of a private individual, except for the payment of reasonable compensation for services rendered; and (2) a church is organized and operated exclusively for religious purposes. [70]

Ministers who divert church funds to their own benefit in excess of their stated compensation may be personally liable on the basis of several legal theories, including breach of trust, embezzlement, fraud, conversion, and theft. In addition, the tax-exempt status of their church may be jeopardized, and a state investigation could result. Diversion of church funds by a minister can be intentional, but often it is inadvertent. For example, diversion of church funds by a minister to compensate himself for travel or entertainment expenses allegedly incurred on behalf of a church may be considered improper if done without proper authorization.

There have been many notable cases of ministers being found guilty of diversion of church funds in recent years. In 1979, the attorney general of the State of California ordered a financial accounting of the Worldwide Church of God and further directed that the church be placed in receivership. The attorney general, acting pursuant to the general supervisory authority vested in him over charitable trusts, justified his actions on the basis of the need to prevent diversion of church assets from charitable purposes to the personal benefit of a few church leaders. [71]

The Founding Church of Scientology lost its exemption from federal income taxation in 1969 because of unexplained payments to its founder in the form of loans and reimbursement of expenses in excess of his salary, even though the amounts of such payments were small. The court observed that Congress, "when conditioning the exemption upon 'no part' of the earnings being of benefit to a private individual, specifically intended that the amount or extent of benefit should not be the determining factor." [72]

The Reverend Sun Myung Moon was convicted of tax fraud for failure to report interest income on certain bank accounts that were held in his name, despite his allegation that he held the funds as "trustee" for the Unification Church. [73] The court concluded: "[T]he government presented evidence . . . that Moon controlled the [bank] accounts, . . . held them in his name, considered [them] his own, used the accounts in a seemingly personal manner, and was regarded by other Church figures as owning the assets personally. . . .

Because he owned the assets, he should have reported the interest . . . on his tax return. Since he failed to do so, his returns were false."[74] The court rejected Moon's "messiah defense" that the church was exempt from paying taxes on its income and therefore he was too since he was "potentially the new messiah" and therefore personified the church and was indistinguishable from it.

In another case, a church had three checking accounts. Two of the accounts were in the church's name and required checks to be signed by the minister and two other persons. The third account was in the name of the minister and only his signature was required for withdrawals. Over the course of many years, funds from many sources were deposited in each of the accounts and withdrawn for various purposes. The minister was charged with embezzlement and fraudulent conversion to his own use of certain funds in the checking account that was in his name.[75]

In summary, ministers ordinarily should not permit church funds or assets to be placed in their names; bank checking and savings accounts should require the signature of two unrelated persons; ministers should not pay for their personal or business expenses out of church funds without written authorization; and they should refrain from accepting favorable loans and other financial benefits out of church funds in excess of their stated compensation.[76]

[69]*See generally* G. BOGERT, THE LAW OF TRUSTS AND TRUSTEES § 371 (1977 & SUPPL. 1984).

[70]I.R.C. § 501(c)(3).

[71]Worldwide Church of God, Inc. v. State, 623 F.2d 613 (9th Cir. 1980), *cert. denied*, 449 U.S. 900 (1980). *See generally* Note, 53 S. CAL. L. REV. 1277 (1980). The California state legislature enacted a new statute in 1980 giving the attorney general authority to investigate religious corporations whenever he had reasonable grounds to believe that corporate property had been improperly diverted for the personal benefit of any individual, or that a substantial diversion of corporate assets from stated corporate purposes had occurred.

[72]Founding Church of Scientology v. United States, 412 F.2d 1197, 1202 (Ct. Cl. 1969), *cert. denied*, 397 U.S. 1009 (1970).

[73]United States v. Moon, 718 F.2d 1210 (2nd Cir. 1983).

[74]*Id.* at 1222.

[75]Commonwealth v. Nichols, 213 A.2d 105 (Pa. 1965).

[76]*See generally* Comment, 73 J. CRIM. L. & CRIMINOL. 1204 (1982).

§ J. State Regulation of Psychologists and Counselors

One of the principal functions of most ministers is that of a counselor. Many hours each week typically are spent in counseling sessions with church members and others in the pastor's study. Some ministers have left the traditional pulpit ministry to open full-time counseling ministries independent of any church. Some churches employ associate ministers with special training specifically for counseling. Do state laws regulating the practice of psychology or counseling apply in any of these situations?

Since 1946, all fifty states have enacted statutes regulating the practice of psychology.[77] These statutes prohibit persons from practicing psychology or representing that they are psychologists unless they are certified or licensed by the state. The purpose of such statutes has been held to be the protection of the public against "charlatans and quacks who, despite inadequate training and professional experience, guarantee easy solutions to psychological problems."[78]

Psychologist regulation statutes fall into two general categories. Certification laws do not prevent persons from practicing psychology, but rather prohibit use of the title "psychologist" or any of its derivatives by persons who are not certified psychologists. Licensure laws prohibit the practice of psychology by anyone who is not a licensed psychologist. Certification laws have been criticized for not adequately protecting the public against unqualified practitioners. Licensure statutes have been criticized as being too restrictive.

A typical certification statute provides: "No person shall, without a valid, existing certificate of registration as a psychologist issued by the [state] attach the title 'psychologist' to his name and under such title render or offer to render services to individuals, corporations, or the public for remuneration or a fee; or render or offer to render to individuals, corporations, or the public, services if the words 'psychological,' 'psychologic,' 'psychologist,' or 'psychology' are used to describe such services by the person or organization offering to render or rendering them."[79]

Certification is obtained from state authorities through an application process. Applicants ordinarily must demonstrate that they are at least 21 years of age, of good moral character, and a citizen of the United States. In addition, they must have earned a specified degree in psychology and have practiced psychology for a minimum number of years.

Licensure statutes prohibit any person from engaging in the "practice of psychology" without a valid license. A typical licensing statute provides: "No person shall practice as a psychologist . . . unless he is validly licensed and registered."[80] Licensing statutes differ in their definition of the phrase "practice of psychology." Some statutes define the term broadly. For example, one statute provides:

The "practice of psychology" . . . is defined as rendering to individuals, groups, organizations, or the public any psychological service involving the application of principles, methods, and procedures of understanding, predicting and influencing behavior, such as the principles pertaining to learning, perception, motivation, thinking, emotion, and interpersonal relationships; the methods and procedures of interviewing, counseling, behavior modification, and psychotherapy; of constructing, administering, and interpreting tests of mental abilities, aptitudes, interests, attitudes, personality characteristics, emotion, and motivation; and of assessing public opinion.[81]

Other statutes define "practice of psychology" more narrowly.[82]

All licensing statutes exempt certain activities from the definition of *practice of psychology*. Exemptions vary from state to state, but the following exemptions are common: (1) professional activities of lawyers, physicians, clergymen, social workers, sociologists, and counselors; (2) activities of government employees in the ordinary course of their employment; (3) activities of a student, intern, or resident in psychology, pursuing a course of study at an accredited university; (4) educational activities of teachers in public and private schools, or the authorized duties of guidance counselors.[83]

An application for a license to practice psychology must satisfy various requirements. Ordinarily, these are similar to the requirements for obtaining a certificate, and generally include a minimum age (typically 21), good moral character, a resident of the state and citizen of the United States, professional experience of a prescribed duration, and the prescribed academic degree. Some states require that the academic degree be a doctoral degree based on a program of studies that were primarily psychological. Others permit a masters degree in psychology plus a longer number of years of professional experience.[84]

Most psychologist licensing laws permit certain persons to obtain a license without meeting all of the normal requirements if they were engaged in the practice of psychology prior to the enactment of the licensing statute. The courts have been sympathetic to such persons and have frequently invalidated state efforts to deny them the right to continue to engage in the practice of psychology because of noncompliance with even limited professional requirements. To illustrate, one court has suggested that persons who practiced psychology before the enactment of a licensing law must be permitted to continue unless the state can affirmatively demonstrate their incompetence.[85]

Several states have combined certification and licensure statutes. Such statutes prohibit anyone from practicing psychology without a license, and also prohibit use of the term *psychology* or any of its derivatives by any person who is not a licensed psychologist.[86]

Can persons engage in "counseling" if they are not licensed to practice psychology? Counseling certainly would come within an expansive definition of the term *practice of psychology,* and thus would appear to be a prohibited practice. Some courts have reached this conclusion. In one case, a state board of psychological examiners obtained a court order barring an individual who had not applied for or received a license to practice psychology from engaging in the practice of counseling. A state appeals court upheld the court order prohibiting the counselor from engaging in the practice of counseling.[87] This case resulted in the enactment of a separate licensing statute for counselors.

The validity of psychologist licensing laws has been challenged in several cases. Such statutes have been upheld despite the claims that (1) they are unconstitutionally vague; (2) they violate due process of law; (3) boards of psychologist examiners unconstitutionally combine prosecutorial and adjudicative powers; (4) they arbitrarily deny licenses to persons holding doctorate degrees in disciplines related to psychology such as vocational rehabilitation and guidance counseling; and (5) they constitute an unconstitutional delegation of legislative authority to administrative agencies without adequate standards for the agency to follow.[88]

In conclusion, ministers who are employed full-time in a pastoral ministry by a church congregation are free to counsel with church members and others in the course of their employment with their church. The same rule ordinarily will apply to ministers who are hired by a church specifically for a counseling ministry. In neither case, however, may a minister use the term *psychology* or any of its derivatives in connection with his counseling ministry unless he is in fact a licensed psychologist. Ministers who establish a full-time or part-time counseling ministry independent of a church ordinarily should not engage in professional counseling unless (1) they are specifically exempted from the prohibition against the unlicensed practice of psychology; (2) their state board of psychologist examiners does not prosecute unlicensed counselors; (3) the term *practice of psychology* is not defined broadly enough to include counseling; or (4) their state has a professional counselor licensing statute under which the counselor is licensed.

Finally, many churches maintaining counseling ministries do not charge for such services but do require counselees to make a "contribution" to the church. Such contributions, often based on the number of hours of counseling, ordinarily are deductible only to the extent that they exceed the fair market value of the counseling services received in exchange.[89]

[77]*See generally* Note, *State Regulation of Psychologists*, 58 WASH. U. L. Q. 639 (1980).

[78]National Psychologist Association v. University of New York, 203 N.Y.S.2d 821 (1960).

[79]ILL. REV. STAT. CH. 111, § 5303.

[80]MO. REV. STAT. § 337.015.

[81]*Id. See also* COLO. REV. STAT. § 12-43-108; GA. ANN. CODE § 84-3101; KY. REV. STAT. § 319.010; OKLA. STAT. ANN. TITLE 59, § 1352.

[82]*See, e.g.*, ARIZ. REV. STAT. ANN. § 32-2061; MINN. STAT. ANN. § 148.81; N.Y. EDUC. LAW § 7601.

[83]*See, e.g.*, KY. REV. STAT. § 319.020; MO. REV. STAT. § 337.045; OKLA. STAT. ANN. TITLE 59, § 1353.

[84]*See, e.g.*, MO. REV. STAT. § 337.020; OKLA. STAT. ANN. TITLE 59, § 1362.

[85]Whittle v. State Board, 483 P.2d 328 (Okla. 1971).

[86]*See, e.g.*, MO. REV. STAT. § 337.015; KY. REV. STAT. § 319.005.

[87]*See* note 77, *supra.*

[88]*See generally* note 77, *supra.*

[89]*See, e.g.*, Graham v. Commissioner, 83 T.C. 575 (1984); Rev. Rul. 76-232, 1976-1 C.B. 62. *See also* Triune of Life Church, Inc. v. Commissioner 85 T.C. ___ (1985).

5

SOCIAL SECURITY FOR MINISTERS

§ B. Ministers Deemed Self-Employed

p. 81. *Add after the first sentence in the text:*

This is true even if a minister reports his income as an employee for federal income tax purposes. In explaining the reason for this rule, the Tax Court has observed: "Congress chose not to place the onus of participation in the old-age and survivors insurance program upon the churches, but to permit ministers to be covered on an individual election basis, as self-employed, whether, in fact, they were employees or actually self-employed."[2a] Thus, ministers have been treated as self-employed for purposes of social security coverage in order to avoid imposing the FICA tax on churches involuntarily.

[2a]Silvey v. Commissioner, 35 T.C.M. 1812 (1976). *See also* S. Rep. No. 1987, 83rd Cong., 2d Sess. (1954), 1954-2 C.B. 695, 701; H. Rep. No. 2679, 83rd Cong., 2d Sess. (1954), 1954-2 C.B. 712, 714.

p. 81. *Add after the last sentence in the text:*

Since 1984, FICA taxes have applied to all non-minister church employees unless a church files a timely election to have all such employees treated as self-employed for purposes of social security coverage. The availability of this election is further evidence of the reluctance of Congress to impose social security taxes directly on churches without their consent.

p. 81, note 2. *Change "3121(b)(8)" to "3121(b)(8)(A)."*

§ C. Coverage Rules

p. 82. *Add after note 7 in the text:*

One court has suggested that a person who functions as a minister in a church that did not ordain, commission, or license him "in a traditional or legally formal manner" is eligible for the exemption.[7a] This ruling is consistent with other judicial pronouncements that the functional equivalents of "ordained, commissioned, or licensed ministers" are eligible for the same benefits as members of that classification.[7b]

[7a]Ballinger v. Commissioner, 728 F.2d 1287 (10th Cir. 1984).
[7b]*See, e.g.*, Silverman v. Commissioner, 57 T.C. 727 (1972); Rev. Rul. 58-221, 1958-1 C.B. 53.

p. 82, note 5. *Add:*

Ballinger v. Commissioner, 728 F.2d 1287 (10th Cir. 1984) (stating that "the triggering event for measuring the statutory time period is the assumption of ministerial duties, combined with earning a particular amount of income").

p. 83. *Add after the first complete paragraph:*

The IRS recognized that many ministers who automatically had been exempt from social security coverage prior to 1968 would not be aware that the law had been amended and that they would have to file an exemption application by April 15, 1970, to retain their exempt status. Accordingly, the income tax regulations specified that if a minister's last federal tax return filed before the deadline for submitting his exemption application (Form 4361) showed no liability for self-employment tax (presumably because of the minister's ignorance of the change in the law) then that return was treated as an application for exemption provided that the minister filed a Form 4361 by February 28, 1975.[10a] Aside from this limited exception, the filing deadline has been considered absolute. Ministers who fail to file an exemption application by the deadline have consistently been denied relief by the courts.[10b]

[10a]Treas. Reg. 1.1402(e)-2A(b).
[10b]*See, e.g.*, Hess v. Commissioner, 40 T.C.M. 415 (1980).

p. 83. *Add after the second complete paragraph:*

The income tax regulations specify that the filing of an exemption application does *not* in itself qualify a minister for the exemption. The exemption is granted only when the application is approved by the IRS.[11a] Thus, a minister will be denied an exemption if the IRS has no record of ever having received an exemption application even if the minister maintains that he did file the application.[11b]

Ministers whose exemption applications are approved by the IRS are free to participate in retirement programs such as Individual Retirement Accounts, Keogh Accounts, and tax-deferred annuities. While this may not be logical, it is perfectly legal. Form 4361, reflecting federal law, only requires that a minister certify that he is "conscientiously opposed to the acceptance (with respect to services performed by me as a minister . . .) of the benefits of any public insurance that makes payments in the event of death, disability, old-age, or retirement or makes payments toward the cost of, or provides services for, medical care (including the benefits of any insurance system established by the Social Security Act)." Ministers do *not* certify that they are conscientiously opposed to the acceptance of payment of benefits payable under any *private* insurance or retirement program.

[11a]Treas. Reg. § 1.1402(e)-2A(c).

[11b]*See, e.g.,* Le Master v. Commissioner, 47 T.C.M. 1495 (1984); Treadway v. Commissioner, 47 T.C.M. 1375 (1984).

p. 83. *Add after note 12 in the text:*

Several ministers who have failed to file a timely exemption application have argued that their constitutional right to freely exercise their religion is abridged by being forced to pay social security taxes against their will. This contention has been consistently rejected by the courts. The United States Supreme Court has observed that "[i]f we hold that ministers have a constitutional right to opt out of the social security system when participation conflicts with their religious beliefs, that same right should extend as well to persons with secular employment and to other taxes, since their right freely to exercise their religion is no less than that of ministers."[12a] In another case, a minister who was ordained in 1969 by a Baptist congregation and became pastor of the church in the same year filed an exemption application in 1977. When his application for exemption was denied on the ground that it had been submitted after the deadline, the minister was "re-ordained" by another church and submitted a second exemption application. He maintained that he became opposed to social security coverage on the basis of "evolving beliefs" only after his first exemption application had been rejected, and that the time period in which an exemption application must be filed should be measured from the time a minister acquires religious beliefs in opposition to social security coverage. A federal appeals court, in rejecting the minister's contention, observed:

The triggering event for measuring the statutory time period is the assumption of ministerial duties, combined with earning a particular amount of income. Thus, the statute does not provide for an exemption where a minister belatedly acquires a belief in opposition to public insurance apart from conversion to another faith. The [minister] did not file for the exemption within the applicable time frame.[12b]

The court did suggest that an individual who has a change of belief accompanied by a change to another faith may "requalify" for the exemption, although such a concession is contrary to the court's conclusion that the "triggering event" for determining the time period in which to file an exemption application is the "assumption of the duties and functions of a minister."

[12a]United States v. Lee, 455 U.S. 252,281 (1982). *See also* Ballinger v. Commissioner, 728 F.2d 1287 (10th Cir. 1984); Olsen v. Commissioner, 709 F.2d 278 (4th Cir. 1983); Hatcher v. Commissioner, 688 F.2d 82 (10th Cir. 1979).

[12b]Ballinger v. Commissioner, 728 F.2d 1287, 1290 (10th Cir. 1984).

p. 83, note 10. *Add:*

Ministers who are opposed to social security coverage solely on the basis of economic considerations are ineligible for the exemption for two related reasons. First, their opposition is not based on religious principles. Second, their opposition is to the *payment* of social security taxes and not to the *acceptance* of social security benefits. The law conditions the exemption on opposition to the acceptance of benefits.

p. 84. *Add after Example 9:*

Example 10. X, an ordained minister, belatedly acquires a religious belief in opposition to social security coverage after the deadline for filing an exemption application has passed. He is not eligible for the exemption.[17a]

Example 11. X was ordained in 1978 and has served as senior pastor of First Church since that date. He failed to file an application for exemption from social security by the deadline. A tax advisor suggests that if he were "reordained" by his church, the time period for filing the exemption application would begin anew. X will not be eligible for the exemption if he is reordained.[17b]

[17a]Ballinger v. Commissioner, 728 F.2d 1287 (10th Cir. 1984).
[17b]*Id.*

§ D. Services to Which Exemption Applies

p. 86, note 26. *Add:*

See also Pavlic v. Commissioner, 47 T.C.M. 1489 (1984).

p. 87. *Insert the following new § E at the end of § D, and change the former § E to § F:*

§ E. Exemption of Members of Certain Religious Faiths

The Internal Revenue Code permits self-employed *members* (whether ministers or laypersons) of certain religious faiths to exempt themselves from social security coverage if the following conditions are satisfied: (1) the member belongs to a recognized religious sect; (2) the sect is opposed to the acceptance of social security benefits on the basis of its established tenets or teachings; (3) the member adheres to the sect's tenets or teachings relating to social security coverage; (4) the member files an exemption application (Form 4029) by the due date of the member's federal income tax return (Form 1040) for the *first* taxable year for which he has self-employment income, or on or by the last day of the third calendar month following the calendar month in which the member is first notified in writing by the IRS that a timely application for an exemption from social security coverage has not been filed; (5) the member's exemption application is accompanied by evidence of his membership in and adherence to the tenets or teachings of the sect; (6) the member waives his right to all social security benefits; and (7) the Secretary of the Department of Health and Human Services finds that the sect (a) does in fact have established tenets or teachings in opposition to social security coverage, (b) makes provision for the financial support of its dependent members, and (c) has been in existence continually since December 31, 1950.[31a] Such an application, if granted, is irrevocable unless the member ceases to be a member of the sect or no longer adheres to the sect's tenets or teachings pertaining to participation in the social security system.

The regulations interpreting this statute specify that a member is not disqualified for the exemption because he is not opposed to obtaining personal liability or property insurance of a kind that will compensate other persons or property that are injured or damaged either by the member or while on the member's property.

The United States Supreme Court has emphasized that the exemption applies only to self-employed persons. Employers and employees who pay social security taxes under the FICA program are not eligible for the exemption. Accordingly, an Amish employer who employed several persons to work on his farm and in his carpentry shop was not eligible for the exemption despite the fact that both he and his Amish employees were opposed to social security coverage on the basis of well-established Amish religious beliefs.[31b] The Court accepted the contention that compulsory participation in the social security program would interfere with the right of the Amish employer and employees to freely exercise their religion. This, however, was only the beginning and not the end of the Court's inquiry, since "[t]he state may justify a limitation on religious liberty by showing that it is essential to accomplish an overriding governmental interest."[31c] It concluded that the government's interest in "assuring mandatory and continuous participation in and contribution to the social security system" was an interest of sufficient magnitude to override the interest of Amish employers and employees in freely exercising their religion.

The courts have strictly enforced the requirement that the member belong to a religious sect having established tenets or teachings in opposition to social security coverage and that provides for its dependent members. To illustrate, a Seventh-Day Adventist was denied an exemption despite his claim that he was personally opposed to social security coverage on the basis of religious beliefs, since the Seventh-Day Adventist Church had no established tenets or teachings against social security coverage and made no provision for the support of its dependent members.[31d]

The exemption has been challenged on the ground that it unconstitutionally discriminates against persons who personally are opposed on the basis of religious beliefs to social security coverage but who are not members of a religious sect that has established tenets or teachings in opposition to social security coverage and that provides for its dependent members. Such challenges thus far have all failed. One court has stated:

> The limitation by Congress of the exemption of members of certain religious sects with established tenets opposed to insurance and which made reasonable provisions for their dependent members was in keeping with the overall welfare purpose of the Social Security Act. This provision provided assurance that those qualifying for the exemption would be otherwise provided for in the event of their dependency.[31e]

[31a]I.R.C. § 1402(g).

[31b]United States v. Lee, 455 U.S. 252 (1982).

[31c]*Id.* at 257-58.

[31d]Varga v. United States, 467 F. Supp. 1113 (D. Md. 1979). *See also* Jaggard v. Commissioner, 582 F.2d 1189 (8th Cir. 1978); Randolph v. Commissioner, 74 T.C. 284 (1980); Henson v. Commissioner, 66 T.C. 835 (1976) (member of Sai Baba denied exemption because his sect did not provide for its dependent members).

[31e]Palmer v. Commissioner, 52 T.C. 310, 314 (1969).

p. 89. *Change § F to § G.*

p. 89. *Insert the following new § H following the first complete paragraph:*

§ H. Conscientious Objection to the Use of Social Security Numbers

Some Christians believe that social security numbers are the "mark of the beast" described in the New Testament Book of Revelation: "He causeth all, both small and great, rich and poor, free and bond, to receive a mark in their right hand, or in their foreheads: and that no man might buy or sell, save he that had the mark, or the name of the beast, or the number of his name. Here is wisdom. Let him that hath understanding count the number of the beast: for it is the number of a man; and his number is Six hundred three score and six" (Revelation 13:16-18). Can the government deny benefits to persons who refuse to obtain a social security number?

In one case, a father's application for welfare benefits for his minor child was rejected on the ground that the child had no social security number. The father claimed that his religious beliefs prevented him from obtaining a number for his child, since he believed that social security numbers were the "mark of the beast" by which the Antichrist would control mankind. A federal appeals court held that a state could deny welfare benefits to a child because of her parents' refusal, based on sincerely held religious beliefs, to obtain a social security number for her, if the state's interest in requiring such a number was "compelling" and was the "least restrictive means" of furthering that interest.[38a] The court concluded that the state's interest in requiring social security numbers for welfare recipients is compelling, since such a requirement "is by far the most cost-effective means of administering the program" and conversion to a non-numerical system "would cost nearly one billion dollars." However, the court concluded that if the administrative cost of developing a non-numerical system for the small number of persons who were opposed to the acquisition of social security numbers on the basis of religious beliefs was small, then a "less restrictive means" would exist for furthering the state's compelling interest in administrative efficiency.

Another court has ruled that the State of New York could not deny welfare benefits to children whose parents refuse to obtain social security numbers because of their belief that such numbers constitute the "mark of the beast."[38b] The court acknowledged that the use of social security numbers resulted in greater administrative efficiency and in the reduction of welfare fraud, and that such interests were substantial. However, the court concluded that "the deleterious effects of [the parents'] action on the welfare system is miniscule" and accordingly a denial of welfare benefits was not the "least restrictive means" of furthering the state's interests.

A California state court has reached the opposite conclusion, denying welfare benefits to children whose parents refuse to obtain social security numbers.[38c] The court quoted from an earlier decision of the United States Supreme Court: "[I]f the State regulates conduct by enacting a general law within its power, the purpose and effect of which is to advance the State's secular goals, the statute is valid despite its indirect burden on religious observance unless the

State may accomplish its purpose by means which do not impose such a burden."[38d] The court noted the necessity of using social security numbers to reduce the widespread fraud and associated escalation of costs in the welfare system, concluding: "We are persuaded that the state's interest in maintaining the fiscal integrity of the very system whose financial resources [the parent] seeks to partake [sic] is sufficiently compelling to counterbalance the incidental infringement thereby placed on [the parent's] free exercise of religion."[38e]

Religious opposition to social security numbers, if sincere, should not be a basis for denying welfare benefits so long as the number of persons holding such beliefs is small and the cost of a non-numerical substitute for such persons is minimal. If these conditions are present, the government's compelling interest in administrative efficiency and prevention of welfare fraud presumably could be accomplished in a less restrictive manner than an absolute denial of benefits, and therefore is superseded by the constitutional guaranty of the free exercise of religion. As one court has noted:

> The government must shoulder a heavy burden to defend a regulation affecting religious actions. It is usually said that the challenged regulation must be the least restrictive means of furthering a compelling state interest. Commentators have observed that, because of its broad and indefinite nature, this test is often inadvertently reduced to an inquiry which stops after the discovery of a compelling state interest. The purpose of almost any law, however, can be traced to a fundamental concern of government. Balancing an individual's religious interest against such a concern inevitably makes the former look unimportant. It is therefore the "least restrictive means" inquiry which is the critical aspect of the free exercise analysis. This prong forces us to measure the importance of a regulation by ascertaining the marginal benefit of applying it to all individuals, rather than to all individuals except those holding a conflicting religious conviction. If the compelling state goal can be accomplished despite the exemption of a particular individual, then a regulation which denies an exemption is not the least restrictive means of furthering the state interest.[38f]

In 1985, the United States Supreme Court, by an equally divided vote (4-4), upheld a lower court decision holding that the rights of an applicant for a driver's license to freely exercise her religion were violated by a state law requiring that her photograph appear on her license despite her sincerely held religious objections.[38g]

[38a]Callahan v. Woods, 736 F.2d 1269 (9th Cir. 1984).
[38b]Stevens v. Berger, 428 F. Supp. 896 (E.D.N.Y. 1977).
[38c]Mullaney v. Woods, 158 Cal. Rptr. 902 (1979).
[38d]Braunfeld v. Brown, 366 U.S. 599, 606-07 (1961).
[38e]158 Cal. Rptr. at 911.

[38f]Callahan v. Woods, 736 F.2d 1269, 1272-73 (citations omitted). *See also* United States v. Kahane, 396 F. Supp. 687, 703 (E.D.N.Y. 1975) ("It would be more convenient for authorities if all people were the same in religion and outlook.").

[38g]Jensen v. Quaring, 105 S. Ct. 3492 (1985).

p. 89. *Change the former § G to § I.*

p. 90. *Delete the 9th and 10th lines of the first complete paragraph and substitute the following:*

indexed, which historically has meant that a person who attained or exceeded his life expectancy received benefits far exceeding his contributions. Further-

p. 90. *Delete the last two lines of the last paragraph in the text and substitute the following:*

as noted earlier, a person who reaches or exceeds his life expectancy historically has received benefits far in excess of his contributions.

p. 90. *Add after the last paragraph in the text:*

In summary, social security has been a good investment for most workers. But it must be recognized that benefits received in the past were based on a larger percentage of workers and a smaller percentage of benefits. In the future, there will be increasingly fewer workers supporting larger numbers of beneficiaries. Undoubtedly, changes will have to be made in the system. Taxes may increase. Benefits may be cut, their rate of increase retarded, or they may be denied altogether to those in higher income brackets. The minimum retirement age may be increased.[40] These potential changes suggest that social security benefits should be viewed as a supplemental and not an exclusive benefit program.

[40]A little-noticed provision in the Social Security Act amendments of 1983 raises the "full benefit" retirement age from the current sixty-five years of age beginning in the year 2000. For example, the full benefit retirement age for persons who attain the age of sixty-two after the year 2005 is sixty-six, and increases to sixty-seven for persons who attain the age of sixty-two in the year 2022 or thereafter. Thus, a person born in 1960 will have a full benefit retirement age of sixty-seven.

6

INCOME TAXES AND THE MINISTER

§ A. Preliminary Considerations

p. 95, note 3. *Add:*

See also Rev. Rul. 79-78, 1979-1 C.B. 9 (minister assumed to be a common law employee of his congregation).

p. 96. *Delete the third line from the top and substitute the following:*

minister's compensation on Form 1099-MISC (Miscellaneous).

p. 97. *Add at the end of the first incomplete paragraph:*

Finally, since 1984, churches and certain church-controlled organizations have been able to exempt themselves from payment of the FICA employer's tax by filing a timely application (Form 8274).[10a] However, the IRS may permanently revoke an exemption if a church or church-controlled organization (1) neglects to issue W-2 forms to its employees for a period of two years or more and (2) fails to furnish all previously unfurnished forms for the period covered by the exemption following a request to do so by the IRS. A revocation of an exemption relates back to the beginning of the two-year period during which the W-2 forms were not furnished.[10b]

[10a] I.R.C. § 3121(w).
[10b] I.R.C. § 3121(w)(2).

p. 99. *Add at the end of the second sentence in the first complete paragraph:*

, unless the minister has elected a voluntary withholding arrangement with his church.

p. 99. *Delete the second and third sentences in the second complete paragraph, and substitute the following:*

In general, the underpayment penalty with respect to any quarterly installment will apply only to the difference between payments made by the due date of the installment and the lesser of an installment based on 80% of the actual tax shown on the minister's Form 1040 for the current year or 100% of the tax shown on the preceding year's return if such return represented a taxable year of twelve months.[14a] In addition, a penalty will be imposed with respect to any payment only to the extent that the total payments for the year up to the required installment are below 80% of the taxes that would be due if the income already received during the current year was placed on an "annualized basis."[14b] Further, the IRS has the authority to waive the underpayment penalty if "by reason of casualty, disaster, or other unusual circumstances the imposition of such addition to tax would be against equity and good conscience."[14c] The law specifies that each quarterly installment shall be credited against unpaid required installments in the order in which such installments are required to be paid. A penalty is based only on the "period of underpayment," which is defined to mean the earlier of the due date of the current year's Form 1040 of the date on which an underpayment is paid. If an installment exceeds the lesser of an installment based on 80% of the actual tax for the current year or 100% of the preceding year's tax liability, the amount of overpayment is carried back to the earliest installment deadline in the current year for which there is an underpayment. If the amount of the overpayment carried back exceeds a prior period's underpayment, the underpayment is eliminated and the underpayment penalty for the earlier period runs from the deadline of the earlier payment through the date of the overpayment. If there is any excess overpayment, it is carried forward to the next quarterly underpayment, if any. These rules are illustrated by the following examples.

Example 1. X, who is exempt from the self-employment tax, paid $2500 in federal income taxes in 1984. He estimates his 1985 federal income tax to be $3000, and pays four quarterly installments of $750 by April 15, June 15, and September 15, 1985, and January 15, 1986. In March 1986, *X* computes his actual 1985 tax liability by completing Form 1040. His actual tax liability for 1985 was $3500. *X* underpaid his 1985 estimated taxes, but he is not liable for the underpayment penalty since each of his quarterly installments for the 1985 tax year exceeded a quarterly installment based on the lesser of 100% of his preceding year's tax liability or 80% of his actual tax for the current year.

Example 2. Same facts as example 1, except that *X's* actual tax liability for 1985, as calculated on his Form 1040, was $4200. *X* underpaid his 1985 estimated taxes, but he is not liable for the underpayment penalty for the same reason discussed in the preceding example.

Example 3. Same facts as example 1, except that X's 1984 tax liability was $4000 and his actual 1985 tax liability was $4200. In this case, X underpaid his 1985 estimated taxes and is liable for the underpayment penalty on each quarterly installment, since his installments ($750) were less than a quarterly installment based on the lesser of 100% of his preceding year's tax liability ($1000) or 80% of his actual tax for the current year ($840). The penalty for each installment is computed by multiplying the applicable annual penalty rate established by the IRS times the amount by which the total payments made by X as of the date of the installment deadline are less than an installment payment based on the lesser of 100% of the preceding year's tax liability or 80% of his actual tax liability for the current year. The penalty applies only for the period of the underpayment. For example, X's penalty on his first installment would be computed by multiplying the applicable penalty rate times $90 ($840-750) times the period of underpayment. The period of underpayment for the initial installment runs from April 15, 1985, until April 15, 1986, (a full year) unless X cuts if off by means of a subsequent overpayment, in which case the penalty is computed only through the date of such overpayment and not through the due date of X's Form 1040. X therefore cannot avoid the underpayment penalty through a subsequent overpayment, but he can minimize the penalty by cutting off the period of underpayment as of the date of the overpayment.

[14a]I.R.C. § 6654(d).
[14b]*Id.*
[14c]I.R.C. § 6654(e).

p. 99. *Add after the fourth complete paragraph:*

7. CONSTITUTIONALITY

The Supreme Court has held that imposing an income tax on ministers does not violate the principle of separation of church and state embodied in the first amendment to the United States Constitution.[14d]

[14d]Murdock v. Pennsylvania, 319 U.S. 105, 112 (1943). *See also* Ballinger v. Commissioner, 728 F.2d 1287 (10th Cir. 1984).

§ B. Housing Allowance

p. 100. *Add after the second complete paragraph:*

The expansion of the parsonage allowance by Congress in 1954 was designed to abolish the discrimination against churches that could not furnish a parsonage but that did pay a housing or rental allowance.[16a]

[16a]The intent of Congress in enacting section 107(2) of the Code is explained in the report of the Senate Finance Committee:

> Under present law, the rental value of a home furnished a minister of the gospel as part of his salary is not included in his gross income. This is unfair to those ministers who are not furnished a parsonage, but who receive larger salaries (which are taxable) to compensate them for expenses they incur in supplying their own home. Both the House and your Committee has [sic] removed the discrimination in existing law by providing that the present exclusion is to apply to rental allowances paid to ministers to the extent used by them to rent or provide a home.

S. Rep. No. 1622 83rd Cong., 2nd Sess. 16 (1954). *See also* IRS Letter Ruling 8350005.

p. 100. *Delete the third complete paragraph and substitute the following:*

Congress never explained its rationale in enacting the original parsonage allowance exclusion in 1921. Apparently, it was based on the principle that the rental value of lodging furnished to an employee on his employer's business premises should be excluded from gross income if it is furnished "for the convenience of the employer" and the employee must accept the lodging in order to adequately perform his duties.[16b] The expansion of the parsonage allowance by Congress in 1954 to include ministers who were given financial "allowances" to rent or purchase a home ended the discrimination against ministers whose churches did not own parsonages, but it also had the effect of undermining the "convenience of the employer" rationale that apparently was the basis for the original parsonage allowance exclusion.

[16b]I.R.C. § 119.

p. 101, note 22. *Add:*

Lawrence v. Commissioner, 50 T.C. 494 (1968).

p. 101, note 23. *Add:*

See chapter 1 for a discussion of the phrase "ordained, commissioned, or licensed minister."

p. 101, note 24. *Add:*

See also Flowers v. United States, F. Supp. (N.D. Tex.) (Texas Christian University held not to be an "integral agency" of the Christian Church, and thus licensed and ordained faculty members are not eligible for the housing allowance exclusion).

p. 102, note 26. *Add:*

The Tax Court has held that § 1.1402(c)-5 of the income tax regulations is a reasonable and valid interpretation of § 107 of the Internal Revenue Code. *See* Toavs v. Commissioner, 67 T.C. 897 (1977).

p. 104. *Add after line 2 of the text:*

The Tax Court has held that an informal, *oral* designation of a housing allowance is sufficient since neither the Internal Revenue Code nor the income tax regulations require that the designation be in writing.[36a] However, in defining the term *rental allowance*, the regulations do require that the allowance be designated by official action in an employment contract, minutes, resolution, budget, "or in any other appropriate instrument evidencing such official action."[36b] Such language, when interpreted in light of the *ejusdem generis* rule of statutory construction, strongly suggests that the housing allowance should be designated in writing, and such a practice is certainly the safest and most appropriate course of action. Nevertheless, precedent does exist for the recognition of a housing allowance despite a church's failure to memorialize a designated allowance in writing. This questionable exception does not of course relieve a church of the obligation of making a bona fide advance designation.

[36a]Libman v. Commissioner, 44 T.C.M. 370 (1982).
[36b]Treas. Reg. § 1.107-1(b).

p. 104. *Add at the end of the third complete paragraph:*

The application of the housing allowance rules to parsonages frequently causes confusion, since ministers oftentimes think that they should deduct an amount on their Form 1040. Actually, ministers living in parsonages "exclude" a housing allowance by *not* reporting the fair rental value of their parsonage as income on Form 1040. Under the "cash equivalent doctrine," a taxpayer ordinarily must report as income any economic benefit that is the "equivalent" of cash. Accordingly, a taxpayer that is provided rent-free use of a home ordinarily must report the fair rental value of the home as income since such use constitutes the equivalent of cash. Economically, there is no difference between being provided the rent-free use of a home or being given additional compensation to pay for a home. However, the tax law specifies that the fair rental value of a parsonage provided rent-free to a minister is excluded from the minister's income as a housing allowance.

p. 105. *Add after the first complete paragraph:*

Later in 1983, the IRS qualified its prohibition of "double deductions." In Announcement 83-100, it authorized double deductions of mortgage interest and real property taxes through January 1, 1985, for any minister who owned and occupied his present home prior to January 3, 1983, (the date of the 1983 IRS ruling) or who had a contract to purchase a home prior to January 3, 1983, and who subsequently owned and occupied that home and who otherwise was eligible for the housing allowance exclusion. A minister who sold his home on or after January 3, 1983, lost the benefit of the double deduction as of the date of sale. Presumably, the double deduction would be available on a prorated basis up until the date of sale. In the Tax Reform Act of 1984, Congress extended the double deduction until January 1, 1986, for any minister who owned and occupied his present home prior to January 3, 1983, or had a contract to purchase a home prior to that date and in fact later owned and occupied the home. The extension of Revenue Ruling 83-3 by Congress in the Tax Reform Act of 1984 is significant for it can be construed as congressional sanction of the double deduction. Many critics of the double deduction, and the IRS itself in Revenue Ruling 83-3, based much of their criticism of the double deduction on section 265 of the Code. The double deduction, being a creation of administrative regulation rather than statutory enactment, was seen as subordinate to and controlled by section 265. This reasoning was significantly impaired by the provision in the Tax Reform Act of 1984 extending the availability of the double deduction, since the double deduction for the first time took on the dignity of statutory enactment and therefore could be viewed as an exception to section 265 rather than as a violation of it.

In Revenue Ruling 85-96 (July 1985) the IRS suspended the disallowance of the double deduction until January 1, 1987, for ministers who owned and occupied their present home prior to January 3, 1983, or who had a contract to purchase a home prior to that date and in fact later owned and occupied the home.

Thus, the continuing availability of the double deduction benefits a diminishing number of homeowning ministers (i.e., those who continue to reside in the home that they owned and occupied prior to January 3, 1983). The IRS has ruled that a minister whose home was destroyed by fire in September 1982 and who signed a contract to purchase a new home in the same community on January 19, 1983, was not eligible for the double deduction since he purchased a new home after January 3, 1983. [46a]

The reluctance of Congress and the IRS to eliminate the double deduction for ministers is largely attributable to the continuing availability of a similar benefit to military personnel who receive housing allowances from the federal government. Both Congress and the IRS are reluctant to eliminate the double deduction for ministers while continuing the same benefit for military personnel. Certainly, such arbitrary and disparate treatment would be suspect under the due process clause of the federal Constitution. But the strongest argument in support of the double deduction is the principle of detrimental reliance. Since 1962, the IRS has induced countless ministers to purchase homes and assume financial obligations in reliance on the significant benefit provided by the double deduction. For the IRS or Congress to repudiate this benefit twenty years or so later would work a severe hardship on thousands of ministers who justifiably relied on Revenue Ruling 62-212.

[46a]IRS Letter Ruling 8402049.

p. 105. *Delete the first sentence of the second complete paragraph and substitute the following:*

If Congress or the IRS ever does eliminate the double deduction, as it already has done for homeowning ministers who sold their homes on or after January 3, 1983, a minister will be denied any itemized deduction for mortgage interest or property taxes if he is able to fully exclude all of his actual expenses incurred in owning and maintaining a home.

p. 105, note 46. *Add:*

[46]United States v. Skelly Oil Co., 394 U.S. 678 (1969).

p. 106. *Add after the first complete paragraph:*

Only the actual expenses incurred in owning or maintaining a home can be used in computing the housing allowance exclusion of a minister who owns his home. If a minister owns his home debt-free, either because he paid cash for his home or because his mortgage loan has been paid in full, his housing allowance exclusion ordinarily will be reduced significantly. Such a minister can continue to exclude such costs as repairs, utilities, home improvements, property taxes, furnishings, and home insurance. But the major expenses of mortgage payments, including principal and interest, are no longer available. One minister who bought a home with cash, and whose housing allowance exclusion accordingly was reduced significantly, argued that the law unfairly discriminated against him in favor of ministers who either purchased a home on credit or rented their homes. The Tax Court, while acknowledging that this argument had "some surface appeal," upheld the validity of the housing allowance exclusion.[48a]

Several ministers who own their homes debt-free have attempted to increase the amount of their housing allowance exclusion by securing a loan with a home mortgage. This arrangement certainly is permissible if the loan proceeds were used for a home improvement, repairs, or some other expense associated with owning or maintaining a home. If, however, a minister obtains a loan for an expense unrelated to owning or maintaining his home (such as a vacation, college education for a child, or a new car) and secures the loan with a mortgage on his home, a more difficult question is presented. It could be argued that payments of principal and interest in such cases are not includable in computing the minister's housing allowance exclusion since the object or purpose of the payments is unrelated to owning or maintaining a home. On the other hand, since the minister might lose his home through foreclosure if he fails to make such payments, the payments could be viewed as expenses associated with maintaining a home. While the latter view certainly seems tenable and consistent with the requirements of the law, there is no supporting precedent as of this time.

[48a]Swaggart v. Commissioner, 48 T.C.M. 759 (1984).

p. 106, note 47. *Add:*

See also IRS Letter Ruling 8350005.

p. 109. *Add section 5 after the first two lines of text:*

5. FUTURE OF THE HOUSING ALLOWANCE

Present efforts by the IRS to limit the housing allowance exclusion suggest that this benefit may be eliminated entirely at some future date. Elimination of the allowance was proposed by the Treasury Department in its tax simplification plan submitted to President Reagan in November 1984. The president's own plan released in May 1985 retained the housing allowance. Whether efforts to limit or repudiate the housing allowance ultimately are successful will depend on several factors, including the need for federal revenue and the intensity of support for the allowance by clergy and others.

§ C. Special Occasion Gifts to Ministers

p. 109. *Add after the last complete paragraph:*

Similarly, a federal appeals court has held that an annual sum paid to a minister by a former church from which he had to resign because of illness was a gift and not taxable compensation.[50a] The minister had served the church for eighteen years when he was stricken with a severe heart attack. After a prolonged recovery, including eight months in a hospital, the minister was advised by his physician to move from Pennsylvania to Florida. The church congregation, aware of the physician's advice and of the minister's lack of funds to move to Florida, adopted the following resolution:

> Whereas the pastor of this church . . . has become incapacitated for the further service as pastor and has requested the congregation to join in a petition . . . to dissolve the pastoral relation; and whereas the congregation moved by affectionate regard for him and gratitude for his long and valued ministry among them, desire that he should continue to be associated with them in an honorary relation; now, therefore, be it resolved that . . . [the minister] be constituted Pastor Emeritus of this church with salary or honorarium amounting to Two Thousand Dollars ($2000) annually, payable in monthly installments, with no pastoral authority or duty, and that the session of this church be requested to report this action to the presbytery.

The minister made no request to the congregation for such payments, had no knowledge that the resolution would be adopted, did not agree to render any services in exchange for the payments, and in fact performed no pastoral services for the church following his resignation. Under these facts, the court concluded that the payments to the minister were nontaxable gifts rather than taxable compensation. Noting that "a gift is none the less a gift because inspired by gratitude for past faithful service," the court observed that the payments were gifts since they were "bestowed only because of personal affection or regard or pity" and not with the intent to pay the minister what was due him.[50b]

[50a]Schall v. Commissioner, 174 F.2d 893 (5th Cir. 1949).
[50b]*Id.* at 894.

p. 109, note 50. *Add:*

Abernathy v. Commissioner, 211 F.2d 651 (D.C. Cir. 1954).

p. 110. *Add at the end of § C:*

The characterization of special occasion payments to a minister as nontaxable gifts presents two additional problems. First, it is doubtful that church members' contributions designated specifically for the special occasion gift to the minister are deductible as charitable contributions. Such transfers would in effect be direct payments from the members to the minister since the church is acting only as a conduit or intermediary. Therefore, there is no contribution to or for the use of a charitable organization as is required in order for a contribution to be deductible.[52a] Furthermore, to hold otherwise would allow both a charitable contribution deduction and a gift exclusion for essentially the same transaction. A second and more fundamental concern is the effect on the church's tax-exempt status of characterizing church payments to a minister as "gifts." One of the conditions that a church or other charitable organization must satisfy in order to remain exempt from federal income taxes is the avoidance of any "inurement" of its net earnings to private individuals other than reasonable compensation for services rendered.[52b] If special occasion payments to a minister are characterized as taxable compensation to him, there is no problem with inurement, since such payments ordinarily could be construed as reasonable compensation for services rendered. In such a case, church members' contributions that make such a payment possible would be tax-deductible charitable contributions since they are going to or for the use of a charitable organization that is making a legitimate payment of compensation for services rendered. However, if such payments are characterized as nontaxable gifts, and they are funneled through the church, the problem with inurement may be presented since payments other than compensation for services rendered are being made out of church funds to a private individual. The courts have observed that since federal law does not specify how much inurement is needed to disqualify a charitable organization for tax-exempt status, presumably *any* amount of inurement will suffice.[52c] Of course, the objective of church members in such a case is to receive a charitable contribution deduction for their payments to the minister, and this can be accomplished only if their "contributions" appear to have been made to the church. But as noted before, the same transaction ordinarily cannot give rise to both a deductible contribution and an excludable gift. By characterizing the payment to the minister as a gift, the designated "contributions" by church members to the church but for the minister become non-deductible.

[52a] *See* chapter 14, § B, *infra.* The IRS has the authority under federal law to "collapse" any step of a multi-step transaction in order to determine the reality and substance of the transaction. By eliminating the use of a church as an intermediary, the "contributions" of church members are readily perceived to be direct transfers to the minister, and as such would not be deductible.

[52b] I.R.C. § 501(c)(3). *See generally* chapter 14, § B, *infra.*

[52c] *See, e.g.,* The Founding Church of Scientology v. United States, 412 F.2d 1197 (Ct. Cl. 1969), *cert. denied,* 397 U.S. 1009 (1970).

§ D. Travel Expenses

p. 112. *Add after the first sentence in the second complete paragraph:*

Since 1963, taxpayers have been required to substantiate travel expenses with "adequate records by sufficient evidence corroborating [their] own statements."[54a]

[54a]I.R.C. § 274.

p. 112. *Add at the end of the text:*

The Tax Reform Act of 1984 amended the law to require that all travel expenses (including meals and lodging while away from home as well as local travel) be substantiated by adequate *contemporaneous* records. "Reconstruction" of expenses would no longer have been allowed unless a taxpayer's records were lost due to circumstances beyond his control, such as in a fire, flood, or earthquake. In response to a storm of protest, both the Senate and House of Representatives overwhelmingly (92-1 and 412-1) repealed the new, stricter standard. Ministers therefore will be able to substantiate their travel expenses as before.

7

DEFINITIONS

p. 119. *Add before the last paragraph:*

8. election to waive employer FICA participation[7a]

[7a]I.R.C. § 3121(w).

p. 120. *Delete the last two lines in the first complete paragraph and substitute the following:*

offense;[14] describes the benefits available to churches under the National Flood Insurance Act;[15] and exempts churches from the provisions of the Robinson-Patman Act.[15a]

[15a]15 U.S.C. § 13c.

p. 122, note 31. *Add:*

But see G.C.M. 38982.

p. 124, note 40. *Add:*

See also Church of the Visible Intelligence that Governs the Universe v. Commissioner, 83-2 U.S.T.C. ¶ 9726 (Ct. Cl. 1983).

p. 125. *Add after the first incomplete paragraph:*

The fourteen criteria developed by the IRS have been criticized for being so restrictive that many if not most bona fide churches fail to satisfy several of them. In part, the problem results from the apparent attempt by the IRS to draft criteria that apply to both local churches and religious denominations. To illustrate, few if any local churches would meet the seventh, ninth, and fourteenth criteria, since these ordinarily would pertain only to religious denominations. In addition, many newer, independent churches often will fail the first and fifth criteria and may also fail the second, third, fourth, sixth, and eighth. It is therefore possible for a legitimate church to fail as many as ten of the fourteen criteria. The original Christian churches described in the New Testament Book of Acts easily would have failed a majority of the fourteen criteria.[41a]

These criteria clearly are vague and inadequate. Some apply exclusively to local churches, others do not. And the IRS does not indicate how many criteria an organization must meet in order to be classified as a church, or if some criteria are more important than others. The vagueness of the criteria necessarily means that their application in any particular case will depend on the discretionary judgment of a government employee. This is the very kind of conduct that the courts repeatedly have condemned in other contexts as unconstitutional. To illustrate, the courts consistently have invalidated municipal ordinances that condition the constitutionally protected interests of speech and assembly upon compliance with criteria that are so vague that decisions essentially are a matter of administrative discretion. The Supreme Court has held that "[i]t is a basic principle of due process that an enactment is void for vagueness if its prohibitions are not clearly defined. . . . A vague law impermissibly delegates basic policy matters to [government officials] for resolution on an *ad hoc* and subjective basis with the attendant dangers of arbitrary and discriminatory application."[41b] This same reasoning should also apply in the context of other fundamental constitutional rights, such as the First Amendment right to freely exercise one's religion. The IRS should not be permitted to effectively limit the right of churches and church members to freely exercise their religion on the basis of criteria that are as vague as the fourteen criteria listed above, and whose application in a particular case is essentially a matter of administrative discretion.

The criteria are also constitutionally suspect on the related ground of "overbreadth." The Supreme Court "has repeatedly held that a governmental purpose to control or prevent activities constitutionally subject to state regulation may not be achieved by means which sweep unnecessarily broadly and thereby invade the area of protected freedoms. The power to regulate must be so exercised as not, in attaining a permissible end, unduly to infringe the protected freedom. Even though the governmental purpose be legitimate and substantial, that purpose cannot be pursued by means that broadly stifle fundamental personal liberties when the end can be more narrowly achieved."[41c] Congress and the IRS may have the authority to identify those churches that are not qualified for the tax benefits afforded by federal law, but they may not do so on the basis of criteria that sweep so broadly as to jeopardize the standing of legitimate churches.

[41a]*See generally* S. SCHLATTER, THE CHURCH IN THE NEW TESTAMENT PERIOD (P. LEVERTOFF TRANS. 1955); R. SCHNECKENBURG, THE CHURCH IN THE NEW TESTAMENT (1965); E. SCHWEIZER, CHURCH ORDER IN THE NEW TESTAMENT (1961); E. SCHWEIZER, THE CHURCH AS THE BODY OF CHRIST (1964).

[41b]Grayned v. City of Rockford, 408 U.S. 104, 108-09 (1972).

[41c]N.A.A.C.P. v. Alabama, 377 U.S. 288, 307-08 (1964).

p. 125. *Add after the last complete paragraph:*

One court has observed that the phrase "conventions or associations of churches" was inserted in the Internal Revenue Code to relieve the concerns of congregational and independent churches that the term *church* included hierarchical religious denominations but not conventions or associations of congregational churches.[46a] Therefore, the term *conventions or associations of churches* pertains to the organizational structures of congregational churches.

An income tax regulation pertaining to the tax on unrelated business activities of churches specifies that the term *church* includes

> a religious order or religious organization of such order or organization (a) is an *integral part* of a church, and (b) is engaged in carrying out the functions of a church, whether as a civil law corporation or otherwise. In determining whether a religious order or organization is an integral part of a church, consideration will be given to the degree to which it is connected with, and controlled by, such church. A religious order or organization shall be considered to be engaged in carrying out the functions of a church if its duties include the ministration of sacerdotal functions and the conduct of religious worship. . . . What constitutes the conduct of religious worship or the ministration of sacerdotal functions depends on the tenets and practices of a particular religious body constituting a church.[46b]

Furthermore, the Supreme Court has held that church-controlled organizations that are not separately incorporated are regarded for tax purposes as part of the church itself.[46c]

[46a]Lutheran Social Service of Minnesota v. United States, 758 F.2d 1283 (8th Cir. 1985).

[46b]Treas. Reg. § 1.511-2(a)(3)(ii) (emphasis added).

[46c]St. Martin Evangelical Lutheran Church v. South Dakota, 451 U.S. 772 (1981) (the Court declined to rule on the status of separately incorporated, church-controlled organizations). *See also* Treas. Reg. § 1.6033-2(g)(5)(iv), example 6; Lutheran Social Service of Minnesota v. United States, 758 F.2d 1283 (8th Cir. 1985).

p. 126. *Add at the end of the text:*

The Lutheran Social Service of Minnesota (LSS) challenged the income tax regulation defining *integrated auxiliary* on the ground that the requirement that an integrated auxiliary's "principal activity" be exclusively religious was unconstitutional.[52a] The LSS is an independent corporation that is affiliated with several Lutheran synods. It provides a variety of services, including child care and adoption, counseling, residential treatment for mentally handicapped persons and felons, nutrition programs for the aged, and a camp for mentally and physically handicapped persons. The LSS argued, and the IRS conceded, that it satisfied the first two parts of the definition of *integrated auxiliary:* exemption from tax as an organization described in section 501(c)(3) of the Internal Revenue Code and affiliation with a church. However, the IRS maintained that LSS did not satisfy the third requirement since many of its functions were "charitable" in nature and as such would serve as a separate basis for exemption under section 501(c)(3). The LSS countered by asserting that this "exclusively religious" requirement for integrated auxiliary status was unconstitutional under the equal protection clause of the United States Constitution and the free exercise of religion clause of the First Amendment. It demonstrated that the Internal Revenue Code itself contains no "exclusively religious" requirement, and that the legislative history supported no such test.

The IRS argued that the courts must defer to income tax regulations that "implement the congressional mandate in some reasonable manner," and that the regulation under consideration clearly furthered section 6033 of the Code in a reasonable way. The trial court agreed with the IRS that the LSS was not an integrated auxiliary. However, this judgment was reversed by a federal appeals court on the ground that the IRS regulation defining the term *integrated auxiliary* was inconsistent with clear congressional policy insofar as it required the principal activity of an integrated auxiliary to be "exclusively religious."[52b] The court observed that Congress specifically required that *religious orders* be "exclusively religious" to qualify for exemption from filing annual information returns under section 6033 of the Internal Revenue Code, but, in the same section, failed to mandate the same requirement with respect to *integrated auxiliaries.* "This omission on the part of Congress," concluded the court, "can only be viewed as an intentional and purposeful decision not to limit the group of integrated auxiliaries qualifying for the filing exception to those that are exclusively religious." To support its conclusion, the court recited the established rule of statutory construction that "[w]here Congress included particular language in one section of a statute but omits it in another section of the same [statute], it is generally presumed that Congress acts intentionally and purposely in the disparate inclusion or exclusion." The court also noted that "once 'exclusively religious' is defined as 'not also charitable or educational' the realm of the 'exclusively religious' becomes very narrow [since] churches themselves are not 'exclusively religious' in the sense that the . . . regulations require of their integrated auxiliaries."

The term *integral agency* occasionally appears in the Internal Revenue Code and associated regulations and refers to agencies that are integrally connected with churches and associations or conventions of churches. For example, ordained, commissioned, or licensed ministers are eligible for the housing allowance exclusion if they are engaged in the "administration and maintenance of religious organizations and their integral agencies."[52c] In a revenue ruling, the IRS has listed the following criteria to be considered in determining whether a church-related institution is an integral agency of a religious organization:

1. whether the religious organization incorporated the institution;
2. whether the corporate name of the institution indicates a church relationship;
3. whether the religious organization continuously controls, manages, and maintains the institution;
4. whether the trustees or directors of the institution are approved by or must be approved by the religious organization or church;
5. whether trustees or directors may be removed by the religious organization or church;
6. whether annual reports of finances and general operations are required to be made to the religious organization or church;
7. whether the religious organization or church contributes to the support of the institution; and
8. whether, in the event of dissolution of the institution, its assets would be turned over to the religious organization or church.[52d]

The IRS has stated that the absence of one or more of these characteristics will not necessarily be determinative in a particular case, and, that if the application of these eight criteria in a particular case does not clearly support an affirmative or negative answer, "the appropriate organizational authorities are contacted for a statement, in light of the criteria, whether the particular institution is an integral agency, and their views are carefully considered."[52e]

Finally, the Internal Revenue Code exempts *religious or apostolic associations or corporations* from federal income taxation if they

have a common treasury or community treasury, even if such associations or corporations engage in business for the common benefit of the members, but only if the members thereof include (at the time of filing their returns) in their gross income their entire pro rata shares, whether distributed or not, of the taxable income of the association or corporation for such year. Any amount so included in the gross income of a member shall be treated as a dividend received.[52f]

Religious or apostolic associations and corporations must file a Form 1065

TABLE 7-1

COMPARISON OF CHURCHES AND CHURCH-RELATED ENTITIES

Entity	Definition	Exempt From Federal Income Taxation	Exempt From Filing Form 990	Qualified Charitable Contribution Recipient
churches	Not defined in the IRC or regulations; the IRS has developed 14 criteria for determining if a particular entity is a church, but these are of doubtful legal validity; a church is composed of its various departments and services (e.g., Sunday school, youth programs) and must be construed to include them; the term *church* also includes hierarchical denominations	yes	yes	yes
conventions or associations of churches	not defined in the IRC or regulations; includes religious denominations or groups of churches that are "congregational" in polity	yes	yes	yes
integral parts of churches	not defined in the IRC or regulations, but Reg. 1.511-2(a)(3)(ii) provides that consideration must be given to the degree to which a particular entity is connected with and controlled by a church; performance of religious worship also required; corporation status not relevant	yes	yes	yes
integral agencies of religious organizations	not defined in the IRC or regulations; Rev. Rul. 72-606 lists 8 criteria to be used in determining if a particular entity is an integral agency of a church	yes, if the religious organization with which it is affiliated is exempt		

Type	Definition			
integrated auxiliaries of churches or of conventions or associations of churches	defined by regulation as an entity that is (1) exempt from federal income taxation under § 501(c)(3) of the IRC, (2) is affiliated with a church, and (3) whose principal activity is exclusively religious. A federal appeals court has ruled that the third requirement is invalid.	yes	yes	yes
separately incorporated church-affiliated organizations	not specifically used in the IRC or regulations	possibly, if they are integral parts of a church		
private schools	not specifically used in the IRC or regulations	yes, if they are not incorporated and affiliated with a church, or if incorporated, or if unincorporated but an integrated auxiliary of a church		
church-controlled organizations	defined by § 3121(w) of the IRC as any church-controlled tax-exempt entity described in § 501(c)(3) that is not engaged in an unrelated trade or business and that does not ordinarily receive more than 25% of its support from (a) governmental sources, or (b) admission receipts, sales of merchandise, performance of services, or furnishing of facilities, in activities that are not a trade or business	yes, if it is an integral part, an integral agency, or an integrated auxiliary of a church		
religious or apostolic associations or corporations	defined by § 501(d) of the IRC as organizations having a common treasury, if members report their pro rata share of the organization's income as gross income on their individual tax returns	no	no, but Form 1065 must be filed annually	yes
all other religious organizations	not applicable	ordinarily no	ordinarily no	ordinarily no

each year, stating the items of gross income and deductions, along with a statement listing the names and addresses of each member and the amount of his distributive share of the organization's taxable income.

Churches and several church-related organizations are compared on the basis of three significant tax benefits in Table 7-1. There is little if any justification for the confusing number of terms employed by the Internal Revenue Code and the income tax regulations in describing church-related organizations. Such terminology suggests a confusion on the part of Congress and the IRS in dealing with church-related organizations. An even more troubling concern is the largely discretionary authority of the IRS to interpret these ambiguously defined or undefined terms.

In summary, there clearly is a need for Congress to (1) reduce the unnecessarily confusing number of terms used in the Internal Revenue Code to describe and define church-related organizations; (2) sufficiently clarify the remaining definitions so as to eliminate discretionary application by the IRS; and (3) demonstrate a greater deference to the legitimate perceptions of bona fide churches concerning those entities that are sufficiently related to their mission to share in their tax benefits.

[52a]Lutheran Social Service of Minnesota v. United States, 583 F. Supp. 1298 (D. Minn. 1984).

[52b]Lutheran Social Service of Minnesota v. United States, 758 F.2d 1283 (8th Cir. 1985).

[52c]Treas. Reg. § 1.107-1(a).

[52d]Rev. Rul. 72-606, 1972-2 C.B. 78.

[52e]Rev. Rul. 72-606, 1972-2 C.B. 78.

[52f]I.R.C. § 501(d). *See also* Riker v. Commissioner, 244 F.2d 220 (9th Cir. 1957); Rev. Rul. 78-100, 1978-1 C.B. 162; Rev. Rul. 77-295, 1977-2 C.B. 196; Rev. Proc. 72-5, 1972-1 C.B. 709.

8

ORGANIZATION AND ADMINISTRATION

§ A. Unincorporated Associations

p. 129. *Add note 11a at the end of the first complete paragraph.*

p. 129. *Delete the third line of the second complete paragraph and substitute the following:*

members or agents of the association, at least if the acts occur in the course

p. 129. *Add at the end of the third complete paragraph:*

The inclusion of unincorporated associations within the definition of the term *corporations* is a well-established principle of federal tax law. Section 7701(a)(3) of the Internal Revenue Code defines *corporation* to include associations, and the federal courts for many years have held that associations possessing at least three of the four principal corporate characteristics of centralized control, continuity, limited personal liability, and transferability of beneficial interests are to be treated as corporations.[13a] The exemption available to religious and charitable corporations under the Internal Revenue Code accordingly should be available to most unincorporated associations that meet all of the other conditions for exempt status.

[13a]*See, e.g.*, Smith's Estate v. Commissioner, 313 F.2d 724 (8th Cir. 1963).

p. 129, note 11a. *Add:*

[11a]*See, e.g.*, Trinity Pentecostal Church v. Terry, 660 S.W.2d 449 (Mo. App. 1983) (unincorporated religious association was "without capacity to hold and pass title to real estate under Missouri law").

p. 131. *Add after the first incomplete paragraph:*

The members of an unincorporated association may vote to incorporate their organization and transfer title to all properties to the new corporation. A minority of the unincorporated association's members are without authority to block such a transfer.[19a]

[19a]Jacobs v. St. Mark's Baptist Church, 415 So.2d 252 (La. App. 1982).

§ B. Corporations

p. 131. *Add after the second complete paragraph:*

The West Virginia constitution specifies that "[n]o charter of incorporation shall be granted to any church or religious denomination." The validity of such a provision is suspect under the prevailing construction of the First Amendment's religion clauses by the United States Supreme Court, for it denies churches a valuable benefit available generally to nonreligious charitable and noncharitable organizations without a sufficiently compelling justification.

Some have maintained that churches should never incorporate since incorporation constitutes a "subordination" of a church to the authority of the state. Before endorsing such a view, one should carefully evaluate two considerations. First, as noted in the preceding section, unincorporated organizations generally are regarded as corporations for tax purposes if they possess most or all of the corporate characteristics of centralized control, continuity, limited personal liability, and transferability of beneficial interests.[20a] Ironically, unincorporated churches are considered to be tax-exempt by the IRS because they generally meet the definition of *corporation* contained in the Internal Revenue Code as interpreted by the courts. Second, and more fundamentally, a corporation is an artificial entity that is entirely separate and distinct from its members. The term *corporation* has been defined as "an association of persons to whom the sovereign has offered a franchise to become an artificial, juridical person, with a name of its own, under which they can act and contract, sue and be sued, and who have . . . accepted the offer and effected an organization in substantial conformity with its terms."[20b] A corporation, then, is entirely distinct from its members and should not be confused with them. A church that incorporates is not "subordinating itself" to the state. Rather, it is subordinating merely the artificial corporate entity to the state, and it is free to terminate that entity at any time. Similarly, under some corporation laws, the state can terminate the corporate status of church corporations that fail to file annual reports. But the termination of the church corporation under such conditions certainly does not mean that the church itself is dissolved, for the church is completely independent of the artificial corporate entity and survives its demise. One legal scholar has observed that the "distinctiveness of the corporate entity from the members . . . is inherent in and exemplified by other corporate attributes, which could not be conceded were they one and the same, e.g., the transfer of shares and change in membership without change in the corporation [and] the right to sue and be sued in the corporate name. . . ."[20c] The distinctiveness of the corporate entity from its members is also the basis for the limitation of personal liability of members for the acts of the corporation. This limitation of personal liability is not an example of social irresponsibility that should be avoided by churches. On the contrary, it is a recognition of the fact that church members should not be personally responsible for the wrongdoing of other members or agents over which they had no control.

In summary, churches wanting to avail themselves of the benefits of the corporate form of organization should not be dissuaded by unwarranted fears of governmental control. In the unlikely event that an incorporated church ever does believe that it is being unduly "controlled" by the state, it can easily and quickly rectify the problem by voluntarily terminating its corporate existence. A number of courts have specifically held that incorporation of a church under a state corporation law does not subject the church to any greater degree of civil scrutiny.[20d]

[20a]*See* note 13a, *supra*, and accompanying text.

[20b]Mackay v. New York, N.H. & H.R. Co., 72 A. 583 (1909) (this definition is still frequently cited by the courts).

[20c]1 W. FLETCHER, CYCLOPEDIA OF THE LAW OF PRIVATE CORPORATIONS § 25 (1974 & Suppl. 1984).

[20d]*See, e.g.*, Bourgeois v. Landrum, 387 So.2d 611 (La. App. 1980), *rev'd on other grounds*, 396 So.2d 1275 (La. 1981).

p. 134. *Add after the first incomplete paragraph:*

Two other objections occasionally are raised to the incorporation of churches under the Model Nonprofit Corporation Act. First, the Act was based largely on the Model Corporation Act for business corporations, and therefore fails to adequately recognize the substantial differences between nonprofit and for-profit enterprises.[32a] Second, some have argued that churches should not incorporate as "nonprofit" organizations, since this would suggest that they are "unprofitable" or of no social or spiritual benefit. In this regard, one court has observed that the term *not-for-profit* refers only to monetary profit and does not include "spiritual profit," and therefore a church properly can be characterized as "not-for-profit" even though it "receives some type of profit from its public works in the form of the feeling of achievement and satisfaction the contributors derive from their good work or the enhancement of the image of the organization and its members in the eyes of the community."[32b]

[32a]*See, e.g.*, OLECK, *supra* note 5, at § 26.

[32b]United States v. 564.54 Acres of Land, More or Less, 576 F.2d 983, 989 (3rd Cir. 1978). *See also* People ex rel. Meiresonne v. Arnold, 553 P.2d 79 (Colo. 1976).

p. 134. *Add note 33a at the end of subsection b.*

p. 134. *Add at the end of subsection b:*

Such statutes have been upheld against the claim that they "entangle" the state in religious matters contrary to the non-establishment of religion clause of the First Amendment to the United States Constitution.[33b] The Supreme Court has upheld the validity of such statutes,[33c] and has approved reference to them as a permissible way to resolve church property disputes.[33d]

[33a]Bible Presbyterian Church v. Harvey Cedars Conference, 202 A.2d 455 (N.J. 1964); Rector, Church Wardens & Vestrymen v. Committee to Preserve St. Bartholomew's Church, 445 N.Y.S.2d 975 (1982).

[33b]Bennison v. Sharp, 329 N.W.2d 466 (Mich. App. 1982).

[33c]Maryland and Virginia Eldership of Churches of God v. Church of God at Sharpsburg, 396 U.S. 367 (1970).

[33d]Jones v. Wolf, 443 U.S. 602 (1979).

p. 137, note 42. *Add:*

In Rev. Proc. 82-2, 1982-3 I.R.B. 9, the IRS held that this paragraph is not required in the articles of incorporation of nonprofit corporations incorporated under the nonprofit charitable corporation laws of Arkansas, California, Louisiana, Massachusetts, Minnesota, Missouri, Ohio, and Oklahoma, since such laws contain adequate dissolution provisions that apply to any organization incorporated under them. *But see* IRS Announcement 82-91 (Missouri has two charitable corporation statutes, and only one contains an adequate dissolution provision).

p. 138, note 44. *Add:*

The IRS has stated that if reference to federal law in articles of incorporation imposes a limitation that is invalid in a particular state, as in California, then the following language may be substituted for the last sentence of the quoted paragraph: "Notwithstanding any other provision of these articles, this corporation shall not, except to an insubstantial degree, engage in any activities or exercise any powers that are not in furtherance of the purposes of this corporation."

p. 139. *Add after the third complete paragraph:*

4. PROPERTY

Since one of the attributes of a corporation is the ability to hold title in the corporate name, it is a good practice for an incorporated church to identify itself as a corporation in deeds, mortgages, contracts, promissory notes, and other legal documents. For example, identifying a church as "First Church, a nonprofit religious corporation duly organized under the laws of the state of Illinois," ordinarily will suffice. Such a practice will be prima facie evidence that the church is incorporated and thus capable of executing legal documents in its name by its appropriate officers. In many states, an unincorporated church must execute such documents in the name of church trustees since the church itself lacks authority to execute legal documents. Unfortunately, it is a common practice for unincorporated churches to execute such documents in the name of the church with the signatures of only the minister and church secretary. Such documents of course will be invalid in many states absent ratification by the church membership through acceptance of the benefits of the transaction. Deeds to property present the greatest problem, and many title examiners will object to a deed executed by an unincorporated church in such a manner even if it is subsequently ratified.

In some states, a business corporation is required to include terminology in its name identifying itself as a corporation. Such terminology may include such words and abbreviations as *corporation, corp., incorporated,* or *inc.* This practice ordinarily does not apply to religious corporations. The absence of such a requirement, of course, makes it imperative for a church corporation to identify itself as a corporation following reference to its name in legal documents to avoid any suggestion that it might be an unincorporated association and thereby incapable of conveying title to property in its own name.

Ownership of church property following a schism or disaffiliation is a complex question that is considered fully in the next chapter.

§ C. Records and Reporting

p. 141. *Delete the first sentence in the last incomplete paragraph.*

p. 141, note 54. *Add:*

Pagano v. Hadley, 100 F.R.D. 758 (D. Dela. 1984).

p. 142. *Delete the last line of the text on page 142, all of pages 143 and 144, and substitute the following:*

Prior to 1985, some churches argued that section 7605(c) prohibited any IRS examination of church records not undertaken to determine whether a church was engaged in an unrelated trade or business. While it is true that section

7605(c) was enacted primarily in response to the application of the unrelated business income tax to churches and religious organizations, it certainly did not suggest that churches and religious denominations could not be examined under any other circumstances. Churches and denominations, for example, remained liable for withholding and paying employment taxes on nonminister employees, and for the payment of certain excise taxes, and they were subject to the IRS examination power to ensure that they were properly complying with such requirements. Section 7605(c) did not negate such authority. On the contrary, the second sentence of that section specifically recognized the authority of the IRS to examine (1) the *religious activities* of a church or denomination to the extent necessary to determine if it were in fact entitled to tax-exempt status, and (2) the *books of account* of a church or denomination to the extent necessary "to determine the amount of tax imposed" under any internal revenue law (including income, employment, and excise taxes). The view that section 7605(c) acknowledged the preexisting authority of the IRS to examine the activities and records of churches and denominations to ensure compliance with income, employment, and excise taxes and entitlement to tax-exempt status was endorsed by the courts[58] and legislative history,[59] and was embodied in the income tax regulations.[60]

Section 7605(c) was criticized for its failure to provide adequate guidelines and for its insensitivity to the unique protections afforded churches by the First Amendment's free exercise of religion clause. Such criticism led to the repeal of section 7605(c) in the Tax Reform Act of 1984 and the enactment of the Church Audit Procedures Act as section 7611 of the Internal Revenue Code. Section 7611 imposes detailed limitations on IRS examinations of churches for tax years beginning in 1985 or thereafter. The limitations can be summarized as follows:

1. The IRS may begin a *church tax inquiry* (defined as any inquiry to determine whether a church is entitled to tax-exempt status as a church or is engaged in an unrelated trade or business) only if
   a. an *appropriate high-level Treasury official* (defined as a regional IRS commissioner or higher official) *reasonably believes* on the basis of written evidence that the church is not exempt[61] (by reason of its status as a church), may be carrying on an unrelated trade or business, or is otherwise engaged in activities subject to taxation; and
   b. the IRS sends the church written *inquiry notice* containing an explanation of
      (1) the specific concerns which gave rise to the inquiry,
      (2) the general subject matter of the inquiry, and
      (3) the provisions of the Internal Revenue Code that authorize the inquiry and the applicable administrative and constitutional provisions, in-

cluding the right to an informal conference with the IRS before any examination of church records, and the First Amendment principle of separation of church and state.

2. The IRS may begin a *church tax examination* of the church records or religious activities of a church only under the following conditions:

a. the requirements of a church tax inquiry have been met, and

b. an *examination notice* is sent by the IRS to the church at least fifteen days *after* the day on which the inquiry notice was sent, and at least fifteen days *before* the beginning of such an examination, containing the following information:

(1) a copy of the inquiry notice;

(2) a specific description of the church records and religious activities which the IRS seeks to examine;

(3) an offer to conduct an informal conference with the church to discuss and possibly resolve the concerns giving rise to the examination; and

(4) a copy of all documents collected or prepared by the IRS for use in the examination and the disclosure of which is required by the Freedom of Information Act.

3. *Church records* (defined as all corporate and financial records regularly kept by a church, including corporate minute books and lists of members and contributors) may be examined only to the extent necessary to determine the liability for and amount of any income, employment, or excise tax.

4. *Religious activities* may be examined only to the extent necessary to determine whether an organization claiming to be a church is in fact a church.

5. Church tax inquiries and church tax examinations must be completed *not later than two years* after the examination notice date.[62]

6. Church tax inquiries not followed by an examination notice must be completed *not later than ninety days* after the inquiry notice date.[63]

7. The IRS can make a determination based on a church tax inquiry or church tax examination that an organization is not a church that is exempt from federal income taxation or that is qualified to receive tax-deductible contributions, or that otherwise owes any income, employment, or excise tax (including the unrelated business income tax), only if the appropriate regional legal counsel of the IRS determines in writing that there has been substantial compliance with the limitations imposed under section 7611 and approves in writing of such revocation of exemption or assessment of tax.

8. Church tax examinations involving tax-exempt status or the liability for any tax other than the unrelated business income tax may be begun only for any one or more of the *three most recent taxable years* ending before the examination notice date. For examinations involving unrelated business taxable income, or if a church is proven not to be exempt for any of the preceding three years, the IRS may examine relevant records and assess tax as part of

the same audit for a total of *six years* preceding the examination notice date. For examinations involving issues other than revocation of exempt status or unrelated business taxable income (such as examinations pertaining to employment taxes), no limitation period applies if no return has been filed.

9. If any church tax inquiry or church tax examination is completed and does not result in a revocation of exemption or assessment of taxes, then no other church tax inquiry or church tax examination may begin with respect to such church *during the five-year period beginning on the examination notice date* (or the inquiry notice date if no examination notice was sent) unless such inquiry or examination is (a) approved in writing by the Assistant Commissioner of Employee Plans and Exempt Organizations of the IRS, or (b) does not involve the same or similar issues involved in the prior inquiry or examination. The five-year period is suspended if the two-year limitation on the completion of an examination is suspended.

10. The limitations upon church tax inquiries and church tax examinations do not apply to

   a. inquiries or examinations pertaining to organizations other than churches (*Churches* is defined by section 7611 as any organization claiming to be a church, and any convention or association of churches. The term does not include separately incorporated church-affiliated schools or other separately incorporated church-affiliated organizations.)

   b. any case involving a knowing failure to file a tax return or a willful attempt to defeat or evade taxes[63a]

   c. criminal investigations

   d. the tax liability of a contributor to a church, or inquiries regarding assignment of income to a church or a vow of poverty by an individual followed by a transfer of property

   e. routine IRS inquiries, including

      (1) the filing or failure to file any tax return or information return by the church;

      (2) compliance with income tax or FICA tax withholding;

      (3) supplemental information needed to complete the mechanical processing of any incomplete or incorrect return filed by a church;

      (4) information necessary to process applications for exempt status, letter ruling requests, or employment tax exempt requests; or

      (5) confirmation that a specific business is or is not owned by a church.

11. If the IRS has not complied substantially with (a) the notice requirements, (b) the requirement that an appropriate high-level Treasury official approve the commencement of a church tax inquiry, or (c) the requirement of informing the church of its right to an informal conference, the church's exclusive remedy is a stay of the inquiry or examination until such requirements are satisfied.

[58]*See, e.g.*, United States v. Coates, 692 F.2d 629 (9th Cir. 1982); United States v. Dykema, 666 F.2d 1096 (7th Cir. 1981); United States v. Life Science Church of America, 636 F.2d 221 (8th Cir. 1980); United States v. Holmes, 614 F.2d 985 (5th Cir. 1980); United States v. Freedom Church, 613 F.2d 316 (1st Cir. 1979).

[59]H.R. Rep. No. 413, 91st Cong., 1st Sess. (1969).

[60]Treas. Reg. § 301.7605-1(c).

[61]Since only organizations that are exempt from federal income tax ordinarily are qualified recipients of deductible charitable contributions, an IRS inquiry into the deductibility of contributions to a particular church is the equivalent of an inquiry into the church's tax-exempt status.

[62]The two-year limitation can be suspended (a) if the church brings a judicial proceeding against the IRS, (b) if the IRS brings a judicial proceeding to compel compliance by the church with any reasonable request for examination of church records or religious activities, (c) for any period in excess of twenty days (but not more than six months) in which the church fails to comply with any reasonable request by the IRS for church records, or (d) if the IRS and church mutually agree.

[63]The ninety-day limitation can be suspended for the same reasons listed in the preceding footnote.

[63a]The Conference Committee Report to the Tax Reform Act of 1984 contains the following information: "In Fiscal Year 1983, the IRS closed 6,612 examinations involving alleged church tax avoidance schemes, assessing $23,803,200 in taxes and penalties (an average assessment of $3,600 per return) and leaving a calendar year-end inventory of 15,296 church tax avoidance cases (in addition to approximately 200 criminal investigations). In the first six months of Fiscal 1984 alone . . . the IRS assessed $25,620,178 in taxes and penalties in 5,498 cases relating to church tax avoidance schemes. The conferees specifically intend that nothing in the church audit procedures will inhibit IRS inquiries, examinations, or criminal investigations of tax protestor or other tax avoidance schemes posing as religious organizations, including (but not limited to) tax avoidance schemes posing as mail-order ministries or storefront churches. . . ."

p. 145. *Delete the first line of the first complete paragraph and substitute the following:*

The fact that the IRS has the authority to examine *church records* and the

p. 145, note 64. *Add:*

The necessity test should apply to church inquiries or examinations conducted under section 7611 since the same language is employed.

p. 146. *Delete the second and third lines and the indented paragraph.*

p. 147. *Add after the first incomplete paragraph:*

The limitations of section 7611 may be illustrated by the following examples:

Example 1. First Church receives substantial rental income each year from several residential properties it owns in the vicinity of the church. The IRS has learned of the rental properties and would like to determine whether the church is engaged in an unrelated trade or business. It sends the church an inquiry notice in which the only explanation of the concerns giving rise to the inquiry is a statement that "you may be engaged in an unrelated trade or business." This inquiry notice is defective since it does not specify the activities which may result in unrelated business taxable income.

Example 2. The IRS receives a telephone tip that First Church may be engaged in an unrelated trade or business. A telephone tip cannot serve as the basis for a church tax inquiry since such an inquiry may commence only if an appropriate high-level Treasury official reasonably believes on the basis of written evidence that a church is not tax-exempt, is carrying on an unrelated trade or business, or otherwise is engaged in activities subject to taxation.

Example 3. The IRS sends First Church written notice of a church tax inquiry on March 1, 1985. On March 10, it sends written notice that it will examine designated church records on April 15. The examination notice is defective. While it was sent at least fifteen days before the beginning of the examination, it was sent less than fifteen days after the date the inquiry notice was sent. The church's only remedy is a stay of the examination until the IRS sends a valid examination notice.

Example 4. An IRS inquiry notice does not mention the possible application of the First Amendment principle of separation of church and state to church audits. Such a notice is defective. A church's only remedy is a stay of the inquiry until the IRS sends a valid inquiry notice.

Example 5. An IRS examination notice specifies that the "religious activities" of First Church will be examined as part of an investigation into a possible unrelated business income tax liability. Such an examination is inappropriate since the religious activities of a church may be examined by the IRS under section 7611 only to the extent necessary to determine if a church is in fact a bona fide church entitled to tax-exempt status.

Example 6. The IRS sends First Church written notice of a church tax inquiry on August 1, 1985. As of October 20, 1985, no examination notice had been sent. The church tax inquiry must be concluded by November 1, 1985.

Example 7. The IRS sends an examination notice to First Church on September 1, 1985. On November 1, as part of its examination, the IRS requests several documents that it reasonably believes are necessary. The church refuses to disclose the documents, and the IRS seeks a court order compelling disclosure. Such an order is issued on October 1, 1987. The two-year limitation on completing church examinations is suspended during the legal proceeding instituted by the IRS, and therefore the examination need not be terminated.

Example 8. In 1985, the IRS conducts an examination of the tax-exempt status of First Church. It concludes that the church was properly exempt from federal income taxation. In 1987, the IRS commences an examination of First Church to determine if it is engaged in an unrelated trade or business, and if it has been withholding taxes from nonminister employees. Such an examination is not barred by the prohibition against repeated examinations within a five-year period, since it does not involve the same or similar issues.

Example 9. First Church knowingly fails to withhold federal income taxes from wages paid to its nonminister employees despite its knowledge that it is legally required to do so. The limitations imposed upon the IRS by section 7611 do not apply.

Example 10. The IRS commences an examination of a separately incorporated private school that is controlled by First Church. The limitations of section 7611 do not apply.

p. 148. *Add after the last complete paragraph:*

A federal appeals court affirmed this determination on the grounds that (1) the government has a compelling interest in preventing the diversion of funds contributed for specific, identified purposes, especially when such funds are obtained through the use of the public airwaves, which, by congressional mandate, must be operated in the public interest; (2) the allegations of diversion of funds were made by a former employee and therefore they were entitled to a "greater inference of reliability"; (3) the government's investigation was narrow and avoided unnecessary interference with the free exercise of religion; and (4) the government's request for records was necessary to serve its compelling interest in investigating the alleged diversion of funds.[76a]

One court has held that the right to associational privacy extends to private lawsuits as well as governmental investigations, and thus a litigant has no right to compel disclosure of the membership list of a church unless he can establish a compelling state interest justifying disclosure.[76b]

[76a]Scott v. Rosenberg, 702 F.2d 1263 (9th Cir. 1983).
[76b]Church of Hakeem, Inc. v. Superior Court, 168 Cal. Rptr. 13 (1980).

p. 149. *Add after the first incomplete paragraph:*

As noted previously, section 7611 of the Internal Revenue Code defines those *church records* that are subject to the IRS subpoena power to include church membership and donor lists.

Finally, neither the Privacy Act of 1974 nor the Freedom of Information Act applies to church records.[77a]

[77a]*See generally* chapter 4, § D, *supra.*

p. 149. *Add after the last paragraph:*

This case is discussed in detail in another chapter.[80a]

[80a]*See* chapter 11, § A, *infra.*

p. 150. *Add after the first complete paragraph:*

This case is discussed in detail in another chapter.[81a]

[81a]*See* chapter 11, § A, *infra.*

p. 150. *Delete note 82 and substitute the following:*

[82]*See* chapters 11 and 18, *infra.*

p. 151. *Delete the caption "Pre-1984 Rules" just before the last incomplete paragraph.*

p. 151. *Delete the fifth line of the last incomplete paragraph and substitute the following:*

Churches are exempted from paying federal and state unemployment taxes on their

p. 151, note 86. *Add:*

See also chapter 10, § C, *infra.*

p. 152. *Change "941E" in the first incomplete and the first complete paragraphs to "941."*

p. 152. *Delete the last incomplete paragraph and substitute the following:*

Social security (FICA) taxes must also be withheld by employers from employee wages. The withheld taxes are combined with withheld income taxes, and they are reported and paid by the employer as summarized above. In general, the amount of social security taxes to be withheld for any payroll period is determined by multiplying the current FICA-Medicare combined tax rate times the employee's taxable wage base. A maximum annual taxable wage base is determined each year by the Secretary of the Department of Health and

Human Services. The employer is also responsible for paying an additional employer's FICA tax on behalf of each employee. The employer's and employee's FICA taxes were both 7.05% of taxable wages in 1985, and they are scheduled to increase progressively to 7.65% by 1990.

Until 1984, services performed in the employ of a church or other religious organization were excepted from liability for social security taxes, although a church or other religious organization could elect to extend social security coverage to its employees by filing Forms SS-15 and SS-15a with the IRS or by paying, either inadvertently or intentionally, social security taxes for at least three consecutive calendar quarters for any nonminister employee. In 1983, Congress removed the automatic exemption of churches and church employees from FICA coverage, effective January 1, 1984. The mandatory inclusion of churches and church employees in the social security program was criticized as a violation of the constitutional principle of separation of church and state, since churches were required to pay the FICA employer's tax to the federal government. Congress responded to this criticism in the Tax Reform Act of 1984 by giving churches and certain other religious organizations the right to waive mandatory inclusion in the FICA program by filing a waiver application (Form 8274) with the IRS before the deadline of the next Form 941 quarterly employer's tax return after October 17, 1984. For churches with nonminister employees, as of October 17, 1984, the waiver had to be filed before the deadline of the church's next Form 941 (October 31, 1984). For churches organized after October 30, 1984, or existing churches that retained their first nonminister employee after that date, the deadline for the waiver is the day before the due date of the first Form 941 that must be filed to report wages withheld from nonminister employees.

The waiver is available only to churches that are opposed to the payment of the employer's FICA tax on the basis of "religious reasons." Churches that file the election are exempted from payment of the employer's FICA tax, but all nonminister church employees thereafter are treated as self-employed for purposes of social security coverage. As a result, such employees must pay the self-employment tax (the social security tax for self-employed persons). The effective self-employment tax rate was 11.8% in 1985, and it progressively increases to 13.02% in 1989. Churches that file the waiver application use Form 941E to report withheld income taxes. The rules that apply to the exemption of churches and other religious organizations from mandatory social security coverage are complex, and they are discussed in detail in another chapter.[89a]

[89a]*See* chapter 10, § A, *infra*.

p. 153. *Delete the first incomplete and the first complete paragraphs.*

p. 153. *Delete the fourth complete paragraph and substitute the following:*

Although a church that has no nonminister employees is not required to withhold taxes or file a Form 941, it may wish to file a Form 941 each quarter if its minister is treated as an employee in order to reconcile the church's W-2 forms. Of course, this procedure must be followed if the minister has elected voluntary withholding.

p. 153. *Delete caption (b) and the last incomplete paragraph.*

p. 154. *Delete the first incomplete paragraph and the first and second complete paragraphs.*

§ D. Church Names

p. 158. *Add after the first complete paragraph:*

A local church congregation that votes to disaffiliate from a parent denomination may lose the right to use the denominational name. One court has observed:

> The local name of a church is of great value, not only because business is carried on and property held in that name, but also because millions of members associate with the name the most sacred of their personal relationships and the holiest of their family traditions. And, since the right to use the name inheres in the institution, not in its members . . . when they cease to be members of the institution, use by them of the name is misleading and, if injurious to the institution, should be enjoined.[103a]

[103a]Carnes v. Smith, 222 S.E.2d 322, 329 (Ga. 1976).

§ E. Officers, Directors, and Trustees

p. 159. *Delete the third sentence in the second complete paragraph under § E and substitute the following:*

Directors of church corporations occasionally are called trustees. This terminology is perfectly appropriate if it is intended to suggest that the business and spiritual oversight of the church is delegated "in trust" to such individuals, or where it is required by law.[105a] However, it often happens that such terminology is simply a holdover from a church's pre-incorporation status when title to church property was held in the name of church trustees. If this is the case, the continued use of the title *trustee* can be misleading.

Unincorporated churches that are required by law to hold title to church property in the name of trustees should add the words "or their successors" following the names of the church trustees in deeds, mortgages, and other legal documents of continuing relevance. Incorporated churches of course hold title to property in the name of the corporation. Incorporated churches that retain the use of the term *trustee* should be careful to refrain from listing the names of the trustees as either the transferor or transferee on a deed.

[105a]Osnes v. Morris, 298 S.E.2d 803 (W.Va. 1982).

p. 160, note 109. *Add:*

See also Trinity Pentecostal Church v. Terry, 660 S.W.2d 449 (Mo. App. 1983).

p. 160, note 110. *Add:*

See also Smith v. Riley, 424 So.2d 1166 (La. App. 1982).

p. 168. *Add after the third complete paragraph:*

The civil courts often have been called upon to review the removal from office of a church officer, director, or trustee. Most courts are willing to review such cases if no "strictly and purely ecclesiastical" question is presented. For example, the claim of a dismissed church director that his dismissal was not in accordance with the church's bylaws ordinarily is reviewable by a civil court. The authority of the courts to review church determinations is fully considered in another chapter.[143a]

[143a]*See* chapter 11, § J, *infra.*

§ F. Members

p. 171. *Delete the first three lines of the first complete paragraph and substitute the following:*

A majority of courts, however, have been willing to review church determinations involving members as long as no "strictly and purely ecclesiastical" question is presented. For example, the courts commonly review such determinations in the following situations: (1) if the church determination

p. 171. *Add after the first complete paragraph:*

The authority of the courts to review church determinations is fully considered elsewhere.[155a]

[155a]*See* chapter 8, § F.4, *infra*, and chapter 11, § J, *infra*.

p. 171, note 155. *Add:*

Smith v. Riley, 424 So.2d 1166 (La. App. 1982) (in the absence of any evidence to the contrary, the term *members* as used in a church charter included females).

p. 172. *Add after the first complete sentence:*

The United States Supreme Court similarly has observed that "[m]ajority rule is generally employed in the governance of religious societies."[157a]

[157a]Jones v. Wolf, 443 U.S. 595, 607 (1979).

p. 172. *Delete line 10 of the text and substitute the following:*

to adopt bylaws;[163] to authorize church activity and direct or control disposition of church property;[163a] and to select and remove a minister.[163b] The general authority possessed by the members of a

[163a]Pilgrim Evangelical v. Lutheran Church–Missouri Synod Foundation, 661 S.W.2d 833 (Mo. App. 1983).
[163b]LeBlanc v. Davis, 432 So.2d 239 (La. 1983).

p. 172. *Add after the first complete paragraph:*

On the other hand, while no court has so held, it would seem reasonable to regard a church's bylaws, like the United States Constitution, as a "delegated powers" instrument. The Tenth Amendment to the Constitution states that "[t]he powers not delegated to the United States by the Constitution, nor prohibited by it to the States, are reserved to the States, respectively, or to the people." In essence, the citizenry has delegated certain powers to the federal government in the Constitution, reserving unto itself all powers not expressly or impliedly delegated. Similarly, it could be said that the members who organize a church delegate various powers to the church and its officers, directors, and committees, and that any powers not specifically delegated are reserved unto the membership.

p. 172, note 161. *Add:*

Smith v. Lewis, 578 S.W.2d 169 (Tex. App. 1979).

p. 172, note 162. *Add:*

Foss v. Dykstra, 342 N.W.2d 220 (S.D. 1983).

p. 172, note 163. *Add:*

First Baptist Church v. State of Ohio, 591 F. Supp. 676 (S.D. Ohio 1983).

p. 172, note 164. *Add:*

See also Smith v. Lewis, 578 S.W.2d 169 (Tex. App. 1979).

p. 172, note 165. *Add:*

First Baptist Church v. State of Ohio, 591 F. Supp. 676 (S.D. Ohio 1983).

p. 175, note 181. *Add:*

First Baptist Church v. State of Ohio, 591 F. Supp. 676 (S.D. Ohio 1983); Church of God in Christ, Inc. v. Stone, 452 F. Supp. 612 (D. Kan. 1976); Chavis v. Rowe, 459 A.2d 674 (N.J. 1983); African Methodist Episcopal Zion Church v. Union Chapel A.M.E. Zion Church, 308 S.E.2d 73 (N.C. App. 1983).

p. 176, note 189. *Add:*

First Baptist Church v. State of Ohio, 591 F. Supp. 676 (S.D. Ohio 1983).

p. 176, note 190. *Add:*

LeBlanc v. Davis, 432 So.2d 239 (La. 1983); Wilkerson v. Battiste, 393 So.2d 195 (La. App. 1980).

p. 177, note 196. *Add:*

First Baptist Church v. State of Ohio, 591 F. Supp. 676 (S.D. Ohio 1983) (noting that the "higher burden of proof typically applied to cases of fraud" is applicable); Hatcher v. South Carolina District Council of the Assemblies of God, Inc., 226 S.E.2d 253 (S.C. 1976).

p. 178. *Add after the first incomplete paragraph:*

The authority of the civil courts to review church determinations is considered fully in another chapter.[203a]

[203a] *See* chapter 11, § J, *infra.*

p. 178, note 200. *Add:*

See generally W. TORPEY, JUDICIAL DOCTRINES OF RELIGIOUS RIGHTS IN AMERICA (1948) (while this text is obsolete in most particulars, it presents a principled analysis that is of continuing utility); Bernard, *Churches, Members and the Role of the Courts,* 51 NOTRE DAME LAWYER 545 (April 1976) (provides useful suggestions regarding judicial involvement in church membership determinations).

p. 179. *Add after the indented paragraph in the text:*

In a subsequent decision, the Court apparently limited the rule of judicial deference to the determinations of hierarchical church tribunals to those determinations involving "religious doctrine or polity."[205a]

[205a]Jones v. Wolf, 443 U.S. 595 (1979).

p. 179, note 204. *Add:*

First Baptist Church v. State of Ohio, 591 F. Supp. 676 (S.D. Ohio 1983).

p. 181. *Add after the first complete paragraph:*

Members who are expelled from a church ordinarily are no longer responsible for the church's debts and liabilities.[212a]

[212a]Smith v. Lewis, 578 S.W.2d 169 (Tex. App. 1979).

§ G. Meetings

p. 183, note 222. *Add:*

Brooks v. January, 321 N.W.2d 823 (Mich. App. 1982); Old Folks Mission Center v. McTizic, 631 S.W.2d 433 (Tenn. 1981).

p. 185. *Delete the third line of the second complete paragraph and substitute the following:*

meeting regardless of age[230] or sex.[230a] And, where the signing of a church's bylaws was

[230a]Smith v. Riley, 424 So.2d 1166 (La. App. 1982).

p. 186. *Add after the second complete paragraph:*

If a church's charter, constitution, or bylaws do not designate the required percentage of votes for an affirmative action, then there is a presumption of majority rule. The United States Supreme Court has observed that "[m]ajority rule is generally employed in the governance of religious societies."[233a] Other courts have similarly held that majority representation is presumed to apply to church determinations unless such a presumption is overcome by express provision in the church's organizational documents, or by a provision in the constitution or bylaws of a parent denomination.[233b]

[233a]Jones v. Wolf, 443 U.S. 595, 607 (1979).
[233b]Foss v. Dykstra, 342 N.W.2d 220 (S.D. 1983).

p. 188. *Add after the first incomplete paragraph:*

Once it is determined that a particular body of parliamentary procedure has been adopted by a church, the civil courts have expressed willingness to apply and enforce that procedure on the ground that no doctrine or substantive ecclesiastical question is involved.[241a]

[241a]Umberger v. Johns, 363 So.2d 63 (Fla. App. 1978).

p. 188, note 242. *Add:*

Old Folks Mission Center v. McTizic, 631 S.W.2d 433 (Tenn. 1981).

p. 189. *Add after the second complete paragraph:*

7. SUNSHINE LAWS

Who is entitled to be present at a church meeting? Who may lawfully be excluded? These questions often cause confusion, particularly in the context of schismatic churches in which one or more factions desire to prevent attorneys, news media personnel, or members of the public from attending. The following considerations will determine to what extent a church can exclude nonmembers from attending church membership meetings:

First, the charter, constitution, and bylaws of the church should be consulted to determine if they address the question. Ordinarily, they do not.

Second, determine what body of parliamentary procedure has been adopted by the church. Many systems of parliamentary procedure permit nonmembers to be excluded from a membership meeting. One authority states the rule as follows:

Nonmembers, on the other hand—or a particular nonmember or group of nonmembers—can be excluded any time from part or all of a meeting of a society, or from all of its meetings. Such exclusion can be effected by a ruling of the chair in cases of disorder, or by the adoption of a rule on the subject, or by an appropriate motion as the need arises—a motion of the latter nature being a question of privilege.[250a]

Third, many states and the federal government have enacted public meeting laws which generally provide that meetings of specified governmental agencies, commissions, and boards, at which official acts are taken, must be open to the public. Such laws, often called sunshine acts, ordinarily do not apply to private, nonprofit organizations,[250b] and they certainly do not apply to entities, such as churches, receiving no tax revenues and having no regulatory authority or relationship with any governmental body. The fact that a church is incorporated will not subject it to the provisions of public meeting laws.[250c]

[250a]Robert's Rules of Order, Newly Revised § 60 (1970).

[250b]See, e.g., Marston v. Wood, 425 So.2d 582 (Fla. App. 1982) (public meeting law did not apply to a law school committee organized to select a new dean); Perlongo v. Iron River Co-op TV Antenna Corp., 332 N.W.2d 502 (Mich. App. 1983) (state public meeting law did not apply to a nonprofit, nonstock corporation).

[250c]Perlongo v. Iron River Co-op TV Antenna Corp., 332 N.W.2d 502 (Mich. App. 1983).

p. 189, note 249. *Add:*

LeBlanc v. Davis, 432 So.2d 239 (La. 1983); Rector, Church Wardens and Vestrymen of St. Bartholomew's Church v. Committee to Preserve St. Bartholomew's Church, 56 N.Y.2d 71 (1982).

§ H. Powers

p. 190. *Add note 251a at the end of the first incomplete paragraph:*

[251a]See, e.g., Jacobs v. St. Mark's Baptist Church, 415 So.2d 253 (La. App. 1982).

p. 190, note 254. *Add:*

Babcock Memorial Presbyterian Church v. Presbytery of Baltimore, 464 A.2d 1008 (Md. App. 1983); Old Folks Mission Center v. McTizic, 631 S.W.2d 433 (Tenn. 1981).

p. 191, note 261. *Add:*

Babcock Memorial Presbyterian Church v. Presbytery of Baltimore, 464 A.2d 1008 (Md. App. 1983).

§ I. Merger and Consolidation

p. 193. *Add after the third complete paragraph:*

However, an unincorporated church and an incorporated church will not be permitted to merge under a state nonprofit law requiring that both of the merging churches be incorporated.[268a]

[268a]Trinity Pentecostal Church v. Terry, 660 S.W.2d 449 (Mo. App. 1983).

p. 197. *Add note 278a at the end of the first complete paragraph:*

[278a]*See, e.g.,* Presbytery of the Covenant v. First Presbyterian Church, 552 S.W.2d 865 (Tex. App. 1977).

p. 197. *Add after the last complete paragraph in the text:*

However, one court held that riots and violence within a church that lasted for only two weeks was not a frustration of the church's purposes and did not constitute an adequate basis for involuntary dissolution.[281a]

[281a]Hill v. Abyssinia Missionary Baptist Church, 370 So.2d 389 (Ala. 1979).

9

CHURCH PROPERTY DISPUTES

p. 210. *Insert a "3." before the first complete paragraph.*

p. 210. *Add at the end of "Method 3" in the text:*

Method 4. Civil courts may resolve the dispute on the basis of any other methodology that they may devise "so long as it involves no consideration of doctrinal matters, whether the ritual and liturgy of worship or the tenets of faith."[37a]

[37a]*See* note 33, *supra.*

p. 213. *Add after the last complete paragraph in the text:*

Nevertheless, a majority of courts have either adopted the principle of *Jones* that the compulsory deference rule is limited to "issues of religious doctrine or polity,"[44a] or have applied a neutral principles approach to the resolution of church property disputes involving hierarchical churches.[44b]

[44a]*See, e.g.,* Graffam v. Wray, 437 A.2d 627 (Me. 1981); Beaver-Butler Presbytery v. Middlesex Presbyterian Church, 489 A.2d 1317 (Pa. 1985).

[44b]*See, e.g.,* Bishop and Diocese of Colorado v. Mote, 668 P.2d 948 (Colo. App. 1983); Grutka v. Clifford, 445 N.E.2d 1015 (Ind. App. 1983); Foss v. Dykstra, 319 N.W.2d 499 (S.D. 1982).

p. 213, note 44. *Add:*

Townsend v. Teagle, 467 So.2d 772 (Fla. App. 1985); First Presbyterian Church v. United Presbyterian Church in the United States, 461 N.Y.S.2d 903 (1983) (dissenting justice urged adherence to *Jones*); Church of God v. Noel, 318 S.E.2d 920 (W. Va. 1984) (dissenting justice urged adherence to *Jones*).

p. 214. *Add after § 1.c:*

Alternatively, a reverter clause could specify that a church's property immediately reverts to a parent religious body upon an attempted conveyance of property by the church. Such a provision would prevent a church from deleting a reverter clause in its deed by reconveying property to itself, either outright or through an intermediary, by a deed not containing the reverter clause. However, it must be recognized that any reverter clause conditioned on an attempted conveyance of church property would automatically vest title in a parent denomination upon *any* attempted conveyance, even those unrelated to a disaffiliation. Most conveyances of church property are not associated with a disaffiliation. Rather, they are prompted by a desire for a new location or a larger facility. But unless the church obtains a written release or renunciation of the reverter clause from the parent denomination and has it recorded in the office of the recorder of deeds for the county in which the property is located, the property will automatically revert to the denomination whenever a church conveys its property. Alternatively, in many states the parent denomination could execute a quitclaim deed in favor of the local church. The parent denomination of course could condition the execution of a release or quitclaim deed upon the inclusion of a reverter clause in the deed by which the local church receives title to its new property.

A church deed could contain a reverter clause conditioned on either an attempted conveyance of church property or disaffiliation. Such a clause presumably would be effective if it involved no interpretation of church doctrine.

A church whose property is held subject to a reversion in favor of a parent religious body, whether through a provision in a deed, charter, bylaw, or constitution, ordinarily is not permitted to borrow money from a commercial lending institution unless the parent body signs a "subordination agreement" agreeing to subordinate its interests under the reversionary clause to the mortgage securing the lender's loan. If such an agreement is not signed, a church mortgage may inadvertently trigger the reverter clause in favor of the parent religious body since a mortgage constitutes a conveyance of a church's legal or equitable interest in its property to the lending institution (or, in the case of a deed of trust, to a trustee) until such time as the loan is repaid. In addition, any attempt by the lender to foreclose on a church mortgage may also inadvertently trigger the reverter clause. Many commercial lending institutions remain unaware of the danger of failing to secure a subordination agreement from the beneficiary of a reverter clause.

p. 215. *Add after the indented paragraph:*

Section 2503 of the *Book of Discipline* similarly requires that the following "trust clause" be incorporated in any deed transferring real estate to a church:

> In trust, that said premises shall be used, kept, and maintained as a place of divine worship of the United Methodist ministry and members of the United Methodist Church; subject to the Discipline, usage, and ministerial appointments of said church as from time to time authorized and declared by the General Conference and by the Annual Conference within whose bounds the said premises are situated. This provision is solely for the benefit of the grantee, and the grantor reserves no right or interest in said premises.

p. 215. *Add at the end of § 2:*

Churches that receive title to property subject to an express trust ordinarily must release the trust when the property is sold. For example, if a deed to church property specifies that the property is held by the church in trust for the use and benefit of a particular denomination, this trust attaches to the property and must be released upon a sale of the property in order to relieve the transferee of the terms of the trust.

p. 216. *Add after the first complete paragraph:*

6. *Resulting trusts.* In many states, a "resulting trust" arises by operation of law in favor of the person who purchases property in the name of another. The law presumes that it ordinarily is not the intention of a person paying for property to make a gift to the one receiving title. This presumption is rebuttable, however. Similarly, if a person contributes only a part of the purchase price of a piece of property placed in the name of another, a resulting trust will arise in favor of the payor on a prorata basis. In such cases, however, the courts often require the payor to demonstrate the precise percentage he contributed toward the entire purchase price.

A local church that acquires property because of the contributions of a parent church body may hold title subject to a resulting trust in favor of the parent body in proportion to the parent's contribution. For example, a parent body contributing all or substantially all of the funds used to purchase a local church property should be entitled to the benefit of a resulting trust interest in the entire property.[46a]

7. *Constructive trusts.* A constructive trust may be imposed whenever it is established that one person holds property which in equity and good conscience should be held by another. A constructive trust may arise as a result of several factors, including misrepresentation, failure to use property or funds for stated

purposes, refusal to carry out the terms of an express trust, frustration of the terms of a will, or wrongful conveyance of another's property. It is possible for the law of constructive trusts to apply to church property so long as no inquiries into church doctrine or polity are involved.[46b]

8. *Arbitration.* A church could insert a provision in its charter, constitution, or bylaws specifying that any dispute concerning title to any of its properties will be resolved through binding arbitration. Such provisions occasionally are contained in the organizational documents of nonprofit corporations, and they ordinarily are upheld as binding agreements on the part of the membership.

9. *Buy-sell agreements.* A buy-sell, or "preemption," agreement requires the owner of a specified tract of property to offer the property to a designated person at a stipulated price before selling it to another. Religious denominations wanting to maintain control over the property of dissident churches could require churches to execute such an agreement, giving the parent denomination a preemptive right to purchase the church's property at a specified price at or below market value. Such an agreement obviously would be of no value unless a dissident church wanted to sell its property. Alternatively, a denomination could enter into a purchase agreement with a local church giving the denomination the right to purchase the church's property in the event of a disaffiliation. Such agreements, if supported by adequate consideration, ordinarily will be enforceable.[46c]

[46a]Grace Evangelical Lutheran Church v. Lutheran Church–Missouri Synod, 454 N.E.2d 1038 (Ill. App. 1983).

[46b]*Id.*

[46c]*Id.*

10

THE CHURCH AS EMPLOYER

§ A. Income Taxation

p. 221. *Delete the first line of the last paragraph and substitute the following:*

In summary, the wages of nonministerial church employees and ministers who have requested voluntary withholding are subject to

p. 221, note 5. *Add:*

Schultz v. Stark, 554 F. Supp. 1219 (D. Wis. 1983) (constitutional right to freedom of religion not abridged by mandatory withholding of taxes from the wages of employees of a religious order).

p. 222. *Delete line 5 of the text and substitute the following:*

managers, or to teachers in a private school operated by a church, provided that such persons do not satisfy the definition of a "common law employee" (discussed in chapter 1). However, a person who is paid by the job rather than by the hour, and who decides when and how to perform the work, ordinarily will be considered to be an independent contractor. For example, a church custodian who is paid a flat fee each month to perform a church's custodial work, and who is free to determine his own hours, ordinarily will be considered to be an independent contractor. Churches are under no legal obligation to withhold income or social security taxes from compensation paid to independent contractors, since such persons are considered to be self-employed for tax purposes. The IRS

p. 222. *Delete the first line of the first complete paragraph and substitute the following:*

If a church has nonministerial employees to whom it pays wages, or if its minister has requested a voluntary withholding arrangement, the following

p. 223. *Delete paragraphs numbered "5" and "6" on pages 223 and 224, and substitute the following:*

5. *Until 1984*, churches that were exempt from social security and that withheld federal income taxes from the wages of any employees filed quarterly returns with the IRS on Form 941E (Quarterly Return of Withheld Federal Income Taxes). Form 941E reported income taxes withheld from employee wages. It was due on April 30, July 31, October 31, and the following January 31 of each year. Churches with less than $500 of withheld income taxes at the end of any calendar quarter simply submitted the taxes each quarter with their Form 941E. Employers with withheld taxes of $500 but less than $3,000 at the end of any month deposited the taxes with an authorized financial institution by the fifteenth day of the following month. Employers with withheld taxes of $3,000 or more at the end of any "eighth-monthly" period (eighth-monthly periods end on the 3rd, 7th, 11th, 15th, 19th, 22nd, 25th, and last day of each month) deposited the taxes with an authorized financial institution within three banking days after the close of the eighth-monthly period. All deposits with authorized financial institutions had to be accompanied by a federal tax deposit form. Employers that were subject to the deposit rules still had to file quarterly returns on Form 941E. Churches could waive their exemption from social security coverage by filing a Form SS-15 and a Form SS-15a with the IRS. Churches that inadvertently paid social security taxes for at least three consecutive calendar quarters on any nonministerial employees were deemed to have filed Forms SS-15 and SS-15a. Churches that waived their exemption from social security coverage were permitted to revoke their waiver by giving written notice two years in advance of the proposed date of revocation, provided that their waiver certificate was in effect for not less than eight years. Churches that waived their exemption from social security had to withhold social security taxes as well as income taxes from nonministerial employee wages. Churches that waived their exemption were required to file their quarterly returns on Form 941 rather than Form 941E.

6. *Since 1983*, churches and their nonminister employees have been automatically subject to the social security (FICA) tax unless the church elects to become exempt from the employer's FICA tax liability by filing an exemption application (Form 8274) with the IRS. The exemption is available only to those churches that are opposed for religious reasons to the payment of social security

taxes, and that file the exemption application within the time limit prescribed by law. These rules are considered fully in the next section of the present chapter. Churches that file the application will be exempted from the payment of the employer's share of FICA taxes, but its employees will be treated as self-employed for social security purposes. This means that the employee will be responsible for estimating and prepaying the self-employment tax through use of the estimated tax procedure (Form 1040-ES). Alternatively, an employee could request that an additional amount be withheld from his wages to cover the estimated self-employment tax liability.[7a] Unless an employee makes such a request, however, a church that has elected to exempt itself from the payment of FICA taxes has no obligation to withhold social security taxes from the wages of its employees. Churches that do not file a timely exemption application are automatically subject to the payment of FICA taxes, and in addition must withhold and pay FICA taxes on the wages of all nonminister employees. The amount of social security tax to be withheld from a particular employee's wages is determined by multiplying the current FICA-Medicare combined tax rate by the employee's taxable wage base. A maximum taxable wage base is determined each year by the Secretary of the Department of Health and Human Services on the basis of wage indexes. The projected combined FICA-Medicare tax rates based on the 1983 Social Security Act amendments are as follows:

	Tax on Employee	Tax on Employer
1985	7.05%	7.05%
1986	7.15%	7.15%
1987	7.15%	7.15%
1988	7.51%	7.51%
1989	7.51%	7.51%
1990	7.65%	7.65%

The church must withhold the employee's social security tax from each wage payment. Churches not filing a timely exemption application must use Form 941 rather than Form 941E in reporting income and social security taxes withheld from employee wages. The pre-1984 deposit rules discussed above generally apply after 1984. Congress of course may amend the amount of withheld taxes that will trigger the monthly or eighth-monthly deposit rules, so these rules should be checked at least annually.

[7a]Treas. Reg. 31.3402(i)-2.

p. 225. Delete § B and substitute the following:

§ B. Social Security Taxes

Since the beginning of the social security program in 1937, the employees of churches and most other nonprofit organizations were exempted from mandatory coverage.[10] The exemption was designed to encourage nonprofit enterprises by freeing them from an additional tax burden that they ordinarily could not pass along to customers through price increases.[11] Churches and other nonprofit organizations were permitted to waive their exemption by filing Forms SS-15 and SS-15a with the IRS.[11a]

In 1983, Congress repealed the exemption for calendar years beginning with 1984. The repeal of the exemption was controversial with many church leaders because it required churches to report and pay the employer's share of social security (FICA) taxes. This "tax on churches" was denounced by some as a violation of the constitutional principle of separation of church and state. Several clergymen publicly defied the law and declared that their churches would not comply.

In the Tax Reform Act of 1984, Congress responded to such criticism by again amending the Social Security Act, this time to give churches a one-time irrevocable election to exempt themselves from social security coverage.[11b] The election is claimed by filing a Form 8274 (reproduced at the end of this chapter) with the IRS prior to the first date more than ninety days after the enactment date of the Tax Reform Act of 1984 (July 17, 1984) on which a church's quarterly tax return (Form 941) reporting the employer's share of social security taxes is due or would be due but for the election. Since an employer's quarterly tax return is due on the last day of the month following the end of each calendar quarter (i.e., April 30, July 31, October 31, and January 31), the election application for churches in existence on July 17, 1984, was due prior to October 31, 1984 (the due date of the first employer's quarterly tax return following ninety days after the enactment date).

The ninety-day period has relevance only for churches that were organized prior to July 31, 1984. To illustrate, a church organized on August 15, 1984, and that has nonminister employees must have filed an election prior to October 31, 1984. A church organized on October 15, 1984, and that has nonminister employees, must have filed an election prior to January 31, 1985. A church organized on June 1, 1985, must have filed the election prior to July 31, 1985.

It must be emphasized that there is no deadline until a church has nonminister employees, since the deadline corresponds to the next filing date of a church's quarterly tax return reporting the employer's share of social security taxes, and no tax or return is due until a church has nonminister employees. Churches with no nonminister employees but whose minister has elected voluntary withholding of income taxes are required by law to file the quarterly Form 941. However, they do not report the employer's share of FICA taxes on the form since a minister in the exercise of his ministry is never considered to be an employee for social security purposes. Therefore, the deadline for filing the election is not triggered.

Clearly, the deadline rules will work a hardship on many new churches that in some cases will be required to file an election in a matter of a few days or weeks following their organization. Many churches will inadvertently fail to file the election before the deadline. The arbitrarily short deadline renders this provision suspect under the due process and free exercise of religion clauses of the federal Constitution. It is doubtful that the federal government can condition the enjoyment of constitutionally protected interests such as the free exercise of religion upon such an arbitrary and unreasonable election deadline.

The effect of the election is to have all church employees treated as self-employed for purposes of social security. This means that church employees will be required to use the estimated tax procedure (Form 1040-ES) to report and pay their estimated self-employment tax in quarterly installments. It also means that church employees will have to pay the entire self-employment tax themselves. The self-employment tax rates are substantial, and range from 14.1% in 1985 (with an offsetting credit of 2.3%) to 15.02% in 1989 (with a 2% credit). The nonminister employees of churches not filing a timely election are automatically subject to social security coverage as self-employed individuals, and they are liable for the self-employment tax on annual compensation in excess of $100. Since ministers are treated as self-employed in the exercise of their ministry, they are not affected by a church's failure to file a timely election.

The election, once claimed, is irrevocable, and applies to all present and future employees. It also covers all services performed after December 31, 1983. This means that a church that filed an election prior to October 31, 1984, was considered to be exempt from social security coverage for all of 1984. Churches that paid social security taxes earlier in 1984 could receive a full refund of such taxes (without interest) if they agreed to pay to their present and former employees that portion of the refund attributable to their share of social security taxes.

Churches that file a timely election application remain subject to income tax withholding and reporting requirements with respect to all nonminister employees and to ministers who have requested voluntary withholding. They must continue to issue W-2 forms to all nonminister employees and to ministers who are treated as employees for income tax purposes and who have requested voluntary withholding. In addition, they must file the employer's quarterly federal tax return with the IRS. Form 941E is the appropriate quarterly return for churches that have filed a timely election to be exempt from social security coverage. Other churches should use Form 941. The law specifies that the IRS can revoke a church's exemption from social security coverage if the church fails to issue W-2 forms for a period of two years or more to nonminister employees and to ministers who have requested voluntary withholding.

Only churches that are opposed "for religious reasons" to the payment of social security taxes are eligible for the exemption. Apparently, a local church will qualify for the exemption if it is opposed for religious reasons to the payment of social security taxes even if it is affiliated with a religious denomination that has no official position on the subject.[11c] Churches, conventions or associations of churches, and elementary and secondary schools that are controlled, operated, or principally supported by a church are all eligible for the exemption. "Qualified church-controlled organizations" also are eligible for the exemption. Such organizations are defined as any church-controlled tax-exempt organization described in section 501(c)(3) of the Internal Revenue Code except for organizations that (1) offer goods, services, or facilities for sale, other than on an incidental basis, to the general public, other than goods, services, or facilities which are sold at a nominal charge which is substantially less than the cost of providing such goods, services, or facilities; and (2) normally receive more than twenty-five percent of their support from either (a) governmental sources, or (b) receipts from admissions, sales of merchandise, performance of services, or furnishing of facilities, in activities that are not unrelated trades or businesses, or both.[11d]

The election is available to a church even if it waived its exemption from social security coverage prior to 1984 by filing Forms SS-15 and SS-15a. Of course, not many churches in good faith could certify that they were opposed on religious grounds to the payment of social security taxes if they previously waived their exemption from mandatory social security coverage. Furthermore, most churches that filed Forms SS-15 and SS-15a prior to 1984 had employees in 1984. As a result, they had to file their elections on or before the initial deadline of October 30, 1984.

The constitutionality of the election procedure has been challenged in a federal court proceeding on the ground that churches electing to be exempt from FICA coverage in effect continue to pay social security taxes because of the increased salaries that ordinarily must be paid to employees to compensate for their liability for the higher self-employment tax. In enacting the 1984 Tax Reform Act, Congress made no judgment concerning the constitutionality of the 1983 amendments that had eliminated entirely any exemption for churches and other religious organizations. The report of the joint House-Senate conference committee to which the 1984 Act was assigned states:

> The conferees agreed to the amendment in order to provide mandatory coverage under social security for employees of churches and at the same time allow the religious convictions of certain employing churches to be reflected in the choice not to be subject to the employer tax. In adapting the amendment, it is not the

intention of the conferees to express an opinion on the constitutionality of the original coverage provision of the 1983 amendments.[11e]

The rules summarized in this section are illustrated by the following examples:

Example 1. A church had two nonminister employees for all of 1984. The church had until October 30, 1984, to file Form 8274.

Example 2. A church was organized in 1960. It has no nonminister employees, but since 1981 its minister has requested voluntary withholding. The church's deadline for filing Form 8274 has not expired since it has no nonminister employees and therefore is not required to report FICA taxes on Form 941. The minister is treated as self-employed for social security purposes.

Example 3. A church was organized in May 1985. It employs a full-time office secretary as well as its minister. It had until July 30, 1985, to file Form 8274.

Example 4. A church files a timely Form 8274. It should use Form 941E rather than Form 941 to report withheld income taxes to the IRS.

Example 5. A church with two nonminister employees files a timely election. The church's employees are treated as self-employed for purposes of social security coverage. The employees must estimate and prepay their self-employment tax by using Form 1040-ES and submitting quarterly payment vouchers to the IRS. The employees do not use the FICA employee tax rate.

Example 6. A church having one nonminister employee filed a timely election in 1984. In 1985, it hired a second employee. The second employee automatically is treated as self-employed for purposes of social security coverage.

Example 7. A church with three nonminister employees filed a timely election in 1984. The church does not issue its employees W-2 forms. The IRS can revoke the church's exemption from social security taxes if the church neglects to issue W-2 forms for a period of two years and disregards an IRS request to furnish employees with such forms for the period during which its election has been in effect.

Example 8. A church having two nonminister employees filed a timely election in 1984. In 1986, it opens an elementary school that is controlled and operated by the church. The school's employees are covered by the church's exemption.

Example 9. An evangelistic association has a staff of four nonminister employees. It cannot file an election unless it is controlled by a church and normally receives less than twenty-five percent of its support from admissions receipts, sales of merchandise, performance of services, or furnishing of facilities other than in an unrelated trade or business.

Example 10. A theological seminary would like to exempt itself from social security coverage. It can do so if it is controlled by a church or convention or association of churches and it is exempt from federal income taxation under section 501(c)(3) of the Internal Revenue Code.

[10]*See* I.R.C. § 3121(b)(8)(B) prior to its deletion by the 1983 amendments. In explaining the purpose of this exemption, one court observed: "Congress chose not to place the onus of participation in the old-age and survivor insurance program upon the churches, but to permit ministers to be covered on an individual election basis, as self-employed, whether, in fact, they were employees or actually self-employed." Silvey v. Commissioner, 35 T.C.M. 1812 (1976). Of course, with the repeal of this provision, there is no longer any basis for the irrebuttable presumption that ministers are self-employed for social security purposes with respect to services performed in the exercise of their ministry.

[11]Jones v. Better Business Bureau, Inc., 123 F.2d 767 (10th Cir. 1948).

[11a]*See* I.R.C. § 3121(k)(1).

[11b]I.R.C. § 3121(w). It is interesting to note that § 3121(w) conditions the exemption on religious objection to the *payment* of social security taxes, whereas § 1402(e) conditions the ministerial exemption from social security coverage on religious objection to the *receipt of social security benefits.* This difference of course was necessitated in part by the fact that churches receive no benefits under the social security system and accordingly cannot be opposed to the receipt of benefits. On the other hand, many ministers who file for exemption do so because of opposition to the *payment* of social security taxes, and not because of opposition to the receipt of social security benefits.

[11c]*See* Grant.v. Spellman, 664 P.2d 1227 (Wash. 1983).

[11d]I.R.C. § 3121(w)(3)(B).

[11e]H.R. REP. NO. 861, 98TH CONG., 2D SESS. (1984).

p. 226. *Delete § C and substitute the following:*

§ C. Unemployment Taxes

Congress enacted the Federal Unemployment Tax Act in 1935 in response to the widespread unemployment that accompanied the great depression. The Act called for a cooperative federal-state program of benefits to unemployed workers. It is financed by a federal excise tax on wages paid by employers in covered employment. An employer, however, is allowed a credit of up to ninety percent of the federal tax for "contributions" paid to a state fund established under a federally approved state unemployment compensation law. All fifty states have employment security laws implementing the federal mandatory minimum standards of coverage. States are free to expand their coverage beyond the federal minimum.

From 1960 to 1970, the Act unrestrictedly excluded from the definition of covered employment all "service performed in the employ of a religious, charitable, educational, or other organization described in section 501(c)(3) which is exempt from income tax under section 501(a)."[12] A 1970 amendment in effect narrowed this broad exemption of nonprofit organizations by conditioning federal approval of *state* compensation plans on the coverage of all nonprofit organizations except those specifically exempted. The Act was then amended to exempt service performed

> (1) in the employ of (A) a church or convention or association of churches, or (B) an organization which is operated primarily for religious purposes and which is operated, supervised, controlled, or principally supported by a church or convention or association of churches; (2) a duly ordained, commissioned, or licensed minister of a church in the exercise of his ministry or by a member of a religious order in the exercise of duties required by such order; (3) in the employ of a school which is not an institution of higher education.[13]

The Act continues the exemption of "service performed in the employ of a religious . . . organization" from the federal tax. Thus, while the exemption afforded religious organizations under federal law remains broad, the requirement imposed upon states has been significantly narrowed.

In 1976, Congress eliminated the exemption of services performed "in the employ of a school which is not an institution of higher education" from the categories of employment that could be exempted from coverage under state programs without loss of federal approval. In 1978 the Secretary of the Department of Labor announced that the elimination of this exemption required mandatory coverage of all the employees of church-related schools. This ruling was followed by many states, prompting a number of lawsuits.

In 1981, the United States Supreme Court ruled that the elimination of service performed "in the employ of a school which is not an institution of higher education" did *not* require the coverage of the employees of unincorporated church-related schools, since the continuing exemption of church employees was broad enough to cover the employees of unincorporated church-controlled elementary and secondary schools.[13a] The Court concluded that the employees of separately incorporated church schools are exempt from coverage only if the school is operated primarily for religious purposes and is operated, supervised, controlled, or principally supported by a church or convention or association of churches.[13b] One state court has held that these additional requirements are unconstitutional as applied to interdenominational religious schools, for they improperly favor religious schools linked with established schools or denominations over those that are not.[13c]

In summary, the following activities are exempt from state unemployment taxes:

1. Service performed in the employ of a church, a convention or association of churches, or an organization that is operated primarily for religious purposes and that is operated, supervised, controlled, or principally supported by a

church or convention or association of churches. The exemption is not limited to employees performing strictly "religious" duties.[13d]

2. Service performed in the employ of an unincorporated church-controlled elementary or secondary school.[13e] This exemption may apply to some interdenominational religious schools.[13f]

3. Service performed in the employ of an incorporated religious elementary or secondary school if it is operated primarily for religious purposes and is operated, supervised, controlled, or principally supported by a church or a convention or association of churches.[13g]

4. Service performed by a duly ordained, commissioned, or licensed minister of a church in the exercise of his ministry or by a member of a religious order in the exercise of duties required by such order.

[12]I.R.C. § 3306(c)(8).

[13]I.R.C. § 3309(b).

[13a]St. Martin Evangelical Lutheran Church v. South Dakota, 451 U.S. 772 (1981). *Accord* Community Lutheran School v. Iowa Department of Job Service, 326 N.W.2d 286 (Iowa 1982); Employment Security Administration v. Baltimore Lutheran High School Association, 436 A.2d 481 (Md. 1981); Ursuline Academy, Inc. v. Director of Division of Employment Security, 420 N.E.2d 326 (Mass. 1981).

[13b]*Id.* at 620 n.12.

[13c]Salem College and Academy v. Employment Division, 659 P.2d 415 (Or. App. 1983).

[13d]Hickey v. District of Columbia Department of Employment Service, 448 A.2d 871 (D.C. App. 1982).

[13e]*See* note 13a, *supra.*

[13f]*See* note 13c, *supra.*

[13g]*See* note 13a, *supra.*

§ D. Workmen's Compensation

p. 226. *Delete line 2 in the text of § D and substitute the following:*

laws provide compensation to employees for injuries and illnesses resulting from employ-

p. 226. *Delete line 4 in the text of § D and substitute the following:*

is based upon the nature and extent of the employee's disability. In exchange for

p. 226. *Delete line 10 in the text of § D and substitute the following:*

2. Did the injury or illness occur during the course of employment?

p. 226. *Delete line 11 in the text of § D and substitute the following:*

3. What were the nature and extent of the disability?

p. 227. *Add after the indented paragraph in the text:*

One court, in upholding the coverage of church employees under a state workmen's compensation law, held that the state's interest in insuring fair compensation for employees disabled in the course of employment is a "compelling" interest that overrides a church's right to freely exercise its religion.[20a] The court concluded that church employees, while not specifically mentioned in the workmen's compensation law, must be included unless specifically exempted. This conclusion, noted the court, is consistent with the workmen's compensation act's purpose of providing the broadest possible coverage to all classes of employees.

[20a]Victory Baptist Temple v. Industrial Commission, 442 N.E.2d 819 (Ohio 1982), *cert. denied,* 459 U.S. 1086 (1982). *But see* NLRB v. Catholic Bishop of Chicago, 440 U.S. 490 (1979). *See also* Meyers v. Southwest Region Conference Association of Seventh Day Adventists, 88 So.2d 381 (La. 1956).

p. 228. *Add after the first incomplete paragraph:*

Another court, in holding that a church is engaged in a "business" subject to the state's workmen's compensation law when constructing a new sanctuary, observed: "The business of a church is not strictly confined to charitable purposes, spiritual uplift, and the saving of souls. Such, no doubt, is the ultimate object and purpose of all church associations; but it is a matter of common knowledge that, in order to attain such ends, it is also necessary to construct and maintain houses of worship in which the business of the church is carried on."[22a] The court also noted that a church could be a *business* under a state workmen's compensation law since there was no requirement that a covered business be "profit-seeking."

[22a]Greenway Baptist Church v. Industrial Commission, 636 P.2d 1264, 1267 (Ariz. App. 1981).

p. 228. *Delete the last line of the first complete paragraph and substitute the following:*

employee, or may be treated as a "self-insurer" and accordingly be liable for the damages prescribed by the workmen's compensation statute.[23]

p. 228. *Delete the second complete paragraph and substitute the following:*

In summary, churches are subject to workmen's compensation laws in many states. Nevertheless, very few churches have obtained workmen's compensation insurance. This will render some churches directly liable to injured employees. Churches should review their liability insurance policies to ascertain what if any coverage exists for injured employees. Often, general liability policies *exclude* the insured's employees on the assumption that they are covered under a workmen's compensation policy. This can create a dangerous gap in coverage.

§ E. Labor Laws

p. 230. *Add at the end of § 1:*

One federal district court has held that the Age Discrimination in Employment Act does not apply to religious institutions.[32a] In reaching this conclusion, the court applied a test devised by the United States Supreme Court in evaluating the validity of applying the National Labor Relations Act to parochial schools. In 1979, the Supreme Court held that when the application of a federal regulatory statute to a religious institution raises serious First Amendment questions, a court must first determine whether the statute in fact imposes jurisdiction over the religious institution. The test used in making this determination is whether there was a "clear expression of an affirmative intention of Congress" to include religious institutions within the scope of the statute.[32b] The district court concluded that "Congress did not express a clear, affirmative intention" to include religious institutions under the Age Discrimination in Employment Act, and therefore the Act did not apply to such institutions. Unfortunately, the district court failed to address the prior question of whether application of the Act to religious institutions would raise serious First Amendment questions. It is by no means self-evident that such questions would be implicated, especially in light of the uncontroverted application of the 1964 Civil Rights Act's prohibition of discrimination based on race, color, sex, or national origin to religious organizations.

Finally, the Act specifies that "it shall not be unlawful for an employer . . . to observe the terms of . . . a bona fide employee benefit plan such as a retirement, pension, or insurance plan, which is not a subterfuge to evade the purposes of [the Act]." Ordinarily, an employee benefit plan will be considered to be "bona fide" if it is genuine and pays substantial benefits.

[32a]Ritter v. Mount St. Mary's College, 495 F. Supp. 724 (D. Md. 1980).

[32b]NLRB v. Catholic Bishop of Chicago, 440 U.S. 490 (1979). See the following subsection for a complete analysis of the *Catholic Bishop* decision.

p. 231. *Add after the last complete paragraph:*

One court has suggested that permitting a religious organization to discriminate in employment decisions on the basis of race, color, sex, or national origin would violate the equal protection and nonestablishment of religion clauses of the Constitution.[37a]

[37a]Hazen v. Catholic Credit Union, 681 P.2d 856 (Wash. App. 1984).

p. 231, note 37. *Add:*

See, e.g., EEOC v. Pacific Press Publishing Assoc., 676 F.2d 1272 (9th Cir. 1984) (religious publishing company not exempt from prohibition against sex discrimination); Larsen v. Kirkham, 499 F. Supp. 960 (D. Utah 1980); Dolten v. Wahlert High School, 483 F. Supp. 266 (N.D. Iowa 1980) (prohibition against sex discrimination applicable to a Catholic school).

p. 232, note 39. *Add:*

Amos v. Corporation of Presiding Bishop, 594 F. Supp. 791 (D. Utah 1984) (absolute exemption of religious organizations violates nonestablishment of religion clause of First Amendment); Feldstein v. Christian Science Monitor, 555 F. Supp. 974 (D. Mass. 1983) (Christian Science Monitor is a "religious activity" of a religious organization, and thus it could discriminate on the basis of religion in employment decisions).

p. 234, note 49. *Add:*

NLRB v. Bishop Ford Catholic High School, 623 F.2d 818 (2nd Cir. 1980), *cert. denied*, 450 U.S. 996 (1980).

p. 235. *Add after the fourth paragraph:*

NLRB assertions of jurisdiction similarly have been upheld over church-affiliated hospitals[50a] and nursing homes[50b] that (1) receive a substantial percentage of their income from governmental sources; (2) hire employees without regard to religious beliefs; and (3) engage in no specific religious indoctrination of patients or employees. A number of courts have concluded that Congress has "clearly expressed an intention to confer [NLRB] jurisdiction" over church-affiliated hospitals, since in 1974 it removed the pre-existing exemption of all nonprofit hospitals under section 2(2) of the National Labor Relations Act, and rejected an amendment that would have retained the exemption for church-affiliated hospitals.

[50a]St. Elizabeth Community Hospital v. NLRB, 708 F.2d 1436 (9th Cir. 1983); Bon Secours Hospital, Inc., 248 N.L.R.B. 115 (1980). *See also* Catholic Community Services, 247 N.L.R.B. 743 (1980) (Catholic social service agency whose purpose was the provision of social services on a nondenominational basis and that hired employees without regard to religious beliefs held to be subject to NLRB jurisdiction).
[50b]Mid American Health Services, Inc., 247 N.L.R.B. 752 (1980).

p. 235. *Add after the fifth paragraph:*

Significantly, the court emphasized that (1) governmental funding comprised over half of the home's income; (2) the home hired employees without regard to their religious affiliation;[51a] (3) the home accepted only abused children and kept them an average of six weeks during which time they remained wards of the state; (4) all children were referrals from a state agency; and (5) children could not attend religious services contrary to the beliefs of their parents without parental consent. The court concluded that under these facts the home was indistinguishable from a nonreligious institution, and, accordingly, no serious First Amendment questions were implicated.

Many children's homes affiliated with churches are not subject to NLRB jurisdiction because their activities are inherently religious. The New Testament itself states: "Pure religion and undefiled before God and the Father is this, To visit the fatherless and widows in their affliction . . . ."[51b] Children's homes that are affiliated with and controlled by bona fide churches, that receive all or most of their income from nongovernmental sources, that actively propagate the church's religious tenets to their children, and that require employees to be members of the church undoubtedly are exempt from NLRB jurisdiction under the Supreme Court's three-part test. However, church-affiliated children's homes that lack most of these characteristics may be subject to NLRB jurisdiction.

[51a]The court failed to explain how the home, consistently with Title VII of the Civil Rights Act of 1964, could restrict hiring to employees who shared the church's religious beliefs.
[51b]James 1:27.

p. 237. *Add after the first incomplete sentence:*

The Act also requires equal pay for equal work regardless of gender, and restricts the employment of underage children.

p. 237. *Add after the first incomplete paragraph:*

As originally enacted, the Act covered only those employees "engaged in commerce or the production of goods for commerce." Coverage was defined solely in terms of each individual employee's association with interstate commerce. Subsequently, the Act was amended to extend coverage to all of the employees of any "enterprise engaged in commerce or in the production of goods for commerce." An *enterprise* is defined by the Act as any organization meeting the following three conditions: (1) related activities, (2) performed through unified operation or common control, and (3) for a common business purpose.[58a] The term *enterprise engaged in commerce or in the production of goods for commerce* is defined by the Act as either (1) a business that has at least two employees engaged in commerce or in the production of goods for commerce, or engaged in the handling, selling, or otherwise working on goods or materials that have been moved in or produced for commerce by any person, *and* that has annual gross sales in excess of a prescribed amount (currently $362,600); or (2) one of the businesses specifically listed under the Act (e.g., launderers, cleaners, clothing repairers, construction companies, hospitals, and schools) without regard to sales volume or employee participation in commerce.[58b] The Department of Labor maintains that the employees of most private religious schools (preschools, elementary and secondary schools, and institutions of higher learning) are covered under the Act because of the second definition of an enterprise engaged in commerce.[58c]

[58a]29 U.S.C. § 203(r).
[58b]29 U.S.C. § 203(s).
[58c]*See* Donovan v. Shenandoah Baptist Church, 573 F. Supp. 320 (D. Va. 1983).

p. 237. *Add after the last paragraph in the text:*

In 1985, the United States Supreme Court unanimously held that the Fair Labor Standards Act applied to some 300 "associates" who performed commercial work for a religious organization in exchange for lodging, food, transportation, and medical care.[62a] The foundation engaged in several commercial enterprises, including advertising, landscaping, service stations, restaurants, manufacture and sale of candy and clothing, record keeping, construction, plumbing, sand and gravel, electrical contracting, hog farms, feed and farm supplies, real estate development, and freight hauling. Most of the associates who performed such activities were former "derelicts, drug addicts, and criminals" who had been evangelized by the foundation.

The Court observed that the Act would apply to the foundation's commercial activities if two conditions were satisfied: (1) the activities comprised an enterprise engaged in commerce, and (2) the associates were "employees." The Court concluded that both conditions were satisfied, and therefore the foundation's associates were entitled to the protections of the Act. In finding the foundation's commercial activities to be an enterprise engaged in commerce, the Court observed that "[t]he statute contains no express or implied exception for commercial activities conducted by religious or other nonprofit organizations, and the agency charged with its enforcement has consistently interpreted the statute to reach such businesses."[62b] The Court did not apply the *Catholic Bishop* test[62c] (i.e., federal statutes substantially burdening the First Amendment rights of religious organizations can be applied to them only if Congress clearly expressed an affirmative intention to cover them) because it perceived "no significant risk of an infringement of first amendment rights." It also rejected the foundation's assertion that its exemption from federal income taxation constituted governmental recognition of its status as a nonprofit religious and educational organization rather than a commercial one.

As to the second condition, the Court concluded that the foundation's associates were employees despite the foundation's characterization of them as "volunteers" who worked without any expectation of compensation in any form. The Court acknowledged that an individual who "without promise or expectation of compensation, but solely for his personal purpose or pleasure, [works] in activities carried on by other persons either for their pleasure or profit" is not an employee. However, it noted that the Act defines *wages* to include in-kind benefits such as food, lodging, and medical care, and that the associates clearly were compensated employees under this definition. In response to the testimony of several associates that they expected no compensation for their labors and that they considered their work to be "ministry," the Court held that "economic reality" rather than the views of the associates was determinative, and that under this test the associates were employees since they "must have expected to receive in-kind benefits—and expected them in exchange for their services."

The Court rejected the foundation's claim that payment of wages to its associates would violate their right to freely exercise their religion. The Court noted that "[i]t is virtually self-evident that the free exercise of religion clause does not require an exemption from a governmental program unless, at a minimum, inclusion in the program actually burdens the claimant's freedom to exercise religious rights." Since the foundation in fact compensated the associates by providing them with noncash benefits including food and lodging, the Court saw no merit in the associates' assertion that receipt of compensation would violate their religious rights.

The Court emphasized that if a religious organization could engage in a commercial activity in direct competition with ordinary commercial enterprises and remain exempt from the provisions of the Act, it would be free to pay substandard wages and thereby would realize an unfair advantage over its competitors that would jeopardize the right of potentially large numbers of workers to receive minimum wage jobs. The Court also noted that there was no reason "to fear that . . . coverage of the foundation's business activities will lead to coverage of volunteers who drive the elderly to church, serve church suppers, or help remodel a church home for the needy," since none of these activities is commercial in nature and those who perform such services ordinarily do so without any expectation of either cash or in-kind compensation.

[62a]Tony and Susan Alamo Foundation v. Secretary of Labor, 53 U.S.L.W. 4489 (April 23, 1985).

[62b]The Court cited 29 C.F.R. § 779.214: "Activities of eleemosynary, religious, or educational organization [sic] may be performed for a business purpose. Thus, where such organizations engage in ordinary commercial activities, such as operating a printing and publishing plant, the business activities will be treated under the Act the same as when they are performed by the ordinary business enterprise."

[62c]NLRB v. Catholic Bishop of Chicago, 440 U.S. 490 (1979). See note 49, supra, and accompanying text.

p. 238. *Delete the first paragraph and substitute the following:*

In summary, most church employees will not be covered by the Act for at least five independent reasons. First, the authority of Congress and, by delegation, the Department of Labor to regulate wages and hours derives from the constitutional authority of Congress to regulate interstate commerce. Activities not affecting interstate commerce are incapable of federal regulation as a matter of constitutional limitation. One federal appeals court has aptly observed:

> While we realize that casuists can and do spin chains of reasoning which are unending, we are of the opinion that that kind of reasoning is not compatible with proper canons of statutory construction. We are particularly of the view that when the question of the exertion of congressional powers over activities occurring wholly within a state is concerned, courts ought not to, indeed they may not, by spinning a web of casuistry, extend the congressional enactment beyond its reasonable confines.[63]

Second, most churches are not an *enterprise* since a purely nonprofit and noncommercial organization does not have a "common business purpose."[64]

Third, most churches will not satisfy the definition of an *enterprise engaged in commerce or in the production of goods for commerce* since they ordinarily do not have at least two employees who are engaged in commerce, in the production of goods for commerce, or in the handling, selling, or otherwise working on goods or materials that have been moved in or produced for commerce. Further, smaller churches will fail the annual sales volume requirement.

Fourth, the Act exempts employees employed by certain retail or service establishments other than those entities specifically included within the definition of the term *enterprise engaged in commerce or in the production of goods for commerce.*[64a]

Fifth, the Supreme Court's test for determining the validity of NLRB jurisdiction over religious organizations applies to the question of coverage of such organizations under the Fair Labor Standards Act. The test, enunciated in the *Catholic Bishop* decision,[64b] provides that if the exercise of jurisdiction by a federal agency over a religious organization would give rise to serious constitutional questions under the First Amendment religion clauses, then the agency may not exercise jurisdiction without showing an "affirmative intention of the Congress clearly expressed" to confer such jurisdiction. Undoubtedly, serious constitutional questions would arise under the First Amendment's religion clauses by an assertion of jurisdiction by the Department of Labor over a local church that is not engaged in significant commercial activities. At the least, this would constitute an impermissible excessive entanglement of religion between church and state. As noted above, in a few cases the courts have upheld assertions of jurisdiction by the Department of Labor over religious organizations engaged in overtly commercial activities. However, these cases cannot serve as authority or precedent for attempted assertions of jurisdiction over most churches and conventions and associations of churches having few if any "commercial" activities. A more pertinent precedent would be the *Catholic Bishop* decision itself, wherein the Supreme Court refused to extend NLRB jurisdiction over Catholic parochial schools since (1) the schools were organized exclusively for the propagation of religion and therefore the imposition of NLRB jurisdiction over them would raise serious constitutional questions, and (2) there was no showing by the agency of an "affirmative intention of the Congress clearly expressed" to confer jurisdiction.

Some religious organizations will meet the definition of an *enterprise engaged in commerce or in the production of goods for commerce.* Examples include commercial religious publishers and any other religious organization engaged in commercial activities. Even these organizations can adjust their liability for overtime compensation and minimum wage payments in a variety of ways. For example, they can reduce the number of hours worked each week; prohibit all unauthorized overtime work;[64c] reduce hourly compensation (but not below the minimum wage); reduce fringe benefits; or take credit for all indirect and noncash payments made on behalf of employees.

All employers having employees covered by the Act must maintain records documenting covered employees' wages, hours, and the other conditions and practices of employment. Included are payroll records, collective bargaining agreements, employment contracts, pension plans and other employee benefits, and worktime schedules. If an employer intends to claim credit for noncash payments, it must maintain records documenting the value of such payments.

[63]Jenkins v. Durkin, 208 F.2d 941, 945 (5th Cir. 1954).

[64]*See, e.g.*, Wirtz v. Columbian Mutual Life Insurance Co., 380 F.2d 903 (4th Cir. 1967).

[64a]29 U.S.C. § 213(a)(2). More than 50% of the establishment's annual dollar volume of sales of goods or services must be made within the state in which the establishment is located; less than 25% of its annual dollar volume of sales must not be for resale; and the establishment is not an enterprise engaged in commerce or in the production of goods for commerce. The Department of Labor maintains that the exemption of "service establishments" is limited to services rendered by establishments that are traditionally regarded as local retail service establishments such as restaurants and motels. *See* 29 C.F.R. § 778.316.

[64b]NLRB v. Catholic Bishop of Chicago, 440 U.S. 490 (1979). This decision is discussed more fully earlier in this section of chapter 10.

[64c]*See, e.g.*, Fleming v. Stillman, 48 F. Supp. 609 (D. Tenn. 1940). *But see* 29 C.F.R. § 778.316 (announcement by employer that no overtime will be allowed does not affect an employees' right to overtime pay if they are "suffered or permitted" by the employer to perform the additional work.

p. 239. *Delete the second line and substitute the following:*

nection with the Fair Labor Standards Act and the National Labor Relations Act.

§ G. Termination of Employees

p. 241. *Add at the end of the second complete paragraph:*

One court has rejected the argument that the "national policy" against religious discrimination is sufficiently compelling to create an exception to the "terminable-at-will" doctrine in the context of religious employers.[82a]

5. A few courts have eroded an employer's right to fire "at will" any employee hired for an indefinite term by finding that the employer's "employee manual" became a part of the contract of employment and afforded employees certain procedural protections.[82b] This approach has been rejected by other courts.[82c]

[82a]Amos v. Corporation of Presiding Bishop, 594 F. Supp. 791, 829-30 (D. Utah 1984). *See also* Ogilbee v. Western District Guidance Center, Inc., 658 F.2d 257 (4th Cir. 1981) (employer has absolute right to terminate employees hired "at will" for an indefinite term); Fleming v. Mack Truck, Inc., 598 F. Supp. 917 (E.D. Pa. 1981) (Pennsylvania law permits the termination of "at will" employees at any time for any or no reason); Murphy v. American Home Products Corp., 451 N.Y.S.2d 770 (1982) (New York does not recognize a cause of action for retaliatory or abusive discharge); Maus v. National Living Centers, Inc., 633 S.W.2d 674 (Tex. App. 1982) (employer's right to terminate "at will" employees upheld despite employee's claim that she was wrongfully discharged in retaliation for her complaints to supervisors that patients in the nursing home where she worked were being neglected); Brower v. Homes Trans-

portation, Inc., 435 A.2d 952 (Vt. 1981) ("at will" employees can be discharged by employer at any time with or without cause).

[82b] *See, e.g.,* Carter v. Kaskaskia Community Action Agency, 322 N.E.2d 574 (Ill. App. 1975).

[82c] *See, e.g.,* Chin v. American Telephone and Telegraph Co., 410 N.Y.S.2d 737 (1978); Reynolds Manufacturing Co. v. Mendoza, 644 S.W.2d 536 (Tex. App. 1982).

p. 241, note 82. *Add:*

Tameny v. Atlantic Richfield Co., 164 Cal. Rptr. 839 (1980) (employee terminated for refusal to participate in illegal scheme to fix retail gasoline prices); Segal v. Arrow Industries Corp., 364 So.2d 89 (Fla. App. 1978) (employee terminated for filing a workmen's compensation claim); Hughes Tool Co. v. Richards, 610 S.W.2d 232 (Tex. App. 1980) (employee terminated for filing a workmen's compensation claim).

Form **8274**

(July 1984)

Department of the Treasury
Internal Revenue Service

Certification by Churches and Qualified Church-Controlled Organizations Electing Exemption from Employer Social Security Taxes

File in Duplicate

Please type or print

Full name of organization.	Employer Identification number

Address (Number and street)

City, State, and ZIP code

If exemption is based on a group ruling, give full name of central organization	Group exemption number

Purpose of Form.—By filing this form, the organization named above elects exemption from employer social security taxes by certifying that it is a church or church-controlled organization which is opposed for religious reasons to the payment of social security taxes.

Effect of Election.—This election applies to all current and future employees of the electing organization for services performed after December 31, 1983. However, this election does not apply to ministers of a church, members of a religious order, or to services performed in an unrelated trade or business of the church or church-controlled organization. The organization may not revoke the election.

The electing organization is required to continue to withhold income tax and to report the tax withheld and wages, tips, and other compensation paid to each employee on **Form W-2**, Wage and Tax Statement, and to file **Form 941E**, Quarterly Return of Withheld Federal Income Tax (or **Form 941**, Employer's Quarterly Federal Tax Return, if the organization has employees whose wages are not exempted by this election (such as those engaged in unrelated business activities) and remain subject to employer taxes). This election shall be permanently revoked if the organization fails to file Form W-2 for 2 years and fails to furnish the information upon request by the IRS.

Employees receiving compensation of $100 or more in a year from the electing organization are subject to self-employment tax on the compensation. They will be considered employees for all other purposes of the Internal Revenue Code including the withholding of income tax.

Organizations filing this form who have reported and paid social security taxes on Form 941 for services performed in 1984 prior to making this election, can receive a refund of these taxes by filing **Form 843**, Claim, with the Internal Revenue Service Center where they filed Form 941. The refund will be made without interest and is conditioned upon the organization agreeing to pay to each employee (or former employee) the portion of the refund attributable to the employee social security tax. This may be accomplished by adding the following sentence in the explanation section on the Form 843: "I agree to repay promptly any withheld employee social security tax to each employee or former employee covered by the election on Form 8274 on which the claim is based." The Service Center will process the claim faster if it is marked "Section 3121(w)" above the title on Form 843 and if Form 8274 accompanies it.

Who May File.—Churches and qualified church-controlled organizations (defined below) who are opposed for religious reasons to the payment of social security taxes may elect exemption from the taxes by filing this form.

The term church includes conventions or associations of churches. It also includes an elementary or secondary school that is controlled, operated, or principally supported by a church (or conventions or associations of churches).

A qualified church-controlled organization includes any church-controlled tax-exempt organization described in section 501(c)(3) of the Internal Revenue Code except an organization that:

1. offers goods, services, or facilities for sale, other than on an incidental basis, to the general public AND
2. normally receives more than 25 percent of its support from the sum of governmental sources and receipts from admissions, sales of merchandise, or furnishing of facilities in activities that are not unrelated trades or businesses.

Goods, services, or facilities which are sold at a nominal charge substantially less than the cost of providing such goods, services, or facilities are not included in 1 above.

An organization which meets both conditions 1 and 2 above will be excluded from the definition of a qualified church-controlled organization and therefore not eligible to file this form.

For example, a church-controlled hospital will generally meet both conditions and will not qualify to make the election.

However, a seminary, a religious retreat center, or a burial society will generally qualify to make the election regardless of its funding sources because it does not offer goods, services, or facilities for sale to the general public. A church-run orphanage or home-for-the-aged may qualify if not more than 25 percent of its support is from admissions, sales of merchandise, or furnishing of facilities in other than unrelated trades or businesses plus from governmental sources. Auxiliary organizations of a church such as youth groups, women's auxiliaries, church pension boards and fund-raising organizations will generally be eligible to make the election.

When to File.—Any organization in existence on September 30, 1984, must file this form by October 30, 1984. Any organization created after September 30, 1984, must file prior to the first date on which a quarterly employment tax return would otherwise be due from the electing organization.

Where to File.—File with the Internal Revenue Service Center for the State in which the church or church-controlled organization is located, as listed below.

New Jersey, New York City and counties of Nassau, Rockland, Suffolk, and Westchester	Holtsville, NY 00501
New York (All other counties), Connecticut, Maine, Massachusetts, New Hampshire, Rhode Island, Vermont	Andover, MA 05501
District of Columbia, Delaware, Maryland, Pennsylvania	Philadelphia, PA 19255
Alabama, Florida, Georgia, Mississippi, South Carolina	Atlanta, GA 31101
Michigan, Ohio	Cincinnati, OH 45999
Arkansas, Kansas, Louisiana, New Mexico, Oklahoma, Texas	Austin, TX 73301
Alaska, Arizona, Colorado, Idaho, Minnesota, Montana, Nebraska, Nevada, North Dakota, Oregon, South Dakota, Utah, Washington, Wyoming	Ogden, UT 84201
Illinois, Iowa, Missouri, Wisconsin	Kansas City, MO 64999
California, Hawaii	Fresno, CA 93888
Indiana, Kentucky, North Carolina, Tennessee, Virginia, West Virginia	Memphis, TN 37501

Churches or church-controlled organizations in Guam, American Samoa, the Virgin Islands, or Puerto Rico should file this form with the U.S. Internal Revenue Service Center, Philadelphia, PA 19255.

If you are already filing Form 941, file with the Internal Revenue Service Center where you are filing the 941.

Filing Instructions.—Complete this form by supplying the information called for. An authorized official of the church or the qualified church-controlled organization must sign the form. Send two copies to the appropriate IRS address. Keep a copy for your records.

Sign Here ▶

I certify that the above named organization is a church or qualified church-controlled organization, as defined in section 3121(w) of the Internal Revenue Code, which is opposed for religious reasons to the payment of employer social security taxes, and elects not to be subject to such taxes.

-------------------------------- -------------------------------- --------------------------------
(Signature of authorized official)   (Title)   (Date)

11

GOVERNMENT REGULATION OF CHURCHES

p. 243. *Delete the last three lines of the first complete paragraph and substitute the following:*

schools of churches and religious organizations. The amenability of churches to some regulation is not seriously disputed. For example, few would protest the application to churches of laws and regulations prohibiting fraud in the sale of securities, requiring donated funds to be expended for the purposes represented, protecting copyright owners against infringement, or prohibiting activities that cause physical harm, property damage, or material disturbance to others. Similarly, churches routinely comply with municipal building codes and zoning regulations in the construction and location of worship facilities. In summary, most churches have acknowledged that religion should not be used as a means of avoiding laws and regulations that (1) prohibit in the least restrictive way those church activities that pose a clear and imminent threat to the life, health, safety, property, or welfare of others or (2) impose fair and reasonable restrictions on those activities of churches that are not intrinsically religious, provided that the restrictions are reasonably related to a legitimate governmental objective that cannot otherwise be served. The more significant forms of governmental regulation of churches and religious organizations will be summarized in this chapter.

p. 243. *Delete § A on pages 243-246 and substitute the following:*

§ A. Regulation of Charitable Solicitations

1. STATE CHARITABLE SOLICITATION LAWS

Several states have enacted laws regulating the solicitation of charitable contributions. Presumably, the purpose of such laws is "to protect the contributing public and charitable beneficiaries against fraudulent practices in the solicitation of contributions for purportedly charitable purposes."[2] The typical statute requires certain charitable organizations to register with the state government prior to the solicitation of contributions within the state and imposes various reporting requirements. Such statutes ordinarily give the state authority to revoke the registration of any charitable organization upon a finding that the organization has engaged in a fraudulent or deceptive practice, or that it has expended more than a prescribed or "reasonable" amount of solicited funds for administrative and fund raising costs, and that the public interests so require.

Religious organizations, including churches, are insulated from regulation in many states either because of an exemption[3] or because no charitable solicitation law has been enacted.[4] Many charitable solicitation laws exempt only some religious organizations. To illustrate, some laws exempt only those religious organizations (1) that are bona fide religious institutions,[5] (2) that solicit funds solely by means of members acting without compensation,[6] (3) that solicit funds only within the county where the religious organization is located or within an adjoining county that is less than six miles away,[7] (4) that do not employ professional fund raisers,[8] (5) that do not receive their financial support primarily from persons other than members,[9] (6) that have received a declaration of current tax-exempt status from the government of the United States,[10] or (7) that are entitled to receive a declaration of current tax-exempt status from the government of the United States.[11]

The application of state charitable solicitation laws to religious and charitable organizations has been challenged in a few recent cases. In *Larsen v. Valente*[12] the United States Supreme Court invalidated a section of the Minnesota Charitable Solicitation Act that exempted from registration only those religious organizations receiving more than half of their support from members. The Court emphasized that "the clearest command of the Establishment Clause is that one religious denomination cannot be officially preferred over another,"[13] and concluded that "the fifty percent rule . . . clearly grants denominational preference of the sort consistently and firmly deprecated in our precedents."[14] Such a law, observed the Court, must be invalidated unless (1) it is justified by a compelling governmental interest and (2) it is clearly fitted to further that interest. The "tripartite" establishment clause analysis formulated by the Court in *Lemon*[15] was deemed inapplicable in this context, since that analysis was "intended to apply to laws affording a uniform benefit to *all* religions, and not to provisions, like the . . . fifty percent rule, that discriminate among religions."[16]

The Court acknowledged that the State of Minnesota had a significant interest in protecting its citizens from abusive practices in the solicitation of funds for charity, even when the solicitation was conducted by religious organizations.

However, it rejected the State's contention that the fifty percent rule was closely fitted to further that interest.

Would a state charitable solicitation law requiring *all* religious organizations to register be constitutionally permissible? Such a law obviously would avoid the "denominational preference" that tainted the Minnesota statute. The Supreme Court even observed in *Larson* that it was not suggesting that "the burdens of compliance with the Act would be intrinsically impermissible if they were imposed evenhandedly."[16a] This more difficult question was addressed in 1980 by the Supreme Court of North Carolina in the *Heritage Village* decision.[16b]

The Supreme Court of North Carolina, in striking down a state charitable solicitation law exempting all religious organizations except those whose financial support came primarily from nonmembers, concluded that the First Amendment prohibits any state from subjecting religious organizations to the administrative requirements of a charitable solicitation law. The Court noted:

[F]or a statute to pass muster under the strict test of Establishment Clause neutrality, it must pass the three-prong review distilled by the Supreme Court from "the cumulative criteria developed over many years": First, the statute must have a secular purpose; second, its principal or primary effect must be one that neither advances nor inhibits religion . . . ; finally the statute must not foster an excessive government entanglement with religion.[16c]

The court concluded that the first part of the Supreme Court's three-prong test was satisfied, since the Act had a valid secular purpose of protecting the public from fraud. It found, however, that the Act violated both the second and third elements since it inhibited certain religious groups and constituted an impermissible governmental entanglement with religion. As to the second element, the Court observed:

[T]he Act grants an exemption from the licensing and reporting requirements to a broadly defined class of religious organizations. . . . The proviso, however, which immediately follows in the same section denies the benefits of the exemption to those religious organizations which derive their financial support "primarily" from contributions solicited from "persons other than their own members."

. . .

[T]he *effect* of the proviso is to alter the original exemption's religious neutrality. The result is a qualified exemption which favors only those religious organizations which solicit primarily from their own members. The inescapable impact is to accord benign neglect to the more orthodox, denominational, and congregational religions while subjecting to registration those religions which spread their beliefs in more evangelical, less traditional ways. This the state may not do.[16d]

As to the third element of the test, the Court observed:

> Considerations of the excessive entanglement between church and state threatened by the Act's substantive requirements additionally compels us to conclude that plaintiffs may not constitutionally be denied an exemption. . . .
> Should plaintiffs or any other religious organization be subjected to the full panoply of strictures contemplated by the Act, we would be faced with precisely the sort of "sustained and detailed administrative relationships for enforcement of statutory and administrative standards" that have been repeatedly condemned by the Supreme Court.[16e]

Both the *Larson* and *Heritage Village* decisions were based on the establishment clause. Neither court directly addressed the applicability of the First Amendment's free exercise of religion and free speech clauses in analyzing the constitutionality of applying charitable solicitation laws to religious organizations. The free exercise and free speech clauses have been relied upon by several courts in invalidating municipal charitable solicitation ordinances.[16f] In 1980, the Supreme Court observed in the *Village of Schaumburg* decision that:

> Prior authorities, therefore, thoroughly establish that charitable appeals for funds . . . involve a variety of speech interests—communication of information, a dissemination and propagation of views and ideas, and the advocacy of causes—that are within the protection of the First Amendment. Soliciting financial support is undoubtedly subject to reasonable regulation but the latter must be undertaken with due regard for the reality that solicitation is characteristically intertwined with informative and perhaps persuasive speech seeking support for particular causes or for particular views on economic, political, or social issues, or for the reality that without solicitation flow of such information and advocacy would likely cease.[16g]

Such reasoning buttresses the conclusion reached in *Heritage Village*. Not only would a state charitable solicitation law that applies to religious organizations be constitutionally suspect under the establishment clause, but it also would clash with the free exercise and free speech clauses.

As the Supreme Court noted in *Larson*, a state unquestionably has a significant interest in protecting its citizens from abusive practices in the solicitation of funds for charity. However, such an interest alone does not determine constitutional validity. The state must also demonstrate that its charitable solicitation law is "closely fitted to further the interest that it assertedly serves."[16h] As the Court noted in *Village of Schaumburg*, "[t]he Village may serve its legitimate interests, but it must do so by narrowly drawn regulations designed to serve those interests without necessarily interfering with First Amendment freedoms."[16i] Can a state serve its legitimate purpose of preventing fraud in the solicitation of funds by religious organizations in a less drastic way than by registration under a charitable solicitation law? The answer clearly is in the affirmative. In an analogous case, the Supreme Court in the *Village of Schaumburg* decision observed that the government's legitimate interest in preventing fraud can be served by less intrusive measures: "Fraudulent misrepresentations can be prohibited and the penal laws used to punish such conduct directly."[16j] Another court has noted that less restrictive alternative means of fulfilling the government's interests include "enforcement of existing laws against fraud, trespass, breach of the peace, and any other substantive offenses which might be committed. The [government] may adopt appropriate registration and identification procedures to protect its residents against wrongdoing by spurious solicitators. . . ."[16k]

In summary, the *Heritage Village* decision effects a reasonable balance of the competing interests of church and state. It frees religious organizations from entangling administrative supervision by the government; it acknowledges that the government remains capable of asserting that a particular organization is not in fact a bona fide religious organization entitled to exemption; it does not insulate religious organizations from private or penal actions; and it gives due weight to the principle that the act of soliciting funds for the support of religious organizations is often an expression of religious faith.[16l]

A similar result has been reached in the related context of securities regulation. Most state securities laws, while designed primarily to prevent fraud, exempt religious organizations from the securities registration requirement. Religious organizations are not exempted from the anti-fraud provisions of such laws, and thus they remain liable for fraudulent conduct even though they are exempt from registration. Further, the state is free to deny an exemption to religious organizations that have engaged in fraud in the past or that are not bona fide religious organizations. Such a balance between the competing interests of church and state serves as a model for the related contexts of state and municipal charitable solicitation laws. The government's interests can be served by less restrictive means than registration.

2. MUNICIPAL CHARITABLE SOLICITATION LAWS

Several cities have enacted ordinances regulating the solicitation of charitable contributions. These ordinances often are similar in content and purpose to the corresponding state laws. Such laws typically require the licensing of persons who solicit funds for charity. A number of cities have no charitable solicitation ordinance.[16m] Several other cities have adopted charitable solicitation ordinances that exempt certain religious organizations. For example, some cities exempt religious organizations that are exempt from federal income taxation.[16n] Other cities exempt properly authorized solicitors of established and organized churches or other established and organized religious organizations,[16o] organizations conducting a solicitation among their own membership,[16p] solicitations in the form of collections or contributions at a regular assembly or service,[16q] and any church which solicits funds for religious purposes.[16r] Some cities require religious organizations that use professional fund raisers to register under a charitable solicitation ordinance.[16s]

The constitutionality of applying such charitable solicitation ordinances to religious organizations has been challenged in several cases. In *Village of Schaumburg*, the Supreme Court struck down an ordinance prohibiting the solicitation of contributions by charitable organizations that did not use at least 75% of their receipts for charitable purposes. The ordinance excluded solicitation expenses, salaries, overhead, and other administrative expenses from the definition of "charitable purpose." The Court conceded that charitable appeals for funds involve a variety of speech interests that are within the protection of the First Amendment, and that any ordinance interfering with such interests would be constitutionally valid only if it (1) served a compelling governmental interest and (2) was narrowly drawn to serve that interest without necessarily interfering with First Amendment freedoms. The Court acknowledged that a city has a substantial interest in protecting the public from fraud, crime, and undue annoyance. However, it concluded that a municipal ordinance banning solicitations by any charity that did not expend more than 75% of solicited funds for charitable purposes could not be upheld, for the city's legitimate interests could be "better served by measures less intrusive than a direct prohibition on solicitation."[16t] The Court also noted that there was no evidence that "organizations devoting more than one-quarter of their funds to salaries and administrative expenses are any more likely to employ solicitors who would be a threat to public safety than are other charitable organizations."[16u]

In summary, *Village of Schaumburg* may be reduced to the following two principles: (1) The right to solicit funds for religious and charitable purposes is protected by the First Amendment's free speech clause, and (2) this right is not unconditional, but may be limited by a municipal ordinance if the ordinance (a) serves a compelling government interest and (b) is narrowly drawn to serve that interest without unnecessarily interfering with First Amendment freedoms.

Village of Schaumburg has been followed in several other cases.[16v] In most of these decisions, municipal ordinances attempting to regulate charitable solicitations were invalidated. The courts generally concede that a city has a legitimate and substantial interest in preventing fraud, crime, and undue annoyance, but they often conclude that a particular charitable solicitation ordinance too broadly serves that interest since other, less restrictive, alternatives exist which serve the same interest. The Supreme Court in *Village of Schaumburg* noted:

> Frauds may be denounced as offenses and punished by law. Trespasses may similarly be forbidden. If it is said that these means are less efficient and convenient than . . . deciding in advance what information may be disseminated from house to house, and who may impart the information, the answer is that considerations of this sort do not empower a municipality to abridge freedom of speech and press.[16w]

In conclusion, a municipal ordinance purporting to regulate the solicitation of funds by some or all religious organizations should presumptively[16x] be unconstitutional unless the city can demonstrate that the ordinance serves a legitimate and compelling interest *and* that this interest cannot effectively be protected by less intrusive, more narrowly drawn, alternatives. Several courts have concluded that the availability of private causes of action for fraud and trespass, together with penal prohibitions of such conduct, sufficiently protect a city's legitimate interests in safeguarding its citizens from abusive charitable solicitations by religious organizations. A city also of course may make a determination that a particular "religious" organization is spurious and therefore not entitled to an exemption, and it is free to deny an exemption to otherwise bona fide religious organizations that have been proven to have engaged in frauds upon the public.[16y] Further, any municipal charitable solicitation ordinance exempting only some religious organizations from registration would be suspect under the establishment clause, since some religious groups are singled out for favored treatment while others are not. All of these factors indicate that most charitable solicitation laws cannot constitutionally be extended to religious organizations.

Certainly any charitable solicitation law that gives a licensing body or official effective discretion to grant or deny permission to solicit funds for religious purposes is likewise unconstitutional:

> The solicitation of funds for religious purposes is protected by the First Amendment. Any law restricting the exercise of such rights must do so with narrow, objective and definite standards. If a certificate is required for one to solicit funds for religious purposes, the discretion of the official granting the certificate must be bounded by explicit standards. If the decision to issue the certificate "involves appraisal of facts, the exercise of judgment, and the formation of an opinion" the ordinance violates the First Amendment. Ambiguities in the application process which give the licensing official effective power to grant or deny permission to solicit funds for religious purposes is likewise unconstitutional. In other words, it is not enough that an official is directed to issue the license forthwith; if the official may deny the application because of unclear requirements in the appli-

cation process, the law is unconstitutional. Laws allowing an investigation into
the financial affairs of religious institutions have been held unconstitutional as an
impermissible entanglement of the affairs of church and state. Finally, any prior
restraint on the exercise of First Amendment freedoms must be accompanied by
procedural safeguards designed to obviate the dangers of prior restraint.[16z]

Finally, the Supreme Court has held that the fund raising activities of religious organizations, "like those of others protected by the First Amendment,
are subject to reasonable time, place, and manner restrictions."[16aa] It is doubtful
that these restrictions are of any practical relevance in the context of charitable
solicitations by religious organizations. One court specifically held that the
Supreme Court's decision in *Heffron* "has a rather narrow applicability" because
of its "somewhat unusual factual situation" involving solicitation at a state fair.[16ab]
The court observed that "the flow of the crowd and demands of safety are more
pressing in the context of the fair."[16ac] The Supreme Court in *Village of Schaumburg* strongly intimated that "time, place and manner" restrictions do not justify
regulation of charitable solicitations.[16ad]

[2]Larson v. Valente, 102 S. Ct. (1982).

[3]*See, e.g.,* GA. CODE § 35-1003(A); ILL. REV. STAT. CH. 23, § 5103; N.J. REV. STAT.
§ 45:17A-5(A).

[4]For example, Louisiana, Montana, and Missouri have not enacted charitable solicitation laws.

[5]FLA. STAT. § 496.02(B).

[6]CONN. GEN. STAT. § 19-3231.

[7]IOWA CODE § 122.4.

[8]MD. CORPS. & ASS'NS CODE ANN. § 103C.

[9]S.C. CODE § 33-55-60(1).

[10]PA. STAT. ANN. § 160-2(1); R.I. GEN. LAWS § 5-52-1(A); W. VA. CODE § 29-19-2(1).

[11]WASH. REV. CODE § 19.09.030. The exemption of religious organizations recognized by
the Washington Code takes into account the fact that churches, conventions and associations of churches, and integrated auxiliaries of churches are automatically entitled
to tax-exempt status without any formal recognition by the government. The exemption
provisions found in the charitable solicitation laws of Pennsylvania, Rhode Island, and
West Virginia unfortunately overlook this fact.

[12]102 S. Ct. 1673 (1982). The Court invalidated § 309.515-1(b) of the Minnesota
Statutes.

[13]*Id.* at 1683.

[14]*Id.* at 1684.

[15]Lemon v. Kurtzman, 403 U.S. 602 612-13 (1971).

[16]*Id.* at 1687. While the Court concluded that the tripartite test of *Lemon* was inapplicable, it nonetheless observed that the Minnesota statute did not satisfy that test.

[16a]*Id.* at 1688.

[16b]Heritage Village Church and Missionary Fellowship, Inc. v. State, 263 S.E.2d 726
(N.C. 1980).

[16c]*Id.* at 731.

[16d]*Id.* 732-33.

[16e]*Id.*

[16f]Village of Schaumburg v. Citizens for a Better Environment, 444 U.S. 620, 632 (1980).

[16g]102 S. Ct. at 1685.

[16h]444 U.S. at 637.

[16i]*Id.* at 637.

[16j]Alternatives for California Women v. County of Contra Costa, 193 Cal. Rptr. 384, 392 (Cal. App. 1983).

[16k]*See, e.g.*, Heffron v. International Society for Krishna Consciousness, 452 U.S. 640 (1981); Village of Schaumburg v. Citizens for a Better Environment, 444 U.S. 620, 637-39 (1980); Murdock v. Pennsylvania, 319 U.S. 105 (1943); Heritage Village and Missionary Fellowship, Inc. v. State, 263 S.E.2d 726, 734 (N.C. 1980).

[16l]For example, the cities of Cleveland, Boston, Seattle, Tucson, and Miami do not at this time regulate charitable solicitations.

[16m]BALTIMORE CITY CODE, ART. 41, § 103 C(A)(6); EL PASO CITY CODE, § 14-44; SAN FRANCISCO CITY CODE, ART. 9.6, § 660.1.

[16n]OMAHA CITY CODE, § 20-7.

[16o]DENVER CITY CODE, 47-121; INDIANAPOLIS CITY CODE, § 17-111; LOUISVILLE CITY CODE, § 111.481(F); MINNEAPOLIS CITY CODE, § 333.190; NEW ORLEANS CITY CODE, CH. 14, ART. II; SAN ANTONIO CITY CODE, § 28-26.

[16p]BUFFALO CITY CODE, § 192(A); PORTLAND CITY CODE, § 7.16.030; NEW YORK CITY CODE, § 603.11.0.

[16q]EL PASO CITY CODE, § 14-44; FORT WORTH CITY CODE, § 32-4(A); TULSA CITY CODE, CH. 9, § 113.

[16r]ALBUQUERQUE CITY CODE, ART. IX.

[16s]444 U.S. 620, 637.

[16t]*Id.*, at 638.

[16u]*See, e.g.*, ACORN v. City of Frontenac, 714 F.2d 813 (8th Cir. 1983); Pennsylvania Public Interest v. York Township, 569 F. Supp. 1398 (M.D. Pa. 1983); NAACP Legal Defense and Educational Fund, Inc. v. Devine, 567 F. Supp. 401 (D.D.C. 1983); Taylor v. City of Knoxville, 566 F. Supp. 925 (E.D. Tenn. 1982); Optimist Club v. Riley, 563 F. Supp. 847 (E.D.N.C. 1982); Alternatives for California Women v. County of Contra Costa, 193 Cal. Rptr. 384 (Cal. App 1983).

[16v]444 U.S. 620, 639.

[16w]*See, e.g.*, Pennsylvania Public Interest v. York Township, 569 F.Supp. 1398, 140 (M.D. Pa. 1983) ("Because the ordinance impinges on the exercise of free speech, it is presumptively unconstitutional.")

[16x]*See* Larson v. Valente, 102 S.Ct. 1673, 1689 n.30 (1982):
Nothing in our opinion suggests appellants could not attempt to compel the Unification Church to register under the Act as a charitable organization not entitled to the religious-organization exemption, and put the Church to the proof of its bona fides as a religious organization. Further, nothing in our opinion disables the State from denying exemption from the Act, or from refusing registration and

licensing under the Act, to persons or organizations proved to have engaged in frauds upon the public.")

[16y]Taylor v. City of Knoxville, 566 F. Supp. 925, 929 (E.D.Tenn. 1982).

[16z]Heffron v. International Society for Krishna Consciousness, Inc., 452 U.S. 40, 647 (1981).

[16aa]Pennsylvania Public Interests v. York Township, 659 F.Supp. 1398, 1402 (M.D.Pa. 1983).

[16ab]*Id.*

[16ac]444 U.S. 620, 639-40 (1980).

[16ad]*See* note 16f, *supra.*

§ B. Limitations on Charitable Giving

p. 247. *Add after the first incomplete paragraph:*

A few courts have upheld testamentary gifts to charity in a will executed within the legally prescribed period of invalidity if the charitable gifts were identical to those listed in an earlier will executed prior to the statutory period. To illustrate, one court upheld a testamentary gift to the Salvation Army made within six months of death despite a state law voiding most testamentary charitable gifts made within six months of death, since the donor made a comparable gift to the Salvation Army in a previous will executed more than six months prior to her death.[26a] Other courts have rejected this view and invalidated charitable gifts made within the prescribed statutory period despite comparable gifts to the same charity in an earlier will executed prior to the statutory period.[26b]

[26a]In re Estate of Rauf, 213 So.2d 31 (Fla. App. 1968). *Accord* In re Estate of Prynn, 315 A.2d 265 (Pa. 1974).

[26b]*See, e.g.,* Newman v. Newman, 199 N.E.2d 904 (Ohio 1964); In re Estate of Gearhart, 255 A.2d 557 (Pa. 1969).

p. 254. *Add note 47a following the first complete paragraph:*

[47a]*See, e.g.,* In the Matter of Keep the Faith, Inc., Ariz. Corp. Com., Dec. 54503 (April 25, 1985) (issuer incorrectly stated that its securities program did not involve a donation and did not disclose material information to investors, including the interest rate and term of the securities, and the background and financial condition of the issuer); In the matter of Johnson Financial Services, Inc., Ga. Securities Div., No. 50-84-9500 (August 6, 1984) (salesperson falsely represented that he was working with a Presbyterian church to help sell its bonds, that he was a licensed salesperson, and that the church bonds he was offering earned 18% "tax free" for years); In the Matter of Tri-County Baptist Church, Mich. Corp. and Secs. Bureau, No. 84-32-S (June 11, 1984) (church failed to maintain an escrow account for proceeds of bond sales and did not apply proceeds as described in prospectus).

§ D. Copyright Law

p. 264. *Add after the first incomplete paragraph:*

In 1976, a publisher of religious music sued the Catholic Bishop of Chicago as representative of various churches in the archdiocese of Chicago that allegedly were infringing upon the publisher's copyrights by unauthorized duplication and use of its songs in "homemade or pirated hymnals" prepared for use in worship services. As a result of an agreement between the parties, over 80,000 "homemade" hymnals and song collections containing the allegedly infringing materials were collected from parishes in Chicago and impounded by the court. Thereafter, the publisher investigated other large dioceses and archdioceses in the United States to determine if unauthorized copying was occurring elsewhere. The publisher, claiming to have found copyright violations nationwide, notified the bishop in each area that local parishes were violating the copyright law by reproducing the publisher's copyrighted music without permission in the "pirated" songbooks. The publisher requested the bishops' assistance in determining the extent of the violations, and in voluntarily compensating it for the violations. When no assistance or compensation was offered, the publisher sought a court injunction restraining the National Conference of Catholic Bishops (NCCB) and the United States Catholic Conference (USCC) from further violations of the copyright law.[58a] Specifically, the publisher alleged that the NCCB and USCC violated the law by

> [f]ailing to provide adequate direction to the dioceses and parishes concerning the proper use of [the publisher's] copyrighted materials and thereby caused, permitted and materially contributed to the publication, distribution and/or sale in many of the archdioceses and dioceses . . . of songbooks including songs which were copies largely from [the publisher's] aforementioned copyrighted work.[58b]

The court, while refusing to grant an injunction, did recognize that the publisher had stated a claim for which relief could be granted.

[58a]F.E.L. Publications v. National Conference of Catholic Bishops, 466 F. Supp. 1034 (N.D. Ill. 1978), aff'd, 754 F.2d 216 (7th Cir. 1985).
[58b]*Id.* at 1039.

§ E. Zoning Law

p. 269, note 72. *Add:*

Lakewood, Ohio Congregation of Jehovah's Witnesses, Inc. v. City of Lakewood, 699 F.2d 303 (6th Cir. 1983).

p. 270. *Add after the first complete paragraph:*

Sign ordinances regulating the height, size, and number of signs have been applied to churches despite the claim that they violate a church's constitutional right to freely exercise its religion.[78a]

[78a]Temple Baptist Church v. City of Albuquerque, 646 P.2d 565 (N.M. 1982).

p. 270. *Delete the last two lines of text and substitute the following:*

minister's residence;[88] a twenty-eight-acre tract used by a Jewish foundation as a conference center, leadership training center, and a children's retreat;[89] a single-family residence used for organized religious services;[89a] and a college.[89b]

[89a]Grosz v. City of Miami Beach, 721 F.2d 729 (5th Cir. 1983); State v. Cameron, 460 A.2d 191 (N.J. App. 1983).
[89b]Fountain Gate Ministries, Inc. v. City of Plano, 654 S.W.2d 841 (Tex. App. 1983).

p. 270, note 77. *Add:*

Pinski v. Village of Norridge, 561 F. Supp. 605 (N.D. Ill. 1982); Heilman v. Zoning Board, 450 A.2d 318 (Pa. 1982).

p. 271. *Delete the last two lines of the second complete paragraph and substitute the following:*

teachers,[96] a school,[97] a neon sign constructed on church property to inform the public as to the time of worship services,[98] a center for performing arts,[98a] and a sanctuary or shelter for the homeless.[98b]

[98a]North Shore Hebrew Academy v. Wegman, 481 N.Y.S.2d 142 (1984).
[98b]St. John's Evangelical Lutheran Church v. City of Hoboken, 479 A.2d 935 (N.J. App. 1983); Lubavitch Chabad House of Illinois, Inc. v. City of Evanston, 445 N.E.2d 343 (Ill. App. 1982).

p. 271. *Add after the last paragraph of text:*

Several courts have upheld municipal zoning ordinances prohibiting the location of "adult theatres" within a prescribed distance of a church, despite the claim that such ordinances constitute an impermissible establishment of religion.[102a] However, the United States Supreme Court struck down an ordinance giving churches the authority to "veto" applications for liquor licenses by facilities located within a 500-foot radius of a church.[102b] The Court concluded that the ordinance substituted the unilateral and absolute power of a church for the decisions of a public legislative body, and thereby "enmeshed" churches in the process of government.

[102a]*See, e.g.*, Amico v. New Castle County, 101 F.R.D. 472 (D.C. Del. 1984); City of Whittier v. Walnut Properties, Inc., 197 Cal. Rptr. 127 (1983).

[102b]Larkin v. Grendel's Den, Inc., 103 S. Ct. 505 (1982).

p. 271, note 102. *Add:*

Seward Chapel, Inc. v. City of Seward, 655 P.2d 1293 (Alaska 1982).

§ F. Building Codes

p. 272, note 104. *Add:*

City of Solon v. Solon Baptist Temple, Inc., 457 N.E.2d 858 (Ohio App. 1982).

§ I. The Civil Rights Act of 1964

p. 278. *Add at the end of subsection b:*

Nevertheless, the validity of the exemption has been upheld by a few courts. One court, in rejecting a claim that the exemption is valid only insofar as it is limited to teachers whose religious belief is a significant factor in the subject being taught, concluded that

> it is inconceivable that the exemption would purport to free religious schools to employ those who best promote their religious mission, yet shackle them to a legislative determination that all nominal members are equally suited to the task. In short, nothing in the language, history or purpose of the exemption supports such an invasion of the province of a religion to decide whom it will regard as its members, or who will best propagate its doctrine. That is an internal matter exempt from sovereign interference.[129a]

Religious schools that employ more than fifteen employees and that are engaged in commerce remain subject to the prohibitions of discrimination based on race, color, national origin, and sex.[129b]

[129a]Larsen v. Kirkham, 499 F. Supp. 960 (D. Utah 1980).

[129b]*See, e.g.*, Dolter v. Wahlert High School, 483 F. Supp. 266 (N.D. Iowa 1980).

p. 279. *Add after the first incomplete paragraph:*

For many churches and religious organizations, a particular religious faith is a bona fide occupational qualification. Certainly this would be true for the pastor of a church or teachers at a church-affiliated school. But many churches and religious organizations would view administrative and support staff, including secretaries and custodians, to fit within the same category. This is certainly consistent with the Pauline concept of the church as representing the "body of Christ," with each individual member empowered for service, no matter how routine or secular the task, by Christ, the living head. This concept is described more fully in the next subsection of the present chapter.

p. 279. *Add after the last complete paragraph:*

In 1985, the Supreme Court invalidated a state law specifying that "[n]o person who states that a particular day of the week is observed as his Sabbath may be required by his employer to work on such day. An employee's refusal to work on his Sabbath shall not constitute grounds for his dismissal."[134a] The Court concluded that the statute violated the nonestablishment of religion clause, since it "arms Sabbath observers with an absolute and unqualified right not to work on whatever day they designate as their Sabbath," irrespective of the burden or inconvenience imposed on their employer or fellow workers. This "unyielding weighting in favor of Sabbath observers over all other interests contravenes a fundamental principle of the religion clauses," concluded the Court. Two concurring Justices noted that they did not read the Court's opinion as "suggesting that the religious accommodation provisions of Title VII of the Civil Rights Act are similarly invalid," since these provisions require religious accommodation of employee religious observances only if such accommodation does not cause undue hardship to the employer's business.

p. 279, note 132. *Add:*

McDaniel v. Essex International, Inc., 696 F.2d 34 (6th Cir. 1982); Draper v. United States Pipe & Foundry Co., 527 F.2d 515 (6th Cir. 1975).

p. 279. *Add note 132a following the third sentence in the second complete paragraph:*

[132a]*See, e.g.*, T.W.A. v. Hardison, 432 U.S. 63 (1977); Brener v. Diagnostic Center Hospital, 671 F.2d 141 (5th Cir. 1982); Turpen v. Missouri-Kansas-Texas Railroad Co., 573 F. Supp. 820 (N.D. Tex. 1983).

[134a]Estate of Thornton v. Caldor, Inc., 105 S. Ct. 2914 (1985).

p. 280. *Add after the last complete paragraph in the text:*

Those courts that have attempted to restrict the exemption provided by section 702 to employment decisions regarding the "religious activities" of churches and other religious organizations have exhibited an unwarranted insensitivity to legitimate religious beliefs. Many churches take literally the Pauline concept of the church as the "body of Christ." According to this concept, developed in the first epistle to the Corinthians (12:12-26) and in the epistles to the Romans (12:4,5), Ephesians (1:22,23; 4:15,16), and Colossians (1:18; 2:19), the church is a living organism consisting of several members, or "parts," some of which may seem less important, but all of which are in fact of equal significance. Paul compares the church and its constituent members to a human body and declares that the "feeble" parts are as indispensable to the whole as the "comely" parts. All are indispensable and of equal dignity because they all are integral parts of a functioning body. Therefore, the foot, while primarily servile, is of equal dignity to the hand. No one part is of more significance than any other, for they are all interdependent and of no utility individually. Similarly, each member of the church is an integral part of the body of Christ, and each member's contribution is of equal dignity and importance, no matter how routine it may appear. Paul declares that each member of the church is endowed with a gift or special ability from Christ, the head of the body, and that the church could not function without the contributions of each part. Here is an emphatic declaration, going to the very essence of the Christian faith, that each member's service or contribution to the church is of equal significance because each contribution, however mundane, is empowered and inspired by the risen Christ. Paul goes so far as to insist that God gives "more abundant honor to that part which lacked." This point is again emphasized by Paul's enumeration of the gift, or ministry, of "helps" as one of the many manifestations of divine enablement (1 Corinthians 12:28). The point is clear: No position of service within the church can be surgically severed and categorized as being either "religious" or "secular," for every position in the body of Christ—and the ignoble, or "secular," most of all—is completely dependent upon Christ the head. Judicial and administrative efforts to characterize a particular position of service within a church as religious or secular completely overlook and do violence to this Biblical concept of the church.

It is true that many churches do not accept the Pauline concept of the body of Christ and would have no reservation in complying with the Act's prohibition of religious discrimination in most employment decisions. However, it would be a gross violation of religious freedom to insist that churches which do accept literally the Pauline concept of the body of Christ be forced to abandon so fundamental a concept in the selection of functioning members, or parts, of the body.[137a]

When a court is faced with a bona fide religious institution claiming that its religious freedom and mission would be impaired by a requirement that it refrain from religious-based discrimination in any of its employment decisions, then such a claim must be accepted and an exception allowed. The number of such churches and religious institutions will be small, since many religious institutions do not discriminate in employment decisions on the basis of religion, and most of those that do discriminate have fewer than fifteen employees or are not engaged in an industry affecting commerce and therefore are not subject to the prohibition against religion-based discrimination. The government's interest in eradicating discrimination under such circumstances is clearly outweighed by the constitutional right of religious institutions to freely exercise their religion. During the debate on the 1972 amendment to section 702, Senator Sam Ervin observed:

> [U]nder the bill in its present form, the EEOC would have the power to compel a Christian church to employ a Mohammedan or an atheist or an agnostic as secretary. When the federal government begins to grasp the power of things of the Lord, it is reaching a state of governmental intemperance which is alien to the First Amendment. The First Amendment was designed to build a wall of separation between church and state. . . . I cannot understand why the EEOC or those who support it are so anxious to extend its powers so that it will have jurisdiction over who is employed by a church to be a janitor, or who is employed to be a secretary for a church, or who is employed—as is done in many instances where religious organizations have fundraising drives—to raise money for them. Yet this bill would extend the power of the EEOC over these employees of churches; and, as I have said, it would lay the political hands of Caesar upon the things of God. The First Amendment was designed to build a wall of separation between church and state and was designed to keep the state's hands off the church and the church's hands off the state. Certainly, a bill which is designed to lay the hands of the state on the employment practices of religious denominations is not keeping the hands of the state off the church.[137b]

A federal district court, in the most extensive attempt to define those "religious activities" which are exempt from the ban on religious discrimination, gave the following three-part test:

> First, the court must look at the tie between the religious organization and the activity at issue with regard to areas such as financial affairs, day-to-day operations and management. Second, whether or not there is a close and substantial tie between the two, the court next must examine the nexus between the primary function of the activity in question and the religious rituals or tenets of the religious organization or matters of church administration. If there is a substantial connection between the activity in question and the religious organization's religious tenets or matters of church administration and the tie under the first part of the test is close, the court does not need to proceed any further and may declare the activity religious. However, where the tie between the religious entity and activity

in question is either close or remote under the first prong of the test and the nexus between the primary function of the activity in question and the religious tenets or rituals of the religious organization or matters of church administration is tenuous or non-existent, the court must engage in a third inquiry. It must consider the relationship between the nature of the job the employee is performing and the religious rituals or tenets of the religious organization or matters of church administration. If there is a substantial relationship between the employee's job and church administration or the religious organization's rituals or tenets, the court must find that the activity in question is religious. If the relationship is not substantial, the activity is not religious.[137c]

This analysis of course completely disregards the Pauline concept of the church as the "body of Christ," and therefore should not be used in the context of churches that subscribe to that concept.

[137a]The same principle underlies Paul's denunciation of lawsuits involving Christians in 1 Corinthians 6. If Christians will "judge angels" by the enabling power of Christ, how much more should they be capable of resolving disputes among themselves without the aid of pagan magistrates who are not similarly enabled. *See generally* E. SCHWEITZER, THE BODY OF CHRIST (1964); C. K. BARRETT, A COMMENTARY ON THE FIRST EPISTLE TO THE CORINTHIANS (1968); F. F. BRUCE, 1 AND 2 CORINTHIANS (1958); L. MORRIS, THE FIRST EPISTLE OF PAUL TO THE CORINTHIANS (1958).

[137b]118 CONG. REC. 1977-81 (1972).

[137c]*See* Amos v. Corporation of Presiding Bishop, 594 F. Supp. 791 (D. Utah 1984).

p. 281. *Add the following new section at the end of the text:*

§ J. Judicial Resolution of Church Disputes

Should the civil courts ever have the authority to intervene in and resolve church controversies? If so, under what conditions? These are questions that have presented considerable difficulty.

Over a century ago, the Supreme Court observed:

[I]t is a very different thing where a subject matter of dispute, *strictly and purely ecclesiastical* in its character—a matter over which the civil courts exercise no jurisdiction—a matter which concerns theological controversy, church discipline, ecclesiastical government, or the conformity of the members of the church to the standard of morals required of them—becomes the subject of the action. It may be said here, also, that no jurisdiction has been conferred on the tribunal to try the particular case before it, or that, in its judgment, it exceeds the powers conferred upon it.[139]

The Court's denunciation of civil court intervention in "strictly and purely ecclesiastical" church disputes is still followed. To illustrate, the courts have refrained from intervening in disputes involving the appointment or removal of clergy;[140] ecclesiastical discipline;[141] church dogmas, doctrines, and customs;[142] canonicity;[143] controversies between a church and parent denomination;[144] removal of a church's board of directors;[145] church management;[146] excommunication or expulsion of members;[147] members entitled to vote at congregational meetings;[148] or "defrocking" of a deacon.[149] The courts also have refrained from taking over and running the affairs of a church, even on a temporary basis,[150] and from making probing inquiries into the sources and balance of power within church organizations.[151]

The principle of judicial nonintervention in essentially ecclesiastical disputes has been justified on the basis of three considerations. First, the Supreme Court in the *Watson* decision[152] seemed to base the principle on the "implied consent" of church members to the exclusive jurisdiction of the church:

> All who unite themselves to such a body do so with an implied consent to this government, and are bound to submit to it. But it would be a vain consent and would lead to the total subversion of such religious bodies, if anyone aggrieved by one of their decisions could appeal to the secular courts and have them reversed. It is of the essence of these religious unions, and of their right to establish tribunals for the decision of questions arising among themselves, that those decisions should be binding in all cases of ecclesiastical cognizance, subject only to such appeals as the organism itself provides for.[153]

Second, several courts in more recent years have based the principle of nonintervention on the First Amendment's religion clauses.[154] Third, a few courts have based the principle on the "sound policy" that churches should be left free to resolve their own disputes.[155]

The courts have rejected the contention that the controversies of incorporated churches should be subject to a greater degree of judicial supervision because such churches, by becoming incorporated, expose themselves to greater governmental scrutiny.[156]

Unfortunately, a few courts have uttered sweeping statements suggesting that they have no role to play in the resolution of church disputes. However, the great majority of courts have concluded that they may engage in "marginal review" of church controversies not involving "strictly and purely ecclesiastical" questions. For example, the courts have intervened in church controversies in order to prevent interference with civil, contract, or property rights;[157] determine whether an ecclesiastical body had authority to take a particular action such as the expulsion of a minister or church member;[158] ensure that a church acted pursuant to its charter, constitution, and bylaws in taking a particular action;[159] determine if a church ruling was based on fraud or collusion;[160] interpret contested terminology in a church's charter, constitution, or bylaws;[161] ascertain whether a church organization was congregational or hierarchical in polity;[162] determine if an organization was a bona fide church or religious entity;[163] or enforce the duly-adopted actions of a church.[164] Courts also have intervened in church disputes when both sides to a controversy consent to judicial assistance, such as in a declaratory judgment action.[165]

However, the mere assertion that a civil, contract, or property right is involved is not enough to warrant civil court intervention, for this often can be a spurious effort to involve a court in an essentially ecclesiastical controversy.[166]

Courts asserting jurisdiction over church disputes not involving ecclesiastical issues ordinarily require that the persons bringing the action "exhaust" all remedies available to them within the church or religious denomination before applying to the civil courts for relief.[167]

Many cases have involved judicial review of a church's action in expelling a minister or church member. Most courts do resolve such disputes if their review is limited to one of the considerations mentioned above. For example, if an expelled minister or church member claims that the church did not follow its bylaws in expelling him, a civil court ordinarily will intervene in the controversy to determine whether the bylaws were followed. This is a neutral inquiry involving no "strictly and purely ecclesiastical" considerations. Civil courts also commonly resolve church property disputes. The Supreme Court has sanctioned civil court resolution of such disputes so long as no determinations of religious doctrine are required. The civil courts are called upon to resolve church property disputes more often than any other kind of church controversy. Such cases are discussed in detail in another chapter.[168]

In summary, judicial review of church disputes under the circumstances described above ordinarily involves a limited and neutral review of the procedural aspects of church disputes, and thus cannot properly be classified with those disputes that involve "strictly and purely ecclesiastical" considerations and over which the civil courts are forbidden from exercising jurisdiction. They involve no scrutiny of religious doctrine, no displacement of ecclesiastical authority, and no interference in substantive ecclesiastical determinations, and accordingly do not implicate those concerns protected by the First Amendment's religion clauses. Those who advocate an absolute rule of judicial nonintervention in all cases often overlook the fact that nonintervention is not necessarily neutrality, since by refusing to intervene in such disputes the courts would in effect always take the side of defendants and repudiate the contentions of claimants. One commentator has aptly noted: "If the goal is avoidance of judicial involvement in church disputes, it is not achieved by deference to the view of the [church]. Deference is also intervention, since it inserts the authority of the state into an internal church dispute in support of one faction."[169] Finally, it is significant that the Supreme Court has observed that "not every civil court decision . . . jeopardizes values protected by the First Amendment."[170] Indeed, one Supreme Court Justice has observed that "[t]o make available the coercive powers of civil courts to rubber-stamp ecclesiastical decisions . . . when such deference is not accorded similar acts of secular voluntary associations, would . . . itself create far more serious problems under the establishment clause."[171]

Hierarchical denominations often provide tribunals for resolving certain kinds of church disputes. The Supreme Court has held that if such a tribunal has resolved a local church dispute, and acted pursuant to its stated procedures, then the civil courts are compelled to defer to that decision, even if it was arbitrary:

> [T]he First and Fourteenth Amendments permit hierarchical religious organizations to establish their own rules and regulations for internal discipline and government, and to create tribunals for adjudicating disputes over these matters. When this choice is exercised and ecclesiastical tribunals are created to decide disputes over the government and direction of subordinate bodies, the Constitution requires that civil courts accept their decisions as binding upon them.[172]

The Court's decision affirmed its century-old ruling in *Watson*[173] that the decisions of hierarchical church tribunals on ecclesiastical matters, although affecting civil rights, are final and binding on the civil courts. The Court's ruling that civil courts are without authority to invalidate even "arbitrary" decisions of church tribunals was a partial repudiation of an earlier decision in which it had suggested that the determinations of such tribunals could be invalidated by the civil courts on the basis of "fraud, collusion, or arbitrariness."[174] The Court's decision has been criticized on two grounds: (1) It constitutes an unwarranted subordination of the principles of fairness, consistency, and minority rights to the principle of the separation of church and state, and (2) it falsely assumes that the courts are being "neutral" in refusing to resolve such disputes, for by their refusal they in effect always take the side of defendants and repudiate the contentions of claimants.[175] As one Supreme Court Justice has predicted, "If the civil courts are to be bound by any sheet or parchment bearing the ecclesiastical seal and purporting to be a decree of a church court, they can easily be converted into handmaidens of arbitrary lawlessness."[176] Unfortunately, the Court's ruling has effectively barred the claims of those alleging that a church tribunal acted arbitrarily in reaching a particular determination.[177] The Court observed in a subsequent decision, however, that the "compulsory deference rule" (i.e., civil courts are compelled to defer to the rulings of ecclesiastical tribunals in hierarchical churches) applies only to questions of "religious doctrine or polity," and thus does not necessarily apply to the many kinds of controversies mentioned above involving no "strictly and purely ecclesiastical" concerns.[178]

[139]Watson v. Jones, 80 U.S. (13 Wall.) 679, 733 (1872) (emphasis added). Although *Watson* was decided before judicial recognition of the coercive power of the Fourteenth Amendment to protect the limitations of the First Amendment against state actions, it has been endorsed by the Supreme Court in several recent decisions and thereby retains its authority. *See, e.g.*, Kedroff v. St. Nicholas Cathedral, 344 U.S. 94 (1952).

[140]Kaufmann v. Sheehan, 707 F.2d 355 (8th Cir. 1983); Lucas v. Hope, 515 F.2d 234 (5th Cir. 1975), *cert. denied*, 424 U.S. 967 (1975); Serbian Eastern Orthodox Diocese v. Ocokoljich, 219 N.E.2d 343 (Ill. App. 1966); Serbian Eastern Orthodox Congregation v. Serbian Eastern Orthodox Congregation, 254 A.2d 119 (N.J. 1969).

[141]Smart v. Indiana Yearly Conference of Wesleyan Methodist Church, 271 N.E.2d 713 (Ind. 1971); Joiner v. Weeks, 383 So.2d 101 (La. App. 1980).

[142]Merryman v. Price, 259 N.E.2d 883 (Ind. App. 1970), *cert. denied*, 404 U.S. 852 (1970); Joiner v. Weeks, 383 So.2d 101 (La. App. 1980).

[143]Russian Church of Our Lady of Kazan v. Dunkel, 326 N.Y.S.2d 727 (1971), *aff'd*, 341 N.Y.S.2d 148 (1972).

[144]First Presbyterian Church v. United Presbyterian Church in the United States, 430 F. Supp. 450 (S.D.N.Y. 1977); Williams v. Arpie, 405 N.Y.S.2d 437 (1978).

[145]United Pentecostal Church International v. Sanderson, 391 So.2d 1293 (La. App. 1980).

[146]Gervin v. Reddick, 268 S.E.2d 657 (Ga. 1980).

[147]Macedonia Baptist Foundation v. Singleton, 379 So.2d 269 (La. App. 1979); Bowen v. Green, 272 S.E.2d 433 (S.C. 1980).

[148]Mulkey v. Blankenship, 558 P.2d 398 (Okla. 1976).

[149]Chavis v. Nickerson, 444 A.2d 590 (N.J. 1982).

[150]In re Galilee Baptist Church, 186 So.2d 102 (Ala. 1966); Gervin v. Reddick, 268 S.E.2d 657 (Ga. 1980).

[151]Kedroff v. St. Nicholas Cathedral, 344 U.S. 94 (1952).

[152]*See* note 139, *supra*.

[153]*Id.* at 729.

[154]Nolynn Assoc. of Separate Baptists in Christ v. Oak Grove Separate Baptist Church, 457 S.W.2d 633 (Ky. 1970), *cert. denied*, 401 U.S. 955 (1970); Gelder v. Loomis, 605 P.2d 1330 (Okla. 1980); Waters v. Hargest, 593 S.W.2d 364 (Tex. App. 1979).

[155]Wheeler v. Roman Catholic Archdiocese, 389 N.E.2d 966 (Mass. 1979); Gorodetzer v. Kraft, 277 N.E.2d 685 (Mass. 1972).

[156]Henry v. Newman, 351 So.2d 1277 (La. App. 1977).

[157]Church of God in Christ, Inc. v. Stone, 452 F. Supp. 612 (D. Kan. 1976); Abyssinia Missionary Baptist Church v. Nixon, 340 So.2d 746 (Ala. 1976); Chavis v. Rowe, 459 A.2d 674 (N.J. 1983); African Methodist Episcopal Zion Church v. Union Chapel A.M.E. Zion Church, 308 S.E.2d 73 (N.C. App. 1983); Lide v. Miller, 573 S.W.2d 614 (Tex. App. 1978).

[158]Bowen v. Green, 272 S.E.2d 433 (S.C. 1980).

[159]Konkel v. Metropolitan Baptist Church, Inc., 572 P.2d 99 (Ariz. App. 1977); Draskovich v. Pasalich, 280 N.E.2d 69 (Ind. App. 1972); LeBlanc v. Davis, 432 So.2d 239

(La. 1983); Wilkerson v. Battiste, 393 So.2d 195 (La. App. 1980); Mitchell v. Albanian Orthodox Diocese, 244 N.E.2d 276 (Mass. 1969).

[160]Berkaw v. Mayflower Congregational Church, 170 N.W.2d 905 (Mich. App. 1969); Hatcher v. South Carolina District Council of the Assemblies of God, Inc., 226 S.E.2d 253 (S.C. 1976).

[161]Second Baptist Church v. Mount Zion Baptist Church, 466 P.2d 212 (Nev. 1970).

[162]Antioch Temple, Inc. v. Parekh, 422 N.E.2d 1337 (Mass. 1981); State ex rel. Morrow v. Hill, 364 N.E.2d 1156 (Ohio 1977).

[163]People v. Wood, 402 N.Y.S.2d 726 (1978).

[164]Smith v. Riley, 424 So.2d 1166 (La. App. 1982); Antioch Temple, Inc. v. Parekh, 422 N.E.2d 1337 (Mass. 1981); First Presbyterian Church v. United Presbyterian Church in the United States, 461 N.Y.S.2d 902 (1983); Hill v. Sargent, 615 S.W.2d 300 (Tex. App. 1981).

[165]Draughn v. Hill, 186 N.W.2d 855 (Mich. App. 1971).

[166]Eddy ex rel. Pfeifer v. Christian Science Board of Directors, 379 N.E.2d 653 (Ill. App, 1978).

[167]First Baptist Church v. State of Ohio, 591 F. Supp. 676 (S.D. Ohio 1983); United Pentecostal Church v. Morrison, 527 P.2d 1169 (Colo. App. 1974).

[168]See chapter 9, infra.

[169]I. Ellman, Driven From the Tribunal: Judicial Resolution of Internal Church Disputes, 69 CAL. L. REV. 1378, 1411 (1981).

[170]Presbyterian Church in the United States v. Mary Elizabeth Blue Hull Memorial Presbyterian Church, 393 U.S. 440, 449 (1969).

[171]Serbian Eastern Orthodox Diocese v. Milivojevich, 426 U.S. 696, 727 (1976) (dissenting opinion).

[172]Id. at 724-25.

[173]See note 139, supra.

[174]Gonzalez v. Archbishop, 280 U.S. 1 (1929). Whether the courts can invalidate the determinations of hierarchical church tribunals is an unresolved question after the Serbian decision.

[175]See, e.g., I. Ellman, Driven From the Tribunal: Judicial Resolution of Internal Church Disputes, 69 CAL. L. REV. 1378, 1411 (1981).

[176]Serbian Eastern Orthodox Diocese v. Milivojevich, 426 U.S. 696, 727 (1976) (Justice Rehnquist, dissenting).

[177]Kaufmann v. Sheehan, 707 F.2d 355 (8th Cir. 1983); Joiner v. Weeks, 383 So.2d 101 (La. App. 1980).

[178]Jones v. Wolf, 443 U.S. 595 (1979). Four dissenting Justices argued that the compulsory deference rule should apply to all the determinations of hierarchical church tribunals.

12

NEGLIGENCE AND PREMISES LIABILITY

§ B. Premises Liability

p. 290. *Delete line 11 of the last incomplete paragraph and substitute the following:*

the church owed her a duty to exercise ordinary care to keep the premises

p. 294. *Add after the first complete paragraph:*

The parents of an infant whose eye was seriously injured in a church nursery during worship services were denied any recovery since no one witnessed the accident and there was no evidence that it was caused by any negligence on the part of the church.[52a] Similarly, a church member doing volunteer work for his church was denied recovery for injuries sustained when a ladder fell on him. The court noted that the member was an invitee, and that the church owed him a legal duty to correct or give notice of concealed, dangerous conditions of which it was or should have been aware. However, the court denied recovery on the ground that the member was aware of the unsecured ladder and the danger it presented, and this knowledge excused the church from its duty of correcting the condition or notifying the member of its existence.[52b]

[52a]Helton v. Forest Park Baptist Church, 589 S.W.2d 217 (Ky. App. 1979).

[52b]Fisher v. Northmoor United Methodist Church, 679 S.W.2d 305 (Mo. App. 1984).

p. 295. *Add note 55a following the first complete paragraph:*

[55a]*See, e.g.*, Jeffords v. Atlanta Presbytery, 231 S.#.2d 355 (Ga. App. 1976); Heath v. First Baptist Church, 341 So.2d 265 (Fla. App. 1977).

p. 295. *Delete the first line of the first complete paragraph and substitute the following:*

Intervening, superseding causes, assumption of risk, comparative negligence, and general liability

§ C. Denominational Liability

p. 296. *Add after the first complete paragraph:*

In many cases, a judicial finding that a religious denomination is responsible for the alleged wrongs of affiliated churches would force that denomination to alter its organization in order to defend itself against similar charges in the future. To illustrate, the national offices and a regional office of the Assemblies of God were sued in 1981 for failure to supervise the fund-raising activities of an affiliated church. The church had created a trust fund in 1973 as a means of financing a new church building and related facilities. The fund consisted of unsecured deposits solicited from both church members and nonmembers. According to the trust agreements and certificates of deposit used in connection with the fund, the deposits could be withdrawn after one year, with interest. Eventually, the fund had assets of over $7,000,000 which had been deposited by some 1100 persons. In 1978, state banking authorities served the fund with a cease and desist order for operating a bank without a license. A subsequent run on the fund resulted in its collapse. In 1979, the church filed a petition for relief under Chapter 11 of the Bankruptcy Code (the same year the new Code became effective).

In 1981, a class action suit was filed in federal district court naming the national organization ("General Council") of the Assemblies of God and one of its regional divisions ("District Council") as defendants. The suit was brought against the national and regional offices because of an automatic stay by the bankruptcy court prohibiting the plaintiffs from suing the church directly. Specifically, the class action complaint alleged that the church had committed securities fraud in violation of state and federal law by selling securities without proper registration, and that the national and regional offices were derivatively responsible for the securities fraud as "control persons" under section 20(a) of the Securities Exchange Act:

> Every person who, directly or indirectly, controls any person liable under any provision of this title or any rule or regulation thereunder shall also be liable

jointly and severally with and to the same extent as such control person to any person to whom such control person is liable, unless the controlling person acted in good faith and did not directly or indirectly induce the act or acts constituting the violation or cause of action.

To substantiate their allegation of control person liability, the plaintiffs cited several factors, including the following: (1) the General Council and District Council issued ministerial credentials to the church's pastor; (2) the General Council and District Council retained control over the pastor's activities by their power to discipline him and withdraw his credentials; (3) the General Council could withdraw the church's certificate of affiliation for improper conduct, and, by failing to do so, it ratified the church's securities fraud; (4) the General Council and District Council and their missionary activities were beneficiaries of some church contributions; (5) by permitting the church to affiliate itself with the Assemblies of God, the General Council and District Council permitted the church to hold itself out as being under their general supervision; and (6) the church was covered by the group federal income tax exemption issued by the IRS to the General Council and all its "subordinate units."

The plaintiffs conceded that the General Council and District Council did not participate in or even know of the church's activities until the state banking authorities issued the cease and desist order in 1978, and therefore were not liable under a strict reading of section 20(a). However, they relied on cases in which the courts have concluded that "broker-dealers" participate in the securities fraud of agents by failing to enforce a reasonable system of supervision.

The General Council and District Council filed motions for summary judgment on a variety of grounds, including the following: (1) they were not "control persons" within the meaning of section 20(a) since (a) under the organizational documents, practice, and theology of the Assemblies of God, they were powerless to exercise control over local churches, (b) their lack of knowledge and participation constituted a "good faith" defense, (c) the stringent broker-dealer standard had no application to religious organizations, and (2) the First Amendment's free exercise of religion clause prohibited a civil court from requiring a religious denomination to exercise a degree of control over its affiliated churches that was repugnant to its practices, organization, and theology. The General Council noted that judicial imposition of a duty to supervise the financial affairs of its 11,000 churches in the United States, despite long-established practice and theology to the contrary, would force it to change its polity in order to defend against similar suits. It noted that the Supreme Court has frequently observed that judicial manipulation of the polity or internal organization of church bodies violates the First Amendment.[59]

In 1985, a federal district court granted the motion for summary judgment filed by the General Council and District Council.[60] The court concluded that the defendants could not be guilty as control persons under section 20(a) of the Securities Exchange Act since they did not know of or participate in the activities of the church. The court was not willing to extend the more stringent "broker-dealer" standard (e.g., failure to adequately supervise constitutes participation) to the defendants since "there are some significant differences between the broker-dealer context and the church structure at issue here." In particular, the court observed that "it is generally recognized that broker-dealers have a high degree of control over their agents," unlike the relationship between the defendants and local Assemblies of God churches. Further, the defendants were nonprofit entities and thus significantly differed from the typical broker-dealer. Most importantly, however, the court stressed that "the Assemblies of God . . . was founded on the principle that local churches would be sovereign, self-governing units, and are given wide discretion in operating their affairs." This relationship falls short of the "control" contemplated by section 20(a).

[59]*See, e.g.,* Jones v. Wolf, 99 S. Ct. 3020, 3026 (1979); Serbian Eastern Orthodox Diocese v. Milivojevich, 426 U.S. 696, 708-09, 724 (1976); Maryland and Virginia Eldership of the Churches of God v. The Church of God at Sharpsburg, 396 U.S. 367, 369-70 (1970); Presbyterian Church in the United States v. Mary Elizabeth Blue Hull Memorial Presbyterian Church, 393 U.S. 440, 449 (1969); Kedroff v. St. Nicholas Cathedral of Russian Orthodox Church, 344 U.S. 94, 105-06, 116 (1952); Watson v. Jones, 80 U.S. 679, 733 (1872).

[60]Kersh v. The General Council of the Assemblies of God, No. C 84-0252 (N.D. Cal., May 17, 1985). *See also* Hope Lutheran Church v. Chellew, 460 N.E.2d 1244 (Ind. App. 1984).

13

ADMINISTRATION OF PRIVATE SCHOOLS

p. 299, note 5. *Add:*

The United States Supreme Court ruled in 1985 that such laws violate the First Amendment nonestablishment of religion clause if prayer is encouraged over other forms of silent behavior. An analysis of a particular law's history, language, and implementation will help determine if prayer is impermissibly encouraged. *Wallace v. Jaffree*, 105 S. Ct. 2479 (1985).

§ A. Incorporation and Tax Exemption

p. 302. *Add after the first incomplete paragraph:*

However, the Court acknowledged that the law exempted incorporated church schools that were operated primarily for religious purposes and that were "operated, supervised, controlled, or principally supported by a church or convention or association of churches."[12a]

The Church Audit Procedures Act, adopted by Congress in 1984, significantly limits IRS audits of churches and some unincorporated church-controlled activities. The Act does *not* apply to separately incorporated church schools.

[12a]*See generally* chapter 10, § C, *supra.*

p. 302. *Add after the first complete paragraph:*

It could be argued, however, that in some cases an incorporated church school is entitled to tax-exempt status. For example, "integral parts" of churches, as defined in the income tax regulations, are exempted from the federal tax on unrelated business income whether or not they are incorporated. There is no reason why such entities should also not share a parent church's exemption from other federal taxes.[12b]

[12b]See generally chapter 7, supra. Similarly, it is possible for incorporated schools to be classified as "integral agencies" of a church if they satisfy most of the eight conditions set forth in Revenue Ruling 72-606. See chapter 7, supra.

§ B. Proof of Nondiscrimination

p. 304. *Delete the last incomplete paragraph and the first incomplete paragraph on page 305, and substitute the following:*

In 1976, the United States Supreme Court held that private schools may not employ racially discriminatory admissions criteria.[21] In so holding, the Court relied upon a federal statute[22] stipulating that "[a]ll persons within the jurisdiction of the United States shall have the same right . . . to make and enforce contracts as is enjoyed by white citizens. . . ." The Court acknowledged that it was not deciding the issue of the legality of racially discriminatory admissions policies based upon religious beliefs. This narrower question was resolved by the Court in 1983 in the Bob Jones University decision.[23] In *Bob Jones*, the Court upheld the authority of the IRS to revoke the tax-exempt status of Bob Jones University on the basis of the school's prohibition of interracial dating and marriage, despite the school's claim that its policies were founded on Biblical principles. The Court agreed with the university that federal tax law contains no express requirement that tax-exempt organizations refrain from racial discrimination. However, the Court concluded that it was the intent of Congress that "entitlement to tax exemption depends on meeting certain common law standards of charity—namely, that an institution seeking tax-exempt status must serve a public purpose and not be contrary to established public policy," and that it provide a benefit to society.[24] The Court then referred to an "unbroken line of cases" that "establish beyond any doubt" its view that "racial discrimination in education violates a most fundamental national public policy" without conferring a public benefit.[24a] As a result, the university's ban on interracial dating and marriage, which the Court found to be a form of racial discrimination,[24b] disqualified it for tax-exempt status.

In rejecting the university's contention that only Congress and not the IRS could "amend" federal tax law by inserting the "public policy" requirement, the Court referred to the "broad authority" vested in the IRS to interpret the laws enacted by Congress:

> In [the federal tax law] Congress has identified categories of traditionally exempt institutions and has specified certain additional requirements for tax exemption. Yet the need for continuing interpretation of those statutes is unavoidable. For more than 60 years, the IRS and its predecessors have constantly been called upon to interpret these and comparable provisions, and in doing so have referred consistently to principles of charitable trust law.[24c]

The Court also found it relevant that Congress, although aware of lower court and IRS rulings denying tax-exempt status to private schools that engaged in racial discrimination, did nothing to legislatively overrule those rulings.

Finally, while acknowledging that the university's discriminatory practice was based on a genuine belief that the Bible forbids interracial dating and marriage, the Court concluded that those beliefs were "substantially out-weighed" by the government's "compelling interest" in "eradicating racial dis-crimination in education." Further, the Court observed that while its ruling inevitably would have an adverse impact on the university, it would not prevent the university from observing its religious beliefs. The Court emphasized that it was dealing with religious schools, and not with churches or "other purely religious institutions," and that "sensitive determinations" by the IRS regarding the effect of an organization's activities on public policy "should be made only where there is no doubt that the organization's activities violated fundamental public policy."[24d]

In summary, racially discriminatory religious schools are ineligible for tax-exempt status under the Internal Revenue Code because they violate a fun-damental public policy and confer no public benefit. The Court left unanswered the question of whether an organization providing a public benefit could be denied tax-exempt status if certain of its activities violated a law or public policy. An example of the latter question would be the practice of the Catholic Church in barring women from the priesthood. It is doubtful that the church's tax-exempt status is jeopardized by the *Bob Jones* decision, since (1) the Cath-olic Church undeniably provides a variety of public benefits, which distin-guishes it from Bob Jones University under the Court's reasoning; (2) it cannot be said that the church's practice is without doubt "contrary to a fundamental public policy," especially in view of the failure of the "equal rights amendment" to become a part of the federal Constitution; (3) the church's practice relates to the relationship between church and clergy, which the courts have consis-tently found to be exempt from governmental regulation;[24e] and (4) the church's practice relates to a fundamental and essential expression of its religious tra-dition, and therefore the exercise of its religion would be materially impeded by a requirement that it admit women to the priesthood.

[23]Bob Jones University v. United States, 103 S. Ct. 2017 (1983).

[24]*Id.* at 2026. The Court's insistence that tax-exempt organizations provide a "public benefit" is contrary to its opinion in Walz v. Commissioner, 397 U.S. 664 (1970), wherein the Court specifically held that this was not a requirement. In rejecting the university's claim that it automatically was entitled to an exemption without the necessity of a "public policy" analysis because it was organized for educational and religious purposes, the Court observed: "Fagin's school for educating English boys in the art of picking pockets would be an 'educational' institution under that definition" and accordingly entitled to tax-exempt status. "Surely," concluded the Court, "Congress had no thought of affording

such an unthinking, wooden meaning to [the federal tax code] as to provide tax benefits to 'educational' organizations that do not serve a public, charitable purpose." *Id.* at 2029, note 18.

[24a]103 S. Ct. at 2029.

[24b]The Court cited Loving v. Virginia, 388 U.S. 1 (1967) as authority for this proposition.

[24c]103 S. Ct. at 2130.

[24d]*Id.* at 2032.

[24e]*See, e.g.*, McClure v. Salvation Army, 460 F.2d 553 (5th Cir. 1972), *cert. denied*, 409 U.S. 896 (1972).

p. 305. *Add after the first complete paragraph:*

The related question of a private school's right to discriminate in employment decisions on the basis of religion is discussed in chapters 10 and 11.

§ D. The Distinction Between Public and Private Education

p. 307, note 30. *Add:*

Reardon v. LeMoyne, 454 A.2d 428 (N.H. 1982).

§ E. Discharge and Discipline of Students

p. 308. *Add note 34a following the first sentence in the last paragraph of § E:*

[34a]*See, e.g.*, Block v. Hillel Torah North Suburban Day School, 426 N.E.2d 976 (Ill. 1981).

§ G. Tuition Refunds

p. 312. *Add after the first incomplete paragraph:*

A school that dismisses a student for failure to pay tuition may itself breach the enrollment contract thereby, and lose its legal right to claim the tuition. One court has suggested that the school should retain the student under such circumstances and sue for the tuition.[48a]

[48a]Buffalo Seminary v. Tomaselli, 435 N.Y.S.2d 507 (1981).

§ H. Government Regulation of Private Schools

p. 313, note 53. *Add:*

State v. Rivinius, 328 N.W.2d 220 (N.D. 1982).

p. 314, note 56. *Add:*

Accord State ex rel. Kandt v. North Platte Baptist Church, 345 N.W.2d 19 (Nebr. 1984); State ex re. Douglas v. Calvary Academy, 348 N.W.2d 898 (Nebr. 1984). *See also* McCurry v. Tesch, 738 F.2d 271 (8th Cir. 1984) (state court order requiring padlocking of church at all times except during religious services violated First Amendment free exercise of religion clause); Sileven v. Tesch, 326 N.W.2d 850 (Nebr. 1982).

p. 314. *Add after the last complete paragraph:*

The Supreme Court of Hawaii has upheld the constitutionality of a state law requiring private church schools to be licensed.[57a] The court, applying the three-part *Yoder* test,[57b] concluded that the license requirement promoted a compelling state interest and did not unduly burden sincerely held religious beliefs.

[57a]State v. Andrews, 651 P.2d 473 (Hawaii 1982).
[57b]*See* note 54, *supra*, and accompanying text.

pp. 315-316. *Delete the last incomplete paragraph on page 315 and the first incomplete paragraph on page 316, and substitute the following:*

In recent years, a number of courts have held that parents who educate their children at home are not in violation of state compulsory attendance laws requiring minor children to be educated in public or private schools. Ordinarily, this conclusion is based on a finding that a compulsory attendance law is "void for vagueness" since it permits children to attend private schools but does not define the term *private school* with sufficient clarity to enable parents who educate their children at home to determine if they are in compliance.[63] However, a number of other courts have ruled that parents who educate their children at home are in violation of compulsory attendance laws. Such courts typically find that home instruction cannot reasonably be included within the term *school,* and that prosecution of parents for violating the law does not abridge their constitutional right to freely exercise their religion.[63a] These courts often rely on the Supreme Court's dictum in Wisconsin v. Yoder[63b] that "the power of the parent, even when linked to a free exercise [of religion] claim, may be subject to limitation . . . if it appears that parental decisions will jeopardize the health or safety of the child, or have a potential for significant social burdens."

Since the permissibility of home education ordinarily is dependent upon a court's interpretation of the term *private school,* a number of state legislatures have helped resolve the problem by specifying that home education satisfies the state compulsory attendance law. Often, such statutes specify various conditions that must be met in order for a particular home to satisfy the compulsory attendance law. For example, some states require that home-educated children be tested periodically to ensure that they are making satisfactory progress.

[63]*See, e.g.,* Roemhild v. State, 308 S.E.2d 154 (Ga. 1983); State v. Pobanz, 332 N.W.2d 750 (Wis. 1983).

[63a]*See, e.g.,* Burrow v. State, 669 S.W.2d 441 (Ark. 1984); F. & F. v. Duvall County, 273 So.2d 15 (Fla. App. 1973); In Interest of Sawyer, 672 P.2d 1093 (Kan. 1983); State v. Garber, 419 P.2d 896 (Kan. 1966); Delconte v. State, 308 S.E.2d 898 (N.C. 1983); City of Akron v. Lane, 416 N.E.2d 642 (Ohio 1979); State v. Riddle, 285 S.E.2d 359 (W. Va. 1981).

[63b]406 U.S. 205 (1972).

p. 317. *Add after the first complete paragraph:*

A federal district court has invalidated administrative regulations adopted by the Maine State Board of Education which attempted to institute a scheme whereby private schools could operate only if approved by the Board.[69a] The court concluded that the Board's action exceeded the authority vested in it by the state legislature.

[69a]Bangor Baptist Church v. State, 576 F. Supp. 1299 (D. Maine 1983).

p. 317. *Delete the first line of the second complete paragraph of the text, and substitute the following:*

Finally, in Wisconsin v. Yoder the United States Supreme Court ruled

§ J. Safety and Health Regulations

p. 321. *Add after the last complete paragraph:*

In a related case, a church operated a school on church premises that complied with applicable church fire and safety regulations. The state of Michigan maintained that since the property was used primarily as a school, the school fire and safety regulations applied. A state appeals court held that while a church school is an "integral part" of a church's ministry, the school fire and safety regulations must apply to a facility used primarily as a school.[90a] The court quoted Romans 13:1-7 and Matthew 22:19-21, and noted that "these verses clearly delineate a Christian's responsibility to obey his government, except where there is direct conflict with his obedience to God." The court concluded that any burden on religious freedom under these circumstances was outweighed by the state's compelling interest in ensuring the safety of school children.

[90a]State Fire Marshall v. Lee, 300 N.W.2d 748 (Mich. App. 1982).

§ K. Taxation

p. 322. *Add after the first indented paragraph:*

This ruling was qualified by the Supreme Court in an important decision in 1983. In the *Mueller* case,[95a] the Court was asked to review the constitutionality of a Minnesota statute allowing taxpayers, in computing their state income tax, to deduct certain expenses incurred in providing for their children's education. Unlike the state law invalidated by the Court in the *Lemon* case,[95b] the Minnesota law granted a deduction for educational expenses incurred by *all* parents, including those whose children attend public or nonsectarian private schools. The Court found this difference to be critical, noting that "a program . . . that neutrally provides state assistance to a broad spectrum of citizens is not readily subject to challenge under the establishment clause."[95c] The Court rejected the argument that the Minnesota law, while neutral on its face, was in practice unconstitutional since most parents of public school children incur no "education expenses" and 96% of the children in the state's private schools attend church-affiliated institutions. The *Mueller* case is significant because it permits state legislatures to grant tax relief to parents who are compelled to subsidize a system of education that they conscientiously oppose.

[95a]Mueller v. Allen, 103 S. Ct. 3062 (1983).
[95b]Lemon v. Kurtzman, 403 U.S. 602 (1971).
[95c]103 S. Ct. at 3069.

p. 323. *Delete the last paragraph and the indented paragraph of the text and substitute the following:*

Finally, many taxpayers have attempted to claim charitable contribution deductions for payments made to a private school or to a church operating a private school in which the taxpayer's child is enrolled. The IRS has emphasized that a charitable contribution is "a voluntary transfer of money or property that is made with no expectation of procuring a financial benefit commensurate with the amount of the transfer."[103] Therefore, payments made by a taxpayer on behalf of a child attending a church-sponsored school are not deductible as contributions either to the school or to the church operating the school if the payments are earmarked for the child.[104]

The fact that payments are not earmarked for a particular child does not necessarily mean that they are deductible. The IRS has held that the deductibility of undesignated payments by a taxpayer to a private school in which his child is enrolled depends upon

> whether a reasonable person, taking all the facts and circumstances of the case in due account, would conclude that enrollment in the school was in no manner contingent upon making the payment, that the payment was not made pursuant to a plan (whether express or implied) to convert nondeductible tuition into charitable contributions, and that receipt of the benefit was not otherwise dependent upon the making of the payment.[105]

In resolving this question, the IRS has stated that the presence of one or more of the following factors creates a presumption that the payment is not a charitable contribution: (1) the existence of a contract under which a taxpayer agrees to make a "contribution" and which contains provisions ensuring the admission of the taxpayer's child; (2) a plan allowing taxpayers either to pay tuition or to make "contributions" in exchange for schooling; (3) the earmarking of a contribution for the direct benefit of a particular individual; or (4) the otherwise unexplained denial of admission or readmission to a school of children of taxpayers who are financially able, but who do not contribute.[106] The IRS has observed that if none of these factors is determinative, a combination of several additional factors may indicate that a payment is not a charitable contribution. Such additional factors include but are not limited to the following: (1) the absence of a significant tuition charge; (2) substantial or unusual pressure to contribute applied to parents of children attending a school; (3) contribution appeals made as part of the admissions or enrollment process; (4) the absence of significant potential sources of revenue for operating the school other than contributions by parents of children attending the school; (5) other factors suggesting that a contribution policy has been created as a means of avoiding the characterization of payments as tuition.[107] If a combination of such factors is not present, payments by a parent will normally constitute deductible contributions, even if the actual cost of educating the child exceeds the amount of any tuition charged for the child's education.

The IRS has illustrated the application of these principles in the following examples:

Situation 1. A school requests parents to contribute a designated amount (e.g., $400) for each child enrolled in the school. Parents who do not make the $400 contribution are required to pay tuition of $400 for each child. Parents who neither make the contribution nor pay the tuition cannot enroll their children in the school. A parent who pays $400 to the school is not entitled to a charitable contribution deduction because the parent must either make the contribution or pay the tuition in order for his child to attend the school. Therefore, admission to the school is contingent upon making a payment of $400. Such a payment is not voluntary.

Situation 2. A school solicits contributions from parents of applicants for admission during the school's solicitation for enrollment of students or while applications are pending. The solicitation materials are part of the application materials or are presented in a form indicating that parents of applicants have been singled out as a class for solicitation. Most parents who are financially able make a contribution or pledge to the school. No tuition is charged. The school suggests that parents make a payment of $400. A parent making a payment of $400 to the school is not entitled to a charitable contribution deduction. Because of the time and manner of the solicitation of contributions by the school, and the fact that no tuition is charged, it is not reasonable to expect that a parent can obtain the admission of his child to the school without making the suggested payments. Such payments are in the nature of tuition, not voluntary contributions.

Situation 3. A school admits a significantly larger percentage of applicants whose parents have made contributions to the school than applicants whose parents have not made contributions. Parents who make payments to the school are not entitled to a charitable contribution deduction. The IRS ordinarily will conclude that the parents of applicants are aware of the preference given to applicants whose parents have made contributions. The IRS therefore ordinarily will conclude that a parent could not reasonably expect to obtain the admission of his child to the school without making the payment.

Situation 4. A society for religious instruction has as its sole function the operation of a private school providing secular and religious education to the children of its members. No tuition is charged. The school is funded through the society's general account. Contributions to the account are solicited from all society members, as well as from local churches and nonmembers. Persons other than parents of children attending the school do not contribute a significant portion of the school's support. Funds normally come to the school from parents on a regular, established schedule. At times, parents are solicited by the school to contribute funds. No student is refused admittance because of the failure of his or her parents to contribute to the school. Under these circumstances, the IRS generally will conclude that payments to the society are nondeductible. Unless contributions from sources other than parents are of such magnitude that the school is not economically dependent upon parent's contributions, parents would ordinarily not be certain that the school could provide educational benefits without their payments. This conclusion is further evidenced by the fact that parents contribute on a regular, established schedule.

Situation 5. A private school charges a tuition of $300 per student. In addition, it solicits contributions from parents of students during periods other than the period of the school's solicitation for student enrollments. Solicitation materials indicate that parents of students have been singled out as a class for solicitation and the solicitation materials include a report of the school's cost per student. Suggested amounts of contributions based on an individual's ability to pay are provided. No unusual pressure to contribute is placed upon individuals who have children in the school, and many parents do not contribute. In addition, the school receives contributions from many former students, parents of former students, and other individuals. A parent pays $100 to the school in addition to the $300 tuition payment. Under these circumstances, the IRS generally will conclude that the parent is entitled to claim a charitable contribution deduction of $100. Because a charitable organization normally solicits contributions from those known to have the greatest interest in the organization, the fact that parents are singled out for a solicitation will not in itself create an inference that future admissions or any other benefits depend upon a contribution from the parent.

Situation 6. A church operates a school providing secular and religious education that is attended both by children of parents who are members of the church and by children of nonmembers. The church receives contributions from all of its members. These contributions are placed in the church's general operating fund and are expended when needed to support church activities. A substantial portion of the other activities is unrelated to the school. Most church members do not have children in the school, and a major portion of the church's expenses are attributable to its nonschool functions. The methods of soliciting contributions from church members with children in the school are the same as the methods of soliciting contributions from members without children in the school. The church has full control over the use of the contributions that it receives. Members who have children enrolled in the school are not required to pay tuition for their children, but tuition is charged for the children of nonmembers. A church member whose child attends the school contributes $200 to the church for its general purposes. The IRS ordinarily will conclude that the parent is allowed a charitable contribution deduction of $200 to the church. Because the facts indicate that the church school is supported by the church, that most contributors to the church are not parents of children enrolled in the school, and that contributions from parent members are solicited in the same manner as contributions from other members, a parent's contributions will be considered charitable contributions, and not payments of tuition, unless there is a showing that the contributions by members with children in the school are significantly larger than those of other members. The absence of a tuition charge is not determinative in view of these facts.

[103]Rev. Rul. 83-100, 1983-30 I.R.B. 5.

[104]*Id. See also* Rev. Rule 54-580, 1954-2 C.B. 97; Tripp v. Commissioner, 337 F.2d 432 (7th Cir. 1964); Bauer v. United States, 449 F. Supp. 755 (W.D. La. 1978); Lloyd v. Commissioner, 29 T.C.M. 453 (1970); Rev. Rul. 62-113, 1962-2 C.B. 10.

[105]*Id.*

[106]*Id.*

[107]*Id.*

p. 323. *Add at the end of § K:*

§ L. Use of Public School Teachers in Private Schools

In 1985, the Supreme Court invalidated a "shared time" program that allowed public school teachers to teach certain remedial and enrichment courses in nonpublic schools at public expense.[109] The Court, applying the three-pronged *Lemon* test, concluded that the program had a primary effect that impermissibly advanced religion:

> The state-paid instructors, influenced by the pervasively sectarian nature of the religious schools in which they work, may subtly or overtly indoctrinate the students in particular religious tenets at public expense. The symbolic union of church and state inherent in the provision of secular, state-provided instruction in the religious school buildings threatens to convey a message of state support for religion to students and to the general public. Finally, the programs in effect subsidize the religious functions of the parochial schools by taking over a substantial portion of their responsibility for teaching secular subjects.

[109]Grand Rapids School District v. Ball, 53 U.S.L.W. 5006 (July 1, 1985). *See also* Aguilar v. Felton, 53 U.S.L.W. 5013 (July 1, 1985). Both decisions were by a 5 to 4 vote.

14

TAXATION OF CHURCHES

§ B. Federal Income Taxation

p. 328. *Add after the first complete paragraph:*

They have been upheld despite the occasional claim that they constitute impermissible "conditions" on the constitutional right to freely exercise one's religion.[1a]

p. 328. *Add after note 2 in the text:*

This is consistent with the definition of *corporation* contained in section 7701(a)(3) of the Internal Revenue Code, and with federal court decisions interpreting the term *corporation* to mean any organization satisfying at least three of the four principal corporate characteristics of centralized control, continuity, limited personal liability, and transferability of beneficial interests.[2a]

[1a]*See, e.g.*, Church of Scientology v. Commissioner, 83 T.C. 381 (1984) (a 145-page opinion).

[2a]*See, e.g.*, Smith's Estate v. Commissioner, 313 F.2d 724 (8th Cir. 1963).

p. 331. *Add after the first two lines:*

One court has held that a church satisfied the "organizational test" even though its bylaws did not call for the distribution of church assets to other tax-exempt organizations upon dissolution, since (1) the church's minister interpreted his denomination's constitution to call for the distribution of church assets to other churches in the denomination upon dissolution, and (2) state law prohibited church property from being distributed for private use so long as there was someone who would carry on its use for church purposes.[7a]

[7a]Bethel Conservative Mennonite Church v. Commissioner, 746 F.2d 388 (7th Cir. 1984).

p. 331. *Add after note 13 in the text:*

To illustrate, a publishing company that was closely associated (though not legally affiliated) with the Orthodox Presbyterian Church and whose primary purpose was the publication of books furthering the reformed faith was held to be exempt by a federal appeals court.[13a]

[13a]Presbyterian and Reformed Publishing Co. v. Commissioner, 743 F.2d 148 (3rd Cir. 1984).

p. 331, note 12. *Delete the Presbyterian and Reformed decision.*

p. 331, note 13. *Add:*

Presbyterian and Reformed Publishing Co. v. Commissioner, 743 F.2d 148 (3rd Cir. 1984); Universal Church of Scientific Truth v. United States, 74-1 U.S.T.C. ¶ 9360 (N.D. Ala. 1974).

p. 332. *Delete the last line and substitute the following:*

to accumulate monies for its "building fund";[22] a religious organization offering financial and tax advice to its members or to the public concerning tax savings, often through the creation of a spurious "church";[22a] a direct mail religious organization that promised spiritual blessings in exchange for monetary contributions;[22b] and a "church" consisting of

[22a]*See, e.g.*, Church of Ethereal Joy v. Commissioner, 83 T.C. 20 (1984) (alleged religious organization conducted few if any religious activities, and one of its directors engaged in extensive counseling on the use of private churches to reduce taxes); National Association of American Churches v. Commissioner, 82 T.C. 18 (1984) (central religious organization providing assistance to local "family missions" in incorporating under state law and in obtaining tax-exempt status was denied exemption because it was not organized exclusively for exempt purposes); Ecclesiastical Order of the Ism of Am v. Commissioner, 80 T.C. 833 (1983) (organization with unorthodox religious beliefs denied exemption because its extensive tax avoidance counseling services were a substantial nonexempt activity); Christian Stewardship Assistance, Inc. v. Commissioner, 70 T.C. 1037 (1978) (an organization offering financial and estate planning advice to wealthy individuals referred to it by prospective charitable donees was denied exemption because it was not organized exclusively for exempt purposes).

[22b]Church by Mail, Inc. v. Commissioner, 48 T.C.M. 471 (1984).

p. 333, note 23. *Add:*

Basic Bible Church of America v. Commissioner, 739 F.2d 265 (7th Cir. 1984).

p. 334. *Add after the first incomplete paragraph:*

Finally, the income tax regulations specify that an organization can be exempt from taxation even if it engages in activities that are not in furtherance of one or more exempt purposes if such activities compose no more than an "insubstantial" part of the organization's total activities.[29a] Neither the Internal Revenue Code nor the regulations define *insubstantial*. Therefore, this is an issue that must be determined under the facts and circumstances of each case. To illustrate, a charitable organization was determined to be exempt despite its participation in a profit-seeking limited partnership.[29b] Another organization whose primary purpose was to raise funds for missionaries was found to be exempt despite its subordinate and unrelated activity of distributing ten percent of its net income in the form of grants and loans to applicants conducting scientific research in the area of energy resources.[29c] The court emphasized that it was not establishing a general rule that ten percent was insubstantial. In an earlier decision, the Tax Court had ruled that a religious organization which made cash grants of approximately twenty percent of its net income to private individuals including its officers was not exempt since such grants were more than an insubstantial nonexempt activity.[29d] The court stated that "while the facts in the instant case merit a denial of exempt status . . . we do not set forth a percentage test which can be relied upon for future reference with respect to nonexempt activities of an organization. Each case must be decided upon its own unique facts and circumstances."[29e] The Tax Court also denied exempt status to a religious retreat facility on the ground that it was operated primarily for recreational and social purposes, and therefore was engaged to more than an insubstantial degree in nonexempt activities.[29f]

[29a]Treas. Reg. § 1.501(c)(3)-1(b)(1)(i).

[29b]Plumstead Theatre Society, Inc. v. Commissioner, 675 F.2d 244 (9th Cir. 1981).

[29c]World Family Corp. v. Commissioner, 81 T.C. 958 (1983). The payment of "commissions" to fundraisers was not found to be "inurement" of the organization's net earnings to private individuals. Presumably, the commissions constituted reasonable compensation.

[29d]Church in Boston v. Commissioner, 71 T.C. 102 (1978). *See also* Self-Realization Brotherhood, Inc. v. Commissioner, 48 T.C.M. 344 (1984).

[29e]*Id.* at 108.

[29f]The Schoger Foundation v. Commissioner, 76 T.C. 380 (1981).

p. 334. *Add after note 30 in text:*

a church-sponsored insurance company that provided members and their families with financial and casualty insurance,[30a]

[30a]Mutual Aid Association of the Church of the Brethren v. United States, 578 F. Supp. 1451 (D. Kan. 1983).

p. 334. *Add after the last paragraph:*

A federal appeals court has held that "profitability" in and of itself does not necessarily mean that an exempt organization is no longer "operated exclusively" for exempt purposes.[35a] To determine whether such an organization should retain its exemption, the court proposed a two-prong test: first, what is the purpose of the organization, and second, to whose benefit do its activities and earnings inure? The court upheld the tax-exempt status of a profitable religious publisher that continued to adhere to its exempt religious purposes and that diverted none of its net earnings to the personal benefit of any individual. The court concluded that "success in terms of audience reached and influence exerted, in and of itself, should not jeopardize the tax-exempt status of organizations which remain true to their stated goals."[35b]

[35a]Presbyterian and Reformed Publishing Co. v. Commissioner, 743 F.2d 148 (3rd Cir. 1984).
[35b]*Id.* at 158.

p. 334. *Delete note 30 and substitute the following:*

[30]Bethel Conservative Mennonite Church v. Commissioner, 80 T.C. 352 (1983), *rev'd*, 746 F.2d 388 (7th Cir. 1984).

p. 334, note 31. *Add:*

Alive Fellowship of Harmonious Living v. Commissioner, 47 T.C.M. 1134 (1984).

p. 334, note 35. *Delete the last line and substitute the following:*

But see Presbyterian and Reformed Publishing Co. v. Commissioner, 743 F.2d 148 (3rd Cir. 1984).

p. 335. *Add after note 42 in the text:*

a church paid an unreasonable and excessive salary to its pastor;[42a]

[42a]United States v. Dykema, 666 F.2d 1096 (7th Cir. 1981); Unitary Mission Church v. Commissioner, 74 T.C. 507 (1980).

p. 335, note 40. *Add:*

Snyder v. Commissioner, 47 T.C.M. 12 (1983); Church of the Transfiguring Spirit, Inc. v. Commissioner, 75 T.C. 1 (1981); Southern Church of Universal Brotherhood Assembled, Inc. v. Commissioner, 74 T.C. 1223 (1980); Basic Bible Church, Inc. v. Commissioner, 74 T.C. 846 (1980); Unitary Mission Church v. Commissioner, 74 T.C. 507 (1980).

p. 335, note 42. *Add:*

Beth-el Ministries, Inc. v. Commissioner, 79-2 U.S.T.C. ¶ 9412 (D.C. Cir. 1979).

p. 336, note 43. *Add:*

Church of the Chosen People v. United States, 548 F. Supp. 1247 (D. Minn. 1982); Truth Tabernacle v. Commissioner, 41 T.C.M. 1405 (1981).

p. 338. *Delete note 61 and substitute the following:*

⁶¹Bethel Conservative Mennonite Church v. Commissioner, 80 T.C. 352 (1983), *rev'd*, 746 F.2d 388 (7th Cir. 1984).

p. 338, note 62. *Add:*

Church of the Chosen People v. United States, 548 F. Supp. 1247 (D. Minn. 1982).

p. 341. *Add after the first incomplete paragraph:*

The limitations on legislative and political activities are of dubious constitutional validity as applied to bona fide churches. It is doubtful that Congress can force churches to choose between fulfilling their prophetic mission (which necessarily will involve some legislative and political involvement) and maintaining their tax-exempt status. In other contexts, the Supreme Court has held that the Constitution prevents the government from forcing persons to choose between a fundamental constitutional right and an important legal benefit.[69a] The fact is, these limitations are largely useless as applied to churches anyway, since most churches are unaware of them, choose not to heed them, or do not participate in political campaigns or engage in substantial efforts to influence legislation. The lack of enforcement of these limitations against churches and the ambiguity of the term *substantial* are further bases for challenging their legal validity.

[69a]*See, e.g.,* Sherbert v. Verner, 374 U.S. 398 (1963).

p. 342, note 72. *Delete the third line and substitute the following:*

Commissioner, 80 T.C. 352 (1983), *rev'd on other grounds,* 746 F.2d 388 (7th Cir. 1984) ("a bona fide church is not per se exempt from

p. 343. *Add after note 82 in the text:*

The Supreme Court has observed that "[t]here is no genuine nexus between tax exemption and establishment of religion."[82a]

[82a]Walz v. Tax Commission, 397 U.S. 664, 675 (1970).

p. 343, note 82. *Add:*

United States v. Dykema, 666 F.2d 1096 (7th Cir. 1981).

p. 348. *Add after the last complete paragraph:*

Finally, the group exemption procedure technically is available only to "connectional," or hierarchical, church organizations consisting of a "central organization" that exerts "general supervision or control" over "subordinate" local churches and church agencies. There are many conventions and associations of churches, however, that exert little if any "general supervision or control" over "subordinate" churches. Up until now, these "congregational" conventions and associations of churches have had to construe the group exemption requirements very loosely in order to obtain the benefits of a group exemption. Many have done so. A potential problem with such an approach is that the association or convention of churches itself may increase its potential liability for the misconduct and improprieties of affiliated churches and church agencies, since in pursuing the group exemption the association or convention must affirm that it does in fact exercise "general supervision or control" over its affiliates. Such an affirmation could serve as a possible basis of legal liability unless the association or convention could demonstrate that it pursued the group exemption as a matter of expedience and that it construed the "supervision or control" language very loosely. It would also be relevant to indicate that congregational associations and conventions of churches are forced to interpret the "control" language loosely because of the discrimination by the IRS against such organizations in favor of connectional, or hierarchical, church organizations. In the final analysis, substance ordinarily takes priority over form or language.

The current group exemption procedure, granting favored status only to connectional church organizations, is suspect under the Supreme Court's interpretation of the First Amendment's nonestablishment of religion clause. In 1982, the Court invalidated a Minnesota law that imposed certain registration and reporting requirements upon religious organizations soliciting more than fifty percent of their funds from nonmembers.[98a] The Court observed that "when we are presented with a state law granting a denominational preference, our precedents demand that we treat the law as suspect and that we apply strict scrutiny in adjudging its constitutionality." The Court concluded that any law granting a denominational preference must be "invalidated unless it is justified by a compelling governmental interest, and unless it is closely fitted to further that interest."

There is no conceivable governmental interest that would justify the government's stated preference for connectional church organizations in the present group exemption procedure. And even if such an interest were assumed, the government has not used the least restrictive means of effecting it.

[98a]Larson v. Valente, 102 S. Ct. 1673 (1982).

p. 349. *Add after the first incomplete paragraph:*

In Notice 84-2, the IRS announced that certain church-controlled organizations carrying out church-related finance and pension programs are sufficiently related to the church itself to share the church's exemption from filing annual information returns.

p. 349. *Add at the end of subsection e:*

Section 503 of the Internal Revenue Code provides for the revocation of the exempt status of any organization engaged in any one or more "prohibited transactions." Prohibited transactions include the making of unsecured or low interest loans, the payment of unreasonable compensation, and the provision of services on a preferential basis to any substantial contributor or to any family member of a substantial contributor. The prohibited transaction rules do *not* apply to churches or other religious organizations. However, such activities may jeopardize the exempt status of a church or religious organization if they negate one of the preconditions to exempt status set forth in section 501(c)(3) of the Code. For example, the net earnings of a church will impermissibly inure to the private benefit of an individual if the church pays unreasonable compensation to its minister. Prior to 1969, section 504 of the Code provided for the revocation of the exempt status of any organization that had "unreasonable accumulations" of income. This provision was repealed in 1969, and even prior to its repeal did not apply to churches or other religious organizations.

p. 350. *Delete line 9 and substitute the following:*

be exempt from social security (FICA) taxes, unemployment taxes, and certain excise

p. 352, note 109. *Add:*

Granzow v. Commissioner, 739 F.2d 266 (7th Cir. 1984).

p. 352, note 110. *Add:*

Universal Life Church v. Commissioner, 83 T.C. 292 (1984); Church of Ethereal Joy v. Commissioner, 83 T.C. 20 (1984); Self-Realization Brotherhood, Inc. v. Commissioner, 48 T.C.M. 344 (1984).

p. 353. *Add after the first complete paragraph:*

In another case, the Tax Court observed: "Until recent years, a mere declaration that an organization was a church was almost enough to assure its treatment as such under the revenue laws. The cynical abuse of the church concept for tax purposes in recent years, however, has made necessary the same critical analysis of organizations claiming exemption on that ground as organizations engaged in admittedly secular activities."[114a]

[114a]Church of Ethereal Joy v. Commissioner, 83 T.C. 20, 27 (1984). An excellent summary of the abuses of mail order churches is contained in the congressional history to the Church Audit Procedures Act. This material is quoted in chapter 8 of this supplement.

p. 354. *Add after the indented paragraphs:*

The Tax Court has held that "our tolerance for taxpayers who establish churches solely for tax avoidance purposes is reaching a breaking point. Not only do these taxpayers use the pretext of a church to avoid paying their fair share of taxes, even when their brazen schemes are uncovered many of them resort to the courts in a shameless attempt to vindicate themselves."[116a] Similarly, a federal appeals court has lamented that "we can no longer tolerate abuse of the judicial review process by irresponsible taxpayers who press stale and frivolous arguments, without hope of success on the merits, in order to delay or harass the collection of public revenues or for other nonworthy purposes."[116b] The court ordered a mail order church to pay the government's costs and attorneys' fees incurred in contesting the church's claim of exemption, and warned that in the future it would "deal harshly" with frivolous tax appeals involving mail order churches. Other courts have sustained additions to tax for negligence or intentional disregard of tax laws pursuant to section 6653(a) of the Code.[116c]

[116a]Miedaner v. Commissioner, 81 T.C. 272 (1982).

[116b]Granzow v. Commissioner, 739 F.2d 265 (7th Cir. 1984).

[116c]*See, e.g.*, Hall v. Commissioner, 729 F.2d 632 (9th Cir. 1984); Davis v. Commissioner, 81 T.C. 806 (1983).

p. 354. *Add prior to § 2:*

h. *"Social Welfare" Organizations*

Section 501(c)(4) of the Internal Revenue Code exempts nonprofit organizations "operated exclusively for the promotion of social welfare." The regulations amplify this basis for exemption: "An organization is operated exclusively for the promotion of social welfare if it is primarily engaged in promoting in some way the common good and general welfare of the people of the community. An organization embraced within this section is one which is operated primarily for the purpose of bringing about civic betterments and social improvements."[117a]

Some religious organizations have applied for tax-exempt status under section 501(c)(4) either because they were unable or unwilling to comply with the more rigorous requirements of section 501(c)(3). The claim ordinarily is made that the organization promotes social welfare because of its religious purposes. This claim, however, has been rejected. To illustrate, one federal court has observed that while "many churches and religious organizations can and do promote the social welfare," such organizations are not *per se* a promotion of social welfare since in many cases they benefit their members rather than the general public as a whole.[117b] This logic of course ignores the fact that any "social welfare" organizations benefit only small segments of the population.

Section 501(c)(4) also exempts "local associations of employees, the membership of which is limited to the employees of a designated person or persons in a particular municipality, and the net earnings of which are devoted exclusively to charitable, educational, or recreational purposes."

[117a]Treas. Reg. § 1.501(c)(4)-1(a)(2)(i).

[117b]Mutual Aid Association of Brethren v. United States, 578 F. Supp. 1451 (D. Kan. 1983), aff'd, 759 F.2d 792 (10th Cir. 1985).

p. 355. *Add after the first incomplete sentence:*

In addition, certain contributions to charity may be recovered by a bankruptcy court if the donor becomes bankrupt.

p. 355. *Add after the first complete paragraph:*

Similarly, the Tax Court denied a charitable contribution deduction to a minister for that portion of his church salary that he voluntarily canceled, since the claimed contribution represented the cash equivalent of the value of the minister's services and thus was not a gift of cash or other property.[117c]

[117c]Winston v. Commissioner, 48 T.C.M. 55 (1984). *See also* Grant v. Commissioner, 84 T.C. 809 (1985); Rev. Rul. 76-341, 1976-2 C.B. 307.

p. 360. *Add after the first complete paragraph:*

A deduction for contributions to the Church of Scientology was denied by the Tax Court since the donors received substantial benefits in exchange for their "contributions."[151a] The court noted that "members" were required to pay "fixed donations" for the "spiritual auditing" that they received from the church and that comprised the basis of Scientology. Contributions made to a charitable organization by participants in a weekend marriage seminar are deductible only to the extent that the contributions exceed the value of all benefits received.[151b] However, if participants' expenses are paid through the contributions of previous participants, then contributions by current participants toward the defrayal of expenses of future participants may be deductible if those participants are not designated.

[151a]Graham v. Commissioner, 83 T.C. 575 (1984).
[151b]Rev. Rul. 76-232, 1976-2 C.B. 62.

p. 361. *Add prior to the last complete paragraph:*

The list of qualified charitable donees closely parallels the list of exempt organizations contained in section 501(c)(3) of the Code. Congress apparently intended the list to have the same meaning in both sections.[152a]

[152a]Bob Jones University v. United States, 103 S. Ct. 2017, 2026 n.10 (1983). *But see* the dissenting opinion at 2040.

p. 362. *Add after the first incomplete sentence:*

Similarly, gifts made by a taxpayer to his mother which he assumed were conveyed to a church were held to be nondeductible gifts to an individual,[155a] as were contributions to an individual who published a church directory for travelers,[155b] and amounts paid by a taxpayer to an individual for spiritual guidance.[155c]

[155a]Moses v. Commissioner, 32 T.C.M. 306 (1973).
[155b]Rev. Rul. 57-525, 1957-2 C.B. 222.
[155c]Miller v. Commissioner, 40 T.C.M. 243 (1980).

p. 362. note 155. *Add:*

Leonhart v. Commissioner, 27 T.C.M. 443 (1968).

p. 362. *Delete all of page 362 following the first complete sentence, excluding footnotes 154 and 155, and substitute the following:*

In 1962, the IRS clarified the application of this principle in a ruling upholding the deductibility of a taxpayer's contribution to a church fund out of which missionaries, including his son, were compensated:

> If contributions to the fund are earmarked by the donor for a particular individual, they are treated, in effect, as being gifts to the designated individual and are not deductible. However, a deduction will be allowable where it is established that a gift is intended by a donor for the use of the organization and not as a gift to an individual. The test in each case is whether the organization has full control of the donated funds, and discretion as to their use, so as to insure that they will be used to carry out its functions and purposes. In the instant case, the son's receipt of reimbursements from the fund is alone insufficient to require holding that this test is not met. Accordingly, unless the taxpayer's contributions to the fund are distinctly marked by him so that they may be used only for his son or are received by the fund pursuant to a commitment or understanding that they will be so used, they may be deducted by the taxpayer in computing his taxable income.[155d]

This principle has been consistently applied by the courts in determining the deductibility of "designated" contributions to charitable organizations. For example, in 1964 the Tax Court held that checks payable to the Sudan Interior Mission were deductible by a donor despite the listing of four missionaries' names on the lower left-hand corner of each check and a letter from the donor requesting that the checks be used for the missionaries.[155e] After analyzing all of the facts, the court concluded that the donor knew and intended that his contributions would go into a common pool and be administered by the mission and distributed in accordance with stated policies regarding missionary support.

As a result, the donor's designation of four individual missionaries "was no more than a manifestation of [his] desire" to have his donations credited to the support allowance of those individuals. The mission maintained "exclusive control, under its own policy, of both the administration and distribution of the funds."

A taxpayer who sent a bank check to a missionary serving in Brazil with the express instruction that the funds be used for Presbyterian mission work was allowed a deduction by the Tax Court.[155f] The court noted that while the check was payable directly to the missionary, it was not a gift to him personally since it was given for the express purpose of "Presbyterian mission work." In substance, the court concluded, the funds were contributed "to or for the use of the church in its mission work, with the missionary receiving the funds as its agent."

Several other "designated contribution" cases have involved missionaries and ministers. For example, a federal appeals court upheld the deductibility of a contribution to a fund established by three Presbyterian churches for the support of a particular missionary, even though the contribution mentioned the missionary's name, since the contribution was "for the use of" an exempt missions organization.[155g] The court noted that a church officer received donated funds and distributed them for the missions work that the church intended. In another case, a taxpayer made rental payments to provide a home for his evangelist son, and deducted the payments as contributions "for the use of" his son's incorporated evangelistic organization. The taxpayer argued that he was entitled to a charitable contribution deduction since his rental payments relieved the evangelistic organization of the necessity of making such payments itself. The Tax Court, in denying the deductibility of the rental payments, observed that by making the payments directly to the landlord, the taxpayer "took away" the discretion of the evangelistic organization to spend its funds in the manner it chose. Since a charity must have "full control of the funds donated in order for a taxpayer to be entitled to a charitable deduction," the deduction was denied.[155h] The court also found the intent of the donor to be relevant in making a determination. If the donor's intent was to benefit his son, then the deduction would be unavailable.

The Tax Court similarly has denied a charitable contribution deduction to the parents of a Mormon missionary who paid their son's travel expenses to a missionary site and in addition contributed to his support. The court concluded that the Mormon church had no control over the contributed funds, and therefore the funds were not "for the use of" the church.[155i] In a related context, a federal appeals court upheld the deductibility of payments made by parents toward the travel and living expenses of their son, a full-time Mormon missionary.[155j] The court noted that the income tax regulations specifically allow a deduction for "out-of-pocket transportation expenses necessarily incurred in performing donated services" as well as "[r]easonable expenses for meals and lodging necessarily incurred while away from home in the course of performing donated services."[155k] It saw "no rational basis" for allowing the deductibility of such expenses when paid by a missionary himself, but denying the deductibility of such expenses when paid on behalf of a dependent missionary son. The court rejected the government's contention that section 262 of the Internal Revenue Code (which prohibits the deductibility of "personal, living, or family expenses") precluded the parents' deduction of payments toward their son's travel and living expenses incurred in performing missionary service, since such expenses were specifically exempted from the general prohibition of section 262. The court also rejected the government's contention that the Mormon Church itself must have control over the expenditure of funds for a donor to receive a deduction, since "that test has never been applied to expenses incurred by a taxpayer performing services for a bona fide charitable organization." Rather, the courts have focused on "whether the primary purpose of the expenditure was to further the aims of the charitable organization or to benefit the spender." Under this test, the court concluded that payments made by parents toward the travel and living expenses of a missionary son are deductible since the expenditures "primarily benefit the church and not the spender."[156]

Similarly, a contribution given directly to a Jesuit priest was held to be deductible on the theory that members of the Jesuit Order are under a vow of poverty obligating them to give to the Order all property received by them, and thus a gift to a priest in reality is a gift "to or for the use of" the Order.[157]

The related question of the deductibility of payments made to church-sponsored schools is discussed fully in chapter 13.

Contributions to a charitable organization may be earmarked by the donor for specific purposes or uses without jeopardizing the charitable deduction.[158]

[155d]Rev. Rul. 62-113, 1962-2 C.B. 10.

[155e]Peace v. Commissioner, 43 T.C. 1 (1964).

[155f]Lesslie v. Commissioner, 36 T.C.M. 495 (1977). The court cited its observation in an earlier decision that the IRS "has chosen the wrong case to be puristic in [its] effort to collect the sovereign's revenue."

[155g]Winn v. Commissioner, 595 F.2d 1060 (5th Cir. 1979).

[155h]Davenport v. Commissioner, 34 T.C.M. 1585 (1975).

[155i]Brinley v. Commissioner, 82 T.C. 932 (1984). The court's holding is clearly contrary to its own ruling in Lesslie, supra at note 155f, and is only dimly distinguishable from Winn, supra at note 155g. It should be reversed or repudiated.

[155j]White v. United States, 725 F.2d 1269 (10th Cir. 1984).

[155k]Treas. Reg. § 1.170A-1(g).

[156]The court expressed disapproval of the result reached by the Tax Court in Brinley, supra note 155i.

[157]Ratterman v. Commissioner, 11 T.C. 1140 (1948), aff'd, 177 F.2d 204 (6th Cir. 1949).

[158]Winn v. Commissioner, 595 F.2d 1060 (5th Cir. 1979).

p. 363. *Delete the first two lines.*

p. 363. *Add after the first complete paragraph:*

Contributions to foreign charities are permitted deductions on federal estate tax returns.[162a]

[162a]Treas. Reg. § 20.2055-1(a).

p. 365. *Add after the third complete paragraph:*

Beginning in 1982, taxpayers who do not itemize their deductions have been allowed a deduction for a portion of their charitable contributions.[170a] The amount deductible is described in the following table:

Year	Percentage Deductible	Maximum Deduction individual	joint
1982	25	$100	$50
1983	25	100	50
1984	25	300	150
1985	50	none	none
1986	100	none	none

[170a]I.R.C. § 170(i). This provision expires on December 31, 1986.

p. 366. *Delete the entire page following the indented paragraph and substitute the following:*

In April 1983, the Treasury Department issued new regulations dealing with the substantiation of charitable contributions. The regulations, which were formally approved in December 1984, contain the following provisions:[175]

1. *Charitable contributions of money.* No charitable contribution of *money* after 1982 will be allowed unless the taxpayer maintains one of the following:
   a. A canceled check.
   b. A receipt from the donee charitable organization showing the name of

the donee, the date of the contribution, and the amount of the contribution. A letter or other communication from the donee may constitute a receipt.

c. In the absence of a canceled check or receipt from the donee organization, other *reliable written records* showing the name of the donee and the date and amount of the contribution. The burden of proving the reliability of records is on the taxpayer. Factors indicating that written records are reliable include (1) the contemporaneous nature of the writing evidencing the contribution; (2) the regularity of the taxpayer's recordkeeping procedures; and (3) in the case of small contributions, the existence of any written or other evidence from the donee organization evidencing receipt of the donation.

2. *Charitable contributions of noncash property.* No charitable contribution of *noncash property* will be allowed after 1982 unless the taxpayer obtains a receipt from the donee charitable organization showing the name of the donee, the date and location of the contribution, and a description of the property (including the value of the property).[176] In addition, the taxpayer must maintain *reliable written records* (as defined above) showing the following:

a. the name and address of the donee charitable organization;

b. the date and location of the contribution;

c. a detailed description of the property;

d. the fair market value of the property at the time the contribution was made, and the method used to determine fair market value; if it was determined by appraisal, a signed copy of the appraiser's report;

e. the cost or other basis of ordinary income property or short-term capital gain property, and the amount of ordinary income or short-term capital gain that would have been realized had the property been sold at its fair market value;

f. if less than the entire interest in the property is contributed, the total amount claimed as a deduction for the current tax year and the amount claimed as a deduction in any prior years for other interests in the same property;

g. the terms of any agreement or understanding entered into with the donee charitable organization that relates to the use, sale, or disposition of the property contributed, as, for example, the terms of any agreement or understanding that restricts the donee's right to dispose of the donated property; that reserves to or confers upon anyone other than the donee any right to the income from donated property, to the possession of such property, or to acquire such property; or that earmarks donated property for a particular charitable use.

3. *Charitable contributions of noncash property in excess of $500.* No charitable contribution of *noncash property* for which a taxpayer claims a deduction in excess of $500 will be allowed after 1982 unless the taxpayer maintains all

of the records described in the preceding paragraph, and in addition maintains *reliable written records* (as defined above) showing

    a. the manner of acquisition, for example, by purchase, gift, bequest, inheritance, or exchange, and the approximate date of acquisition of the property of the taxpayer;

    b. the cost or other basis of property held by the taxpayer for a period of less than six months preceding the date of contribution, and, if available, the cost or other basis of property held for a period of six months or more preceding the date of contribution.

    4. *Taxpayer's election.* Taxpayers have the option of applying pre-1983 law to any contribution made prior to December 31, 1984.

In lieu of amending section 170 of the Code to set forth additional substantiation requirements for contributions of noncash property with a claimed value of $5,000 or more, a congressional conference committee required the Treasury Department to issue temporary or final regulations prior to January 1, 1985, incorporating the substantiation requirements set forth in the conference committee report to the Tax Reform Act of 1984. On December 26, 1984, the Treasury Department released regulations with the following key provisions:[176a]

    1. *Charitable contributions of noncash property in excess of $5,000.* No charitable contribution of *noncash property* for which a taxpayer claims a deduction in excess of $5,000 for any single item ($10,000 in the case of nonpublicly traded stock) will be allowed after 1984 unless the taxpayer satisfies the following substantiation requirements:

    a. A *qualified appraisal* must be obtained for the contributed property. A *qualified appraisal* is an appraisal document that is made within sixty days of the contribution; prepared, signed, and dated by a qualified appraiser; does not involve a fee based on a percentage of the appraised value; and includes the following information:

    (1) a detailed description of the property;

    (2) in the case of tangible property, the physical condition of the property;

    (3) the date of contribution;

    (4) the terms of any agreement or understanding entered into with the donee charitable organization that relates to the use, sale, or disposition of the property contributed, as, for example, the terms of any agreement or understanding that restricts the donee organization's right to dispose of donated property; that reserves to or confers upon anyone other than the donee any right to the income from donated property, to the possession of such property, or to acquire such property; or that earmarks donated property for a particular charitable use;

    (5) the name, address, and taxpayer identification number of the qualified appraiser and of his employer, if any;

(6) the qualifications of the qualified appraiser, including his background, experience, education, and membership in professional associations;

(7) a statement that the appraisal was prepared for income tax purposes;

(8) the date on which the property was valued;

(9) the appraised fair market value of the property on the date of contribution;

(10) the method of valuation used to determine fair market value;

(11) the specific basis for the valuation, if any, such as any specific comparable sales transactions;

(12) a description of the fee arrangement between the donor and the appraiser.

b. A fully completed *appraisal summary* must be attached to the taxpayer's tax return on which the deduction was claimed. An *appraisal summary* is prepared on IRS Form 8272. The summary must be signed and dated by the donee charitable organization and the qualified appraiser. Signature by a representative of the donee is not construed as acquiescence with the appraisal value. A copy of Form 8272 is contained at the end of this chapter.

2. A *qualified appraiser* is defined by the regulations as anyone who includes on the appraisal summary (Form 8272) a declaration that (1) he holds himself out to the public as an appraiser; (2) he is qualified to make the appraisal; (3) he is not the taxpayer claiming the deduction or a party to the transaction in which the donor acquired the contributed property (unless the property is donated within two months of the date of acquisition and its appraised value does not exceed its acquisition price); (4) he is not the donee of the property; (5) he is not employed by or related to the taxpayer, any party to the transaction in which the donor acquired the contributed property, or the donee; and (6) he does not have a relationship with any of the foregoing persons that would cause a reasonable person to question his independence as an appraiser.

3. The $5,000 threshold may be satisfied by combining similar items of property, such as stock, land, buildings, and books, whether donated to the same or different charitable donees. For example, if a taxpayer claims on his return deductions of $2,000 for books to College A, $2,500 for books to College B, and $900 for books to College C, the $5,000 threshold is exceeded.

4. Taxpayers who fail to attach an *appraisal summary* to a tax return in which a contribution of noncash property in excess of $5,000 is claimed do not lose the deduction if (1) the omission was in good faith and (2) the taxpayer submits an appraisal summary within ninety days of an IRS request.[176b]

Finally, section 6050L of the Code requires the donee charitable organization to file an information return (Form 8273) with the IRS in the event that it sells, exchanges, or otherwise disposes of the property (or any portion thereof) described in the appraisal summary within two years after the date of the receipt of the property. A copy of Form 8273 is contained at the end of this chapter.

[175]Treas. Reg. § 1.170A-13(a).

[176]The regulations specify that a receipt from the donee organization is not required if the contribution is made under circumstances making it impractical to obtain a receipt (e.g., by depositing property at a charity's unattended drop site). However, in all cases the taxpayer must maintain reliable written records with respect to each item of donated property, showing the information described in the text.

[176a]Treas. Reg. § 1.170A-13T.

[176b]Treas. Reg. § 1.170A-13T(c)(4)(iv)(G).

p. 367. *Delete the entire page.*

p. 368. *Delete the first incomplete and the first complete paragraphs.*

p. 368. *Add before § 3:*

g. *Recovery of Certain Contributions by Bankruptcy Courts*

A church or other religious organization can be compelled to transfer donated funds to a bankruptcy trustee if they were given for the purpose of defrauding creditors. The Bankruptcy Act permits a bankruptcy court to repudiate any transfer of property by a debtor within one year before the filing of a bankruptcy petition if (1) the debtor intended thereby to hinder, delay, or defraud his creditors, or (2) the debtor received less than "reasonably equivalent value" in exchange for the transfer of property and (a) was insolvent at the time of the transfer, (b) was engaged in business with an unreasonably small amount of capital, or (c) intended to incur debts beyond his ability to pay.[176c]

Many contributions to charity will not be voidable by a bankruptcy court. While it is true that a debtor receives less than "reasonably equivalent value" for his charitable contributions, this fact alone does not nullify the contributions. In addition, the bankruptcy court must determine that the contributions were made with an attempt to hinder, delay, or defraud creditors, or that the debtor (a) was insolvent at the time of transfer or became insolvent because of the transfer, (b) was engaged in business with an unreasonably small amount of capital, or (c) intended to incur debts beyond his ability to pay. In many cases, these conditions will not be satisfied. For example, many debtors make charitable contributions without knowing that they will declare bankruptcy within one year and thus they lack an actual intent to hinder, delay, or defraud creditors. In addition, many debtors remain solvent following their charitable contributions, they are not unreasonably undercapitalized if in a trade or business, and they have no intention of incurring debts beyond their ability to pay. Under these circumstances, the requirements of the Bankruptcy Act for recovery of transferred property do not apply and the contributions will be upheld.

It is possible of course for a debtor, in making a charitable contribution, to satisfy these conditions. A debtor, for example, may make a substantial charitable contribution in order to divert his assets to charity instead of his lawful creditors. Clearly, such a contribution could be recovered.

[176c]11 U.S.C. § 548.

p. 371. Add at the end of the last complete paragraph:

Occasionally, a church will operate a bookstore. Is such an enterprise an unrelated trade or business subject to the tax on unrelated business income? This will depend on several considerations, including the following: (1) Is the business operated within the church building, or is it located in another facility? (2) Does the bookstore sell only religious merchandise (books, tapes, records, etc.), or does it also sell "nonreligious" items such as pen and pencil sets, radios, stationery, and film? If it sells nonreligious items what percentage of gross sales consists of such sales? (3) Is the bookstore separately incorporated, or does it come under the church's corporate umbrella? (4) If the bookstore is on church premises, is it open only during those times when the church is in use? (5) Is the bookstore open to the general public? (6) Does the bookstore engage in advertising? (7) What is the relative size of the bookstore's revenue in comparison with church revenues? As has been noted previously, the fact that a bookstore's net earnings are used exclusively for religious purposes is not controlling. The tax on unrelated business income is designed primarily to eliminate the unfair competitive advantage that nonprofit organizations would enjoy if they could sell products to the public in direct competition with taxable enterprises selling the same or similar merchandise. Finally, even if a bookstore's activities suggest that it is an unrelated trade or business, it will not be liable for the tax on unrelated business income if it fits within any of the three exceptions described in the following subsection. For example, a church-operated bookstore will not be considered to be an unrelated trade or business if substantially all of its labor is performed by unpaid volunteers; if it exists primarily "for the convenience" of church members; or if it sells merchandise substantially all of which has been received as gifts or contributions.

p. 372. Add after the first complete paragraph:

To illustrate, in one case the IRS argued that a Catholic religious order that owned and maintained a 1600-acre farm that produced crops and livestock for commercial markets was engaged in an unrelated trade or business. The Tax Court, while rejecting the order's contentions that it was not operated for profit and that its farming operation was substantially related to its tax-exempt purpose, concluded that the farm earnings were not unrelated business taxable income since 91% of the labor was provided by members of the order without compensation. The court rejected the government's contention that the members of the order received "noncash compensation" for their labor in the form of room and board, since the members would have received such amenities even if they performed no work or the farm operations ceased.[191a]

[191a]St. Joseph Farms of Indiana Brothers of the Congregation of the Holy Cross v. Commissioner, 85 T.C. ___ (1985).

p. 375. *Delete subsection g and substitute the following:*

g. *IRS Audits*

The authority of the IRS to audit churches and certain church-controlled organizations is restricted by the Church Audit Procedures Act. This Act, which took effect in 1985, is discussed fully in chapter 8.

§ C. Social Security

p. 375. *Delete § C and substitute the following:*

§ C. Social Security

The subject of social security taxes has been discussed fully in other chapters.[200] It will suffice for purposes of the present chapter to repeat that services performed in the employ of a religious, charitable, or educational organization were exempted from social security (FICA) taxes through December 31, 1983, unless the organization waived its exemption by filing Forms SS-15 and SS-15a with the IRS or paid (intentionally or inadvertently) social security taxes on any employee.

The Social Security Act amendments of 1983 removed this exemption as of January 1, 1984. Due to widespread criticism of the mandatory coverage of church employees and the corresponding obligation of churches to pay the employer's FICA tax on all church employees, Congress again amended the Act in 1984 to give churches a one-time election to exempt themselves from the employer's FICA tax if they were opposed on the basis of religious belief to such coverage.[200a] Churches must make the election by filing a Form 8274 with the IRS prior to the due date of their first Form 941 (Employer's Quarterly

Federal Tax Return) following July 30, 1984. The employees of a church that exempts itself from FICA coverage are treated as self-employed for purposes of social security coverage.

[200]See chapter 8, § C, and chapter 10, § B, *supra*.
[200a]I.R.C. § 3121(w).

§ D. Unemployment Taxes

p. 376. *Add at the end of § D:*

The subject of unemployment taxes is discussed fully in chapter 10.

§ E. State Taxes

p. 379. *Add after the second complete paragraph:*

In holding that a parsonage can meet the definition of property "used exclusively for religious purposes," one court observed that "a parsonage qualifies for an exemption even if it reasonably and substantially facilitates the aims of religious worship and religious instruction because the pastor's religious duties require him to live in close proximity to the church or because the parsonage has unique facilities for religious worship and instruction or is primarily used for such purposes."[231a]

[231a]McKenzie v. Johnson, 456 N.E.2d 73 (Ill. 1983). The court cited with approval a dissenting opinion in an earlier case: "The evidence in this case is that the work of the church cannot be carried on efficiently without the constant care and attention of the pastor. The parsonage was paid for with the contributions made by the church congregation. It was erected for the benefit it would be in promoting the work of the church and not for the benefit of the pastor." First Congregational Church v. Board of Review, 98 N.E. 275 (Ill. 1912) (dissenting opinion).

p. 381. *Add after the first incomplete paragraph:*

However, church-owned lots and undeveloped land have qualified for exemption in a few cases where significant church activities occurred there, or where a church was actively working toward the development of such property for exempt uses. For example, a church-owned 15-acre tract of land was granted an exemption by a state court since the land was used for neighborhood recreational activities, Boy Scout and Girl Scout activities, and was reasonably necessary for the convenient use of the church's existing structures.[245a] However, if no religious or charitable activities occur on vacant church-owned property, or such uses are negligible and insignificant, there ordinarily will be no basis for an exemption.[245b] Vacant church-owned property was granted an exemption where the church had prepared plans and raised funds for the construction of a house of worship within a reasonable time after the filing of the application for exemption.[245c]

[245a]Appeal of Southview Presbyterian Church, 302 S.E.2d 298 (N.C. App. 1983).

[245b]First Congregational Church v. Gilmanton, 461 A.2d 128 (N.H. 1983); Welch v. Freewill Baptist Church v. Kinney, 461 N.E.2d 19 (Ohio App. 1983).

[245c]Holy Trinity Episcopal Church v. Bowers, 173 N.E.2d 682 (Ohio 1961).

p. 381. *Add after the second complete paragraph:*

Religious camp grounds have also been denied exemption where they were used to promote Bible study by Christian groups but were not owned or controlled by a church or religious denomination;[250a] and where they accommodated large numbers of groups having no religious program and freely opened their facilities to non-Christian individuals.[250b]

[250a]Highland Lake Bible Conference v. Board of Assessors, 460 N.Y.S.2d 170 (1983).

[250b]West Brandt Foundation, Inc. v. Carter, 652 P.2d 564 (Colo. 1982).

p. 381, note 246. *Add:*

Round Lake v. Commissioner of Tax Equalization, 447 N.E.2d 132 (Ohio App. 1982); Kerrville Independent School Dist. v. Southwest Texas Encampment Assoc., 673 S.W.2d 256 (Tex. App. 1984) (existence of dormitories, cooking facilities, swimming pool, and recreation program were collateral to religious program and did not preclude an entire 64-acre camp grounds from being considered an actual "place of worship").

p. 381, note 247. *Add:*

Moraine Heights Baptist Church v. Kinney, 465 N.E.2d 1281 (Ohio 1984).

p. 383. *Add after the first incomplete paragraph:*

However, a building used to broadcast the Herald of Truth radio and television programs was granted an exemption under a statute exempting property owned by a religious organization that is "used primarily as a place of regular religious worship."[264a] A Salvation Army thrift shop was granted an exemption on the ground that it was used exclusively for carrying out that organization's exempt purposes.[246b] The court emphasized that the generation of profits was a "small part of the purpose" of the shop, which existed primarily to further the owner's purpose of providing meaningful work for those persons seeking to become self-supporting.

[246a]Highland Church of Christ v. Powell, 644 S.W.2d 177 (Tex. App. 1983).
[246b]Salvation Army v. Town of Ellicott, 474 N.Y.S.2d 649 (1984).

p. 383, note 263. *Add:*

Sunday School Board of the Southern Baptist Convention v. Mitchell, 658 S.W.2d 1 (Mo. 1983) (bookstore owned by Southern Baptist Convention sold nondenominational literature to the general public at competitive retail prices).

p. 383, note 270. *Add:*

Village of Oak Park v. Rosewell, 450 N.E.2d 981 (Ill. App. 1983).

p. 383, note 271. *Add:*

Summit United Methodist Church v. Kinney, 455 N.E.2d 669 (Ohio 1983) (education wing of parish center used for Sunday school on Sunday but as a commercial child-care center during the week was not used primarily for public worship and was denied exemption).

p. 384. *Add after the second complete paragraph:*

The fact that a religious organization has received a determination letter from the IRS acknowledging that it is exempt from federal income taxation as an organization described in section 501(c)(3) of the Internal Revenue Code does not necessarily entitle the organization to a property tax exemption.[277a]

[277a]*See, e.g.*, Haas v. Ashland, 451 A.2d 1287 (N.H. 1982); Highland Lake Bible Conference v. Board of Assessors, 460 N.Y.S.2d 170 (1983).

p. 384, note 272. *Add:*

Highland Church of Christ v. Powell, 644 S.W.2d 177 (Tex. App. 1983).

Form **8282**
(February 1985)

Department of the Treasury
Internal Revenue Service

Donee Information Return

(Sale, Exchange, or Trade of Donated Property)

OMB No. 1545-0908
Expires 12-31-87

Give Copy to Donor

	Charitable organization (donee) name	Employer identification number
Please Print or Type	Number and street	
	City or town, state, and ZIP code	

Name of donor(s) who contributed the gift | Donor identification number

Donor address (Number and street)

City, town or post office, state and ZIP code

(a) Description of donated property sold, exchanged, or traded (Attach a separate sheet if more space is needed)	(b) Date item(s) contributed	(c) Date item(s) sold, exchanged, or traded	(d) Amount received

Instructions

Paperwork Reduction Act Notice.—We ask for this information to carry out the Internal Revenue laws of the United States. We need it to ensure that taxpayers are complying with these laws and to allow us to figure and collect the right amount of tax. You are required to give us this information.

New Law.—The Tax Reform Act of 1984 (P.L. 98-369) requires the donee of any **charitable deduction property** who sells, exchanges, or otherwise disposes of the property within two years after the date of receipt of the property to file the information shown on this return with the Internal Revenue Service.

Charitable Deduction Property.—The term "charitable deduction property" means any property (other than money

or publicly traded securities) contributed after December 31, 1984, with respect to which the donee signed **Form 8283,** Noncash Charitable Contributions Appraisal Summary.

When to File.—Form 8282 must be filed with the IRS within 90 days after the donee disposes of the property. Also, the donee must send a copy of this form to the donor.

Where to File.—File this form with the Internal Revenue Service Center in Cincinnati, OH 45944.

Penalties.—Failure to file this information return and failure to furnish a copy of this return to the donor will make the charitable organization liable for a $50 penalty for each failure. See sections 6652, 6676, and 6678 of the Internal Revenue Code.

Form **8283**
(February 1985)

Department of the Treasury
Internal Revenue Service

Noncash Charitable Contributions
Appraisal Summary

▶ **Attach to Tax Return**

OMB No. 1545-0908
Expires 12-31-87

Name(s) as shown on the Tax Return

Identification number

Part I Donee Acknowledgement *(To be completed by the charitable organization)*

1 This charitable organization acknowledges that it is a qualified organization under section 170(c) and that it received the donated property as described in Part II on _____ .

(Date)

Furthermore, this organization affirms that in the event it sells, exchanges, or otherwise disposes of the property (or any portion thereof) within two years after the date of receipt, it will file an information return (**Form 8282**, Donee Information Return) with the IRS and furnish the donor a copy of that return. This does not represent concurrence in the fair market value.

Charitable organization (Donee) name

Employer identification number

Number and street

City or town, state, and ZIP code

Authorized signature

Title

Date

Part II Information on Donated Property *(To be completed by the taxpayer and/or appraiser)*

2	**(a)** Description of donated property (attach a separate sheet if more space is needed)	**(b)** Date acquired by donor (mo., yr.)	**(c)** How acquired by donor	**(d)** Donor's cost or adjusted basis	**(e)** Fair market value of donated property

3 If tangible property was donated, a brief summary of the overall physical condition of the property at the time of the gift.

....
....
....

Part III Certification of Appraiser *(To be completed by the appraiser of the above donated property)*

I declare that I am not the donor, the donee, a party to the transaction, employed by or related to any of the foregoing persons, or a person whose relationship to any of the foregoing persons would cause a reasonable person to question my independence as an appraiser.

Also, I declare that I hold myself out to the public as an appraiser and because of my appraiser qualifications as described in the appraisal, I am qualified to make appraisals of the type of property being valued. I certify the appraisal fees were not based upon a percentage of the appraised property value. Furthermore, I understand that a false or fraudulent overstatement of the property value as described in the qualified appraisal or appraisal summary may subject me to the civil penalty under section 6701(a) (aiding and abetting the understatement of tax liability). I affirm that I have not been barred from presenting evidence or testimony by the Director of Practice.

Please Sign Here

Signature ▶

Title ▶

Date ▶

Business address

Identification number

City, town or post office, state and ZIP code

For Paperwork Reduction Act Notice, see Instructions.

Form **8283** (2-85)

15

A SUMMARY OF CONSTITUTIONAL HISTORY

p. 387, note 2. *Add:*

Kurland, *The Irrelevance of the Constitution: The Religion Clauses of the First Amendment and the Supreme Court,* 24 VILLANOVA L. REV. 3 (1978); R. CORD, SEPARATION OF CHURCH AND STATE (1982) (excellent historical analysis).

p. 388. *Add after the first indented paragraph:*

Similarly, Justice Powell has noted:

At this point in the 20th century we are quite far removed from the dangers that prompted the Framers to include the Establishment Clause in the Bill of Rights. The risk of significant religious or denominational control over our democratic processes—or even of deep political division along religious lines—is remote. . . .[4a]

After a comprehensive analysis of the history of the establishment clause, Justice Rehnquist has concluded that

[i]t seems indisputable from these glimpses into Madison's thinking, reflected by actions on the floor of the House in 1789, that he saw the amendment as designed to prohibit the establishment of a national religion, and perhaps to prevent discrimination among sects. . . . The framers intended the Establishment Clause to prohibit the designation of any church as a "national" one.[4b]

[4a]Wolman v. Walter, 433 U.S. 229, 263 (concurring in part and dissenting in part). This statement was quoted with approval by a majority of the Supreme Court in Mueller v. Allen, 103 S. Ct. 3062, 3069 (1983).

[4b]Wallace v. Jaffree, 105 S. Ct. 2479 (1985) (dissenting opinion).

p. 388. *Add after the last complete paragraph:*

Thomas Cooley, an eminent 19th-century authority on constitutional history, observed that "[n]o principle of constitutional law is violated when thanksgiving or fast days are appointed; when chaplains are designated for the army and navy; when legislative sessions are opened with prayer or the reading of the Scriptures; or when religious teaching is encouraged by a general exemption of the houses of religious worship from taxation for the support of state government."[6a]

[6a]T. COOLEY, CONSTITUTIONAL LIMITATIONS 471 (1851).

p. 388, note 5. *Delete note 5 and substitute the following:*

[5]J. STORY, COMMENTARIES ON THE CONSTITUTION 630 (5TH ED. 1891).

p. 390. *Add after the first incomplete paragraph:*

A single federal district court judge in 1983, in a notable if futile opinion, openly condemned the Supreme Court for its unwarranted extension of the First Amendment religion clauses to the states.[15a] Lamentably, such is the authority of the Supreme Court that it could publicly deride this historically accurate lower court ruling as "remarkable" and aberrant.[15b]

[15a]Jaffree v. James, 554 F. Supp. 1130 (S.D. Ala. 1983).
[15b]Wallace v. Jaffree, 105 S. Ct. 2479 (1985).

p. 391. *Add at the end of the text:*

The continuing and willful frustration by the Supreme Court and lower federal courts of voluntary religious practices that are perceived as legitimate by a substantial public majority may one day prompt a reassessment of the meaning of nonestablishment and free exercise of religion. It is possible that such a reassessment has already begun, for in a few recent decisions the Supreme Court, by narrow majorities, has been willing to tolerate certain religious practices that almost certainly would have been outlawed only a few years before. Significantly, some Supreme Court Justices are even calling for a reconsideration of the Court's present interpretation of the religion clauses.[23a]

[23a]*See, e.g.,* Wallace v. Jaffree, 105 S. Ct. 2479 (1985) (Justices White and Rehnquist, dissenting).

16

LANDMARK SUPREME COURT DECISIONS INTERPRETING THE RELIGION CLAUSES

p. 394, note 4. *Add:*

See Justice Rehnquist's dissenting opinion in Wallace v. Jaffree, 105 S. Ct. 2479 (1985), for a devastating critique of the historical accuracy of this ruling.

p. 404. *Add after the last paragraph in the text:*

This "divisive political potential" test was subsequently limited by the Court to cases involving direct financial subsidies to private religious schools.[41]

§ I. Chambers v. Marsh[42]

For many years, the Nebraska unicameral legislature has begun each of its sessions with a prayer offered by a chaplain chosen biennially and paid out of public funds. This practice was challenged in 1980 by a state senator who claimed that it constituted an establishment of religion in violation of the First Amendment. A federal district court found the practice to be permissible, but a federal appeals court ruled that the practice violated the nonestablishment of religion clause.

In a six to three decision, the Supreme Court reversed the federal appeals court and upheld the constitutionality of the Nebraska legislative chaplaincy program. The Court surveyed the history of legislative chaplains, observing that "[t]he opening of sessions of legislative and other deliberative public bodies with prayer is deeply embedded in the history and tradition of this country," and that this practice "coexisted with the principles of disestablishment and religious freedom." The Court found it especially relevant that the first Congress, which drafted the First Amendment religion clauses, adopted the policy of selecting a chaplain to open each session with prayer:

175

It can hardly be thought that in the same week members of the First Congress voted to appoint and to pay a chaplain for each House and also voted to approve the draft of the First Amendment for submission to the States, they intended the Establishment Clause of the Amendment to forbid what they had just declared acceptable. In applying the First Amendment . . . it would be incongruous to interpret that clause as imposing more stringent First Amendment limits on the States than the draftsmen imposed on the Federal Government.[43]

While acknowledging that "no one acquires a vested or protected right in violation of the Constitution by long use," the Court found the historical precedent to unequivocally establish the constitutionality of legislative chaplaincies.

The Court also rejected the claims that the Nebraska practice was invalidated by one or more of the following factors: a clergyman of only one religious faith had been selected for sixteen consecutive years; the chaplain is compensated at public expense; and the prayers are in the Judeo-Christian tradition. None of these characteristics, concluded the Court, was materially different from the experience of the first Congress.

The true significance of this decision is the Court's willingness to depart from the three-pronged *Lemon* test in evaluating the constitutionality of a practice challenged on establishment clause grounds. In the *Lemon* case, decided in 1971, the Court had formulated the following test as a device to assist in applying the First Amendment's establishment clause:

First, the statute . . . must have a secular legislative purpose; second, its principal or primary effect must be one that neither advances nor inhibits religion; finally, the statute must not foster an excessive governmental entanglement with religion.[44]

This test, unfortunately, was used by many state and federal courts as a cudgel to obliterate many forms of religious expression and practice that were not even remotely considered to be establishments of religion by the framers of the First Amendment. The willingness of the Court to uphold a religious practice without any reference to the *Lemon* test suggests that not every accommodation of the "religious nature of our people"[45] or acknowledgment of religious belief will be summarily invalidated.

[41]Mueller v. Allen, 103 S. Ct. 3062 (1983).

[42]103 S. Ct. 330 (1983).

[43]This evidence would conclusively establish the legitimacy of legislative chaplains to all but the most doctrinaire disestablishmentarians, or to those who adhere to a "progressive understanding" of constitutional provisions. To illustrate, in a dissenting opinion, Justice Brennan urged the Court to disregard history and the original purpose of the First Amendment in favor of a more enlightened view of the proper place of religious

exercise. Of course, one of the deficiencies of such an approach is that once the moorings of history are abandoned, any substitute standard is itself immediately susceptible to revision. Thus, condemnations by Justice Brennan and others of recent majority opinions that have departed from the "settled" meaning of the *Lemon* decision are hollow and unprincipled.

[44]Lemon v. Kurtzman, 403 U.S. 602 (1971).

[45]Zorach v. Clauson, 343 U.S. 306 (1952) (Justice Douglas speaking for the Court).

§ J. Wallace v. Jaffree[46]

In 1981, the Alabama legislature enacted a law specifying:

At the commencement of the first class of each day in all grades in all public schools the teacher in charge of the room in which each class is held may announce that a period of silence not to exceed one minute in duration shall be observed for meditation or voluntary prayer, and during any such period no other activities shall be engaged in.[47]

This law was challenged in 1982 by a parent who asserted that it was an impermissible establishment of religion in violation of the First Amendment. A federal district court, after a lengthy and accurate historical analysis, concluded that the Supreme Court was misguided in its interpretation and application of the First Amendment, and declined to follow its precedents. In particular, the court concluded, correctly, that the First Amendment religion clauses were not applicable to the states, and therefore the State of Alabama was free to accommodate or even establish a religion if it so desired.[48] Predictably, this decision was reversed by a federal appeals court, and ultimately by the Supreme Court as well. Ironically, characterizing the district court's thorough and historically indisputable analysis as "remarkable" and aberrant, the Supreme Court saw nothing improper in its illicit application of the First Amendment to the states contrary to the expressed intention of the framers of that amendment.[49]

The Court concluded that the Alabama law constituted an impermissible "establishment of religion" since it did not have a clearly secular purpose and therefore failed the first prong of the three-pronged *Lemon* test.

The significance of this decision is not the Court's ruling or its facile "historical" analysis. Rather, it is the dissenting opinion of Justice Rehnquist, which presents a compelling and comprehensive historical explication of the establishment clause and in the process calls into question the *Lemon* test, the "wall of separation between church and state" metaphor, and the propriety of applying the First Amendment's proscriptions to state goverments.

Justice Rehnquist began his opinion by exposing the impropriety of the "wall of separation" metaphor allegedly coined by Thomas Jefferson. Justice Rehnquist pointed out that Jefferson was in France at the time the First Amendment was debated, enacted, and ratified, and that his metaphor was contained in a brief letter to the Danbury Baptist Association fourteen years after the First Amendment was drafted. "He would seem to any detached observer," concluded Justice Rehnquist, "as a less than ideal source of contemporary history as to the meaning of the religion clauses of the First Amendment."

Justice Rehnquist then summarized the debates associated with the enactment of the First Amendment by Congress and demonstrated that the concern was "the establishment of a national church, and perhaps the preference of one religious sect over another. . . ." James Madison, the chief architect of the amendment, saw no need for it, but proposed it merely as an expedient to satisfy the concerns of those opponents of the Constitution who insisted that without a Bill of Rights the newly created federal government might become despotic. Justice Rehnquist also cited the early nineteenth-century commentaries of Supreme Court Justice Story and legal historian Thomas Cooley as proof that the purpose of the establishment clause was the prevention of a national religion. He condemned the Court's constitutionalization of the "wall of separation" metaphor in its *Everson* decision in 1947, and suggested that this "theory of rigid separation" be "frankly and explicitly abandoned."

Justice Rehnquist denounced the three-pronged *Lemon* test adopted by the Court in 1971, since it "has no more grounding in the history of the first amendment than does the wall theory upon which it rests." He observed that the Court itself had moved away from the *Lemon* formulation: "[W]e soon began describing the test as only a 'guideline,' and lately we have described it as 'no more than [a] useful signpost. . . . We have noted that the *Lemon* test is 'not easily applied,' under the *Lemon* test we have 'sacrificed clarity and predictability for flexibility. . . .' [and] the *Lemon* test has never been binding on the Court. . . . If a constitutional theory has no basis in the history of the amendment it seeks to interpret, is difficult to apply and yields unprincipled results, I see little use for it."

In place of the "wall of separation" metaphor or the *Lemon* test, Justice Rehnquist proposed that the religion clauses be interpreted consistently with the principles that "the framers inscribed," for "[a]ny deviation from their intentions frustrates the permanence of [the Bill of Rights] and will only lead to the type of unprincipled decisionmaking that has plagued our establishment clause cases since *Everson*" in 1947. The principles inscribed by the framers on the First Amendment's religion clauses were clear:

> The framers intended the establishment clause to prohibit the designation of any church as a "national" one. The clause was also designed to stop the federal government from asserting a preference of one religious denomination or sect over others. Given the "incorporation" of the establishment clause as against the

states via the fourteenth amendment in *Everson*, states are prohibited as well from establishing a religion or discriminating between sects. As its history abundantly shows, however, nothing in the establishment clause requires government to be strictly neutral between religion and irreligion, nor does that clause prohibit Congress or the states from pursuing legitimate secular ends through nondiscriminatory means.

Justice Rehnquist concluded that the Court's decision would come "as a shock to those who drafted the Bill of Rights" as well as to "a large number of thoughtful Americans today." Noting that George Washington himself, at the request of the very Congress that passed the Bill of Rights, proclaimed a day of public thanksgiving and prayer, Justice Rehnquist observed that "[h]istory must judge whether it was the father of his country in 1789, or a majority of the Court today, which has strayed from the meaning of the establishment clause."

[46]105 S. Ct. 2479 (1985).

[47]ALA. CODE § 16-1-20.1.

[48]*See* chapter 15, *supra*.

[49]As noted in chapter 15, the Court has since 1940 assumed that the Fourteenth Amendment's guaranty of "life, liberty and property" against state interference "incorporates" the First Amendment religion clauses. Therefore, the Court believes that it is justified in invalidating *state* legislation even though the First Amendment is by its own terms a limitation solely on the power of the federal government. One can only wonder why it took the Court three-quarters of a century to "discover" that the protections of the First Amendment were "incorporated" into an amendment ratified at the conclusion of the Civil War and designed to protect newly-freed slaves. This untenable construction is convincingly refuted in a number of scholarly works on constitutional law. *See, e.g.*, R. BERGER, GOVERNMENT BY JUDICIARY: THE TRANSFORMATION OF THE FOURTEENTH AMENDMENT (1977).

17

THE PRESENT MEANING OF THE FIRST AMENDMENT RELIGION CLAUSES

§ A. The Establishment Clause

p. 405. *Delete the first ten lines of the text and substitute the following:*

The clearest evidence that the framers of the First Amendment's establishment clause intended only to prohibit the creation of a national church is the virtual absence of any judicial decisions applying the clause in the first century and a half following its adoption despite the existence of innumerable state and federal accommodations of religion.[1] Prior to 1940, the Supreme Court interpreted the establishment clause on only two occasions. In 1890, it rejected a claim that an Idaho law prohibiting polygamy constituted an impermissible establishment of religion.[2] The Court observed that the purpose of the establishment clause was to prohibit federal legislation "for the support of any religious tenets, or the modes of worship of any sect. The oppressive measures adopted, and the cruelties and punishments inflicted, by the governments of Europe for many ages, to compel parties to conform in their religious beliefs and modes of worship, to the views of the most numerous sect, and the folly of attempting in that way to control the mental operations of persons, and enforce an outward conformity to a prescribed standard, led to the adoption of the [first] amendment. . . ."

In 1918, the Court summarily dismissed a claim that the exemption of ministers from military conscription constituted the establishment of a religion.[2a]

In 1940, the Court reaffirmed that the purpose of the establishment clause was to prevent an established church: "[I]t forestalls compulsion by law of the acceptance of any creed or the practice of any form of worship."[2b] However, the Court added that the concept of "liberty" protected against state interference by the Fourteenth Amendment to the federal Constitution "embraces the liberties guaranteed by the first amendment." The significance of this holding cannot be overstated. The First Amendment's liberties, including the free exercise and nonestablishment of religion, intended by the framers of that amendment as a limitation on the *federal* government and so interpreted for a century and a half,[2c] were now also limitations upon state and local governments. Ironically, shortly after this unwarranted expansion of federal authority over the states, the Court remarked that "[j]udicial nullification of legislation cannot be justified by attributing to the framers of the Bill of Rights views for which there is no historic warrant."[2d]

Despite this assurance, the Court largely abandoned the views of the framers of the establishment clause in its landmark *Everson* decision in 1947.[2e] In *Everson*, a case involving a constitutional challenge to a state law authorizing bus transportation for parochial school students at public expense, the Court announced the following interpretation of the establishment clause:

> Neither a state nor the Federal Government can set up a church. Neither can pass laws which aid one religion, aid all religions, or prefer one religion over another. Neither can force nor influence a person to go or to remain away from church against his will or force him to profess a belief or disbelief in any religion. No person can be punished for entertaining or professing religious beliefs or disbeliefs, for church attendance or nonattendance. No tax in any amount, large or small, can be levied to support any religious activities or institutions, whatever they may be called, or whatever form they may adopt to teach or practice religion. Neither a state nor the Federal Government can, openly or secretly, participate in the affairs of any religious organizations or groups and vice versa. In the words of Jefferson, the clause against establishment of religion by law was intended to erect a "wall of separation between church and state."[2f]

Four dissenting justices similarly remarked that the First Amendment's purpose "was not to strike merely at the official establishment of a single sect, creed or religion, outlawing only a formal relation such as had prevailed in England and some of the colonies. Necessarily, it was to uproot all such relationships. . . . It was to create a complete and permanent separation of the spheres of religious activity and civil authority by comprehensively forbidding every form of public aid or support for religion."[2g]

Thus, by 1947, the Court not only had expanded the prohibitions of the establishment clause beyond anything contemplated by its framers, but also had enjoined its interpretation upon state and local governments by means of the Fourteenth Amendment.[2h]

The Court found in Jefferson's "wall of separation" metaphor the philosophical basis for its interpretation of the establishment clause in *Everson*. (However, as Justice Rehnquist demonstrated nearly forty years later, Jefferson's metaphor cannot properly be used as evidence of the meaning of the establishment clause).[2i]

In the years following *Everson*, several longstanding accommodations of religious belief and practice fell victim to this distorted interpretation of the establishment clause. In 1948, the Court, specifically relying on *Everson* and Jefferson's "wall of separation" metaphor, struck down a local school board policy that permitted teachers employed by private religious groups to come weekly into public school buildings during regular school hours and impart religious instruction for thirty minutes to students whose parents requested it.[2j]

In 1962, the Court struck down a New York law requiring the following prayer to be said aloud in each public school classroom at the beginning of each school day: "Almighty God, we acknowledge our dependence upon Thee, and we beg Thy blessings upon us, our parents, our teachers and our country."[2k] The Court concluded that recitation of the prayer in public schools "breaches the wall of separation between church and state," even though children who were opposed to the prayer were not compelled to participate and could be excused from class until the recitation was completed. Similarly, the Court in 1963 invalidated a Pennsylvania law requiring that "[a]t least ten verses from the Holy Bible shall be read, without comment, at the opening of each public school on each school day."[2l] The law permitted children to be excused from attending class during the reading upon the written request of a parent. The Court relied entirely on the expansive interpretation of the establishment clause enunciated in *Everson* in striking down the law.

In 1968, the Court struck down an Arkansas law making it unlawful for public school teachers to "teach the theory or doctrine that mankind ascended or descended from a lower order of animals."[2m] The Court, relying on *Everson*, concluded that the First Amendment does not permit the state to require that teaching and learning must be tailored to the principles or prohibitions of any religious sect or dogma."

In 1971, the Court held that its establishment clause decisions since *Everson* could be embodied in a three-pronged test: "First, the statute must have a secular legislative purpose; second, its principal or primary effect must be one that neither advances nor inhibits religion; finally, the statute must not foster 'an excessive governmental entanglement with religion.' "[2n] This test, known as the three-pronged *Lemon* test, enshrined the dubious interpretation of the establishment clause announced in *Everson* and its progeny. The Court, in amplifying on this test, has observed that "[t]he purpose prong of the *Lemon* test asks whether government's actual purpose is to endorse or disapprove of religion. The effect prong asks whether irrespective of government's actual purpose, the practice under review in fact conveys a message of endorsement or disapproval. An affirmative answer to either question should render the challenged practice invalid."[2o] With regard to the effect prong, the Court has further observed that "not every law that confers an 'indirect,' 'remote,' or 'incidental' benefit upon [religion] is, for that reason alone, constitutionally invalid."[2p] "Excessive entanglement" between church and state connotes "comprehensive, discriminating, and continuing state surveillance."[2q] The Court suggested in Lemon that laws or government practices having the potential for "political divisiveness" may violate the entanglement prong. However, the Court later confined this aspect of entanglement to "cases where direct financial subsidies are paid to parochial schools or to teachers in parochial schools."[2r]

Application of the Lemon standard resulted, predictably, in the invalidation of many additional accommodations of religious practice. For example, the Supreme Court outlawed several programs providing limited assistance to private education,[2s] a Kentucky law requiring a copy of the Ten Commandments to be posted in each public school classroom,[2t] and a state law specifying that each public school day should begin with a minute of silence during which students could pray, meditate, or occupy themselves in any other manner they chose.[2u] Lower federal courts invalidated scores of religious practices on the basis of the Lemon test.

The Supreme Court has often expressed misgivings about the Lemon formulation. In 1971, the Court called the Lemon test a mere "guideline."[2v] It later described the test as "no more than [a] useful signpost,"[2w] and expressed an unwillingness to be "confined to any single test or criterion."[2x] Similarly, the Court has noted that the test "is not easily applied"[2y] and "sacrifices clarity and predictability for flexibility."[2z] The Court has even disregarded the Lemon test on at least two occasions. In 1982, the Court deviated from the Lemon test in striking down a Minnesota statute requiring certain religious organizations to register with the state prior to soliciting contributions.[2aa] The Court, observing that the Lemon test was "intended to apply to laws affording a uniform benefit to all religions," announced the following two-part test to be used in assessing the constitutionality of a law that discriminates "among religions": (1) The law must be justified by a compelling governmental interest, and (2) it must be closely fitted to further that interest.

In 1983, the Court again deviated from the Lemon test in upholding the practice of legislative chaplains,[2ab] reversing a federal appeals court ruling that invalidated the practice on the basis of the Lemon test. The Court, noting that the very Congress that approved the First Amendment establishment clause also voted to appoint and pay a chaplain for both houses, concluded that "it would be incongruous to interpret that clause as imposing more stringent First Amendment limits on the states than the draftsmen imposed on the federal government." Such cases are a repudiation, at least in part, of the hostility that the Court has shown to religious practice since Everson. They suggest that there is hope for a repudiation of Everson and the Lemon test, and a return to an interpretation of the establishment clause that is faithful to its history and purpose. However, until the three-part Lemon test is repudiated, it likely will continue to be the primary analytical tool employed by the courts in establishment clause cases, with the following limitations:

1. Laws that discriminate between religious groups will be upheld against a claim that they violate the establishment clause only if (1) they are justified by a compelling governmental interest, and (2) they are closely fitted to further that interest.[2ac]

2. Certain accommodations of religious custom and practice may be validated by history. For example, in 1984 the Supreme Court upheld the practice of including a nativity scene on public property as part of a Christmas display.[2ad] While the Court validated the practice on the basis of *Lemon*, its application of the *Lemon* test was influenced if not controlled by historical precedent. Noting that the nativity scene had the secular purpose of depicting the origins of Christmas, did not have a primary effect of advancing religion, and did not create an excessive entanglement between church and state, the Court concluded: "It would be ironic, however, if the inclusion of a single symbol of a particular religious event, as part of a celebration acknowledged in the Western World for 20 centuries, and in this country by the people, by the Executive Branch, by the Congress, and the courts for two centuries, would so 'taint' the City's exhibit as to render it violative of the establishment clause." Similarly, the Court upheld the constitutionality of legislative chaplaincies in 1983 on the basis of historical precedent without any reference to the *Lemon* test.[2ae] The Court found controlling the fact that the first Congress, which approved the First Amendment establishment clause, also voted to appoint and pay a chaplain for each House.

3. The benefits of public welfare legislation cannot be denied to any group of persons "because of their faith, or lack of it."[2af] Thus, for example, the establishment clause does not require that a law authorizing free transportation of children to school must exclude children attending private religious schools.

4. As noted in the following section of this chapter, the principles underlying the establishment clause can in some cases conflict with the values embodied in the free exercise of religion clause. Therefore, neither clause should be construed in isolation. The establishment clause, properly construed in light of the free exercise of religion clause, mandates governmental neutrality toward religion. Neither sponsorship nor hostility is permissible.

5. "[N]ot every law that confers an 'indirect,' 'remote,' or 'incidental' benefit upon [religion] is, for that reason alone, constitutionally invalid."[2ag]

The following table summarizes several federal court decisions applying the establishment clause since 1970.

[1]This construction is also amply supported by historical evidence. *See, e.g.*, Wallace v. Jaffree, 105 S. Ct. 2479 (1985) (dissenting opinion of Justice Rehnquist); R. CORD, SEPARATION OF CHURCH AND STATE (1982); chapter 15, *supra*.

[2]Davis v. Beason, 133 U.S. 333 (1890).

[2a]Aver v. United States, 245 U.S. 366 (1918).

[2b]Cantwell v. Connecticut, 310 U.S. 296 (1940).

[2c]*See, e.g.*, chapter 15, *supra. See also* Permoli v. Municipality No. 1 of New Orleans, 44 U.S. 589 (1845) (federal Constitution makes no provision for protecting religious liberties against *state* interference).

[2d]Minersville School District v. Gobitis, 310 U.S. 586 (1940).

[2e]Everson v. Board of Education, 330 U.S. 1 (1947).

[2f]*Id.* at 15-16.

[2g]*Id.* at 31-32.

[2h]Wallace v. Jaffree, 105 S. Ct. 2479 (1985) (dissenting opinion of Justice Rehnquist). The dissenting opinion is an extensive historical analysis that seriously undermines the legitimacy of the Court's *Everson* decision and many subsequent rulings based on that precedent.

[2i]*Id.*

[2j]People of State of Illinois ex rel. McCollum v. Board of Education, 333 U.S. 203 (1948). Justice Reed, in dissent, noted that "the 'wall of separation between church and state' that Mr. Jefferson built at the university which he founded [the University of Virginia] did not exclude religious education from that school." *Id.* at 247.

[2k]Engel v. Vitale, 370 U.S. 421 (1962). In a dissenting opinion, Justice Stewart observed that "the Court's task, in this as in all areas of constitutional adjudication, is not responsibly aided by the uncritical invocation of metaphors like the 'wall of separation,' a phrase nowhere to be found in the Constitution." *Id.* at 445-46.

[2l]School District of Abington v. Schempp, 374 U.S. 203 (1963).

[2m]Epperson v. Arkansas, 393 U.S. 97 (1968).

[2n]Lemon v. Kurtzman, 403 U.S. 602, 612-13 (1971).

[2o]Lynch v. Donnelly, 104 S. Ct. 1355 (1984).

[2p]Committee for Public Education & Religious Liberty v. Nyquist, 413 U.S. 756, 771 (1973).

[2q]Lemon v. Kurtzman, 403 U.S. 602, 619 (1971). *But see* Wallace v. Jaffree, 105 S. Ct. 2479 (1985) (dissenting opinion of Justice Rehnquist).

[2r]Mueller v. Allen, 103 S. Ct. 3062, 3071 n.11 (1983).

[2s]*See, e.g.*, Meek v. Pittinger, 421 U.S. 349 (1975); Wolman v. Walter, 433 U.S. 229 (1977); Levitt v. Committee for Public Education, 413 U.S. 472 (1973).

[2t]Stone v. Graham, 449 U.S. 39 (1980).

[2u]Wallace v. Jaffree, 105 S. Ct. 2479 (1985).

[2v]Tilton v. Richardson, 403 U.S. 672 (1971).

[2w]Mueller v. Allen, 463 U.S. 388 (1983).

[2x]Lynch v. Donnelly, 104 S. Ct. 1355 (1984).

[2y]Meek v. Pittinger, 421 U.S. 349 (1975).

[2z]Committee for Public Education v. Regan, 444 U.S. 646 (1980).

[2aa]Larson v. Valente, 456 U.S. 228 (1982).

[2ab]Marsh v. Chambers, 463 U.S. 783 (1983).

[2ac]Larson v. Valente, 456 U.S. 228 (1982).

[2ad]Lynch v. Donnelly, 104 S. Ct. 1355 (1984).

[2ae]Marsh v. Chambers, 103 S. Ct. 3330 (1983).

[2af]Everson v. Board of Education, 330 U.S. 1 (1947).

[2ag]Committee for Public Education & Religious Liberty v. Nyquist, 413 U.S. 756, 771 (1973). *See also* Widmar v. Vincent, 454 U.S. 263, 273 (1981).

p. 405. *Add the following cases at the beginning of the table and renumber the remaining cases:*

	Constitutional	Unconstitutional
1. State law permitted public schools to begin each day with a minute of silence during which time students could meditate or pray. *Wallace v. Jaffree*, 105 S. Ct. 2479 (1985)		X
2. "Shared time" program permitted public school teachers to teach certain courses in private religious schools. *Grand Rapids School District v. Ball*, 53 U.S.L.W. 5006 (1985)		X
3. A nativity scene was included in a Christmas display on city property. *Lynch v. Donnelly*, 104 S. Ct. 1355 (1984)	X	
4. A state selected and paid a chaplain to serve its legislature. *Marsh v. Chambers*, 463 U.S. 783 (1983)	X	

§ B. The Free Exercise Clause

p. 411. *Delete the first case in the table and substitute the following:*

	Constitutional	Unconstitutional
1. IRS revoked religious university's tax-exempt status because of its rule prohibiting interracial dating and marriage. *Bob Jones University v. United States*, 103 S. Ct 2017 (1983)	X	

§ C. Procedure for First Amendment Analysis

pp. 412-413. *Delete § C.*

18

SIGNIFICANT FIRST AMENDMENT ISSUES

§ B. Prayer on Public Property

p. 418. *Add after the first complete paragraph:*

A state law authorizing a one-minute period of silence in all public schools "for meditation or voluntary prayer" was invalidated by the Supreme Court in 1985 on the basis of the nonestablishment of religion clause.[17a] A majority of the Court, however, expressed a willingness to uphold "moment of silence" laws (even those specifically including silent prayer as a permitted or suggested activity) so long as the language and legislative history of the law, and its actual implementation, do not suggest a preference for prayer. Presumably, several of the twenty-five state moment of silence laws currently in effect would be permissible under this test.

[17a]Wallace v. Jaffree, 105 S. Ct. 2479 (1985).

p. 418. *Delete line 2 of the second complete paragraph and substitute the following:*

and religious exercises prior to, during, or following regular school hours.[18] The Supreme Court has agreed to determine the constitutionality of allowing students to use public high school facilities during regular school hours for religious purposes.[18a] In 1984, Congress enacted the Equal Access Act, which assures public high school students of the right to meet informally for religious purposes on school property before or after regular school hours if the school permits other groups to use the facilities at such times.[18b] The Act provides: "It shall be unlawful for any public secondary school which receives Federal financial assistance and which has a limited open forum to deny equal access or a fair opportunity to, or discriminate against, any students who wish to conduct a meeting within that limited open forum on the basis of religious, political, philosophical, or other content of the speech at such meetings." A public secondary school has a *limited open forum* if it provides an opportunity for one or more noncurriculum-related student groups to meet on school premises during *noninstructional* time.[18c] A school is deemed to offer a *fair opportunity* to students wishing to conduct a meeting on school premises during noninstructional hours if it uniformly provides that (1) the meeting is voluntary and student-initiated; (2) there is no sponsorship of the meeting by the school; (3) employees or agents of the school are present at religious meetings only in a nonparticipatory capacity; (4) the meeting does not materially interfere with the orderly conduct of educational activities within the school; and (5) nonschool persons may not direct, conduct, control, or regularly attend activities of student groups.[18d] However, the assignment of a teacher, administrator, or other school employee to a meeting for custodial purposes does not constitute impermissible sponsorship. The term *noninstructional time* refers to time set aside by the school before actual classroom instruction begins or after actual classroom instruction ends.

[18a]Bender v. Williamsport Area School District, 741 F.2d 538 (3rd Cir. 1984), *cert. granted*, 105 S. Ct. 1167 (1985).

[18b]20 U.S.C. §§ 4071-4074.

[18c]*Id.* at § 4071(b).

[18d]*Id.* at § 4071(c).

p. 418, note 15. *Add:*

Doe v. Aldine Independent School District, 563 F. Supp. 883 (S.D. Tex. 1982).

p. 418, note 18. *Add:*

Nartowicz v. Clayton County School District, 736 F.2d 646 (5th Cir. 1984).

p. 419, note 22. *Add:*

See also Clergy and Laity Concerned v. Chicago Board of Education, 586 F. Supp. 1408 (N.D. Ill. 1984).

p. 420. *Delete all of the text prior to § C and substitute the following:*

The Supreme Court has held that it is permissible for state legislatures to select and compensate legislative chaplains,[24] and other courts similarly have approved congressional chaplains[25] and the practice of opening county board meetings with prayer.[25a]

[24]Marsh v. Chambers, 103 S. Ct. 3330 (1983).

[25]Murray v. Buchanan, 720 F.2d 689 (D.C. Cir. 1983).

[25a]Bogen v. Doty, 598 F.2d 1110 (8th Cir. 1979). The court upheld this practice since no expenditure of funds were involved and the primary purpose and effect of the prayer was public decorum and solemnity at county board meetings. These requirements would not be necessary after the Supreme Court's decision in the *Marsh* case.

§ C. Display of Religious Symbols on Public Property

p. 421. *Delete the last complete paragraph and substitute the following:*

In 1984, the Supreme Court held that a city's practice of including a nativity creche in an annual Christmas display on public property did not violate the establishment clause. Besides the creche, the city's display contained several "secular" objects, including a Santa Claus house, a talking Christmas tree, reindeer, candy-striped poles, and lights. The Court, applying the three-part *Lemon* test "in the context of the Christmas season," concluded that inclusion of the creche in the city's display had the secular purpose of depicting the origin of the Christmas holiday, did not have a primary effect of advancing religion, and did not excessively entangle church and state.[34] Acknowledging that the creche "in a sense" advanced religion, the Court concluded that its previous decisions make it "abundantly clear" that not every law or governmental practice that confers an indirect or incidental benefit upon religion is for that reason alone impermissible. Drawing support from the history and context of the display, the Court noted that "[i]t would be ironic . . . if the inclusion of a single symbol of a particular historic religious event, as part of a celebration acknowledged in the Western World for 20 centuries, and in this country by the people, by the Executive Branch, by the Congress, and the courts for two centuries, would so 'taint' the City's exhibit as to render it violative of the establishment clause." In a similar case, the Court upheld the practice of permitting a nativity scene in a city park during the Christmas season at virtually no expense to the city.[35] Unlike the situation in the *Lynch* case, the nativity scene was not in the context of a larger display containing numerous "secular" objects. Since the ruling was by an equally divided Court (4-4), it is controlling only in the second federal circuit (New York, Vermont, and Connecticut).

[34]Lynch v. Donnelly, 104 S. Ct. 1355 (1984).

[35]Board of Trustees v. McCreary, 105 S. Ct. 1859 (1985).

p. 423. *Delete caption D and substitute the following:*

§ D. Use of Public Property for Religious Purposes

p. 423. *Add after note 46 in the text:*

A federal court has held that "[a] public school is a public forum for its students and teachers," and that "[i]f it is opened to the school district community for meetings and discussions during non-school hours, then it becomes a public forum for the community" that cannot exclude religious groups.[46a] In response to the school's fear that its facilities would be used by "snake cults, groups that practice animal sacrifices, groups that wear odd clothes, and groups that use smoke and fire in their worship services," the court observed that if such activities ever did occur the First Amendment would "pose no obstacle" to their regulation.

[46a]Country Hills Christian Church v. Unified School District, 560 F. Supp. 1207 (D. Kan. 1983).

§ F. The Right to Refuse Medical Treatment

p. 426, note 60. *Add:*

Matter of Hamilton, 657 S.W.2d 425 (Tenn. App. 1983) ("Where a child is dying with cancer and experiencing pain which will surely become more excruciating as the disease progresses . . . we believe is one of those times when humane considerations and life-saving attempts outweigh unlimited practices of religious belief.").

p. 427. *Add after the first incomplete paragraph:*

In a number of cases, parents have refused medical treatment for a dependent child because of their belief in the power of prayer to effect a healing. For example, one court found a mother guilty of neglect who believed that healing of her son's arthritic knee condition was possible only through prayer.[63a] Another court held that parents could be guilty of neglect if they relied on prayer rather than medical technology and drugs for the healing of their child's life-threatening medical condition.[63b]

Some states have enacted statutes to provide guidance in this area. For example, Colorado has a statute that provides:

Notwithstanding any other provision of this title, no child who in good faith is under treatment solely by spiritual means through prayer in accordance with the tenets and practices of a recognized church or religious denomination by a duly accredited practitioner shall, for that reason alone, be considered [neglected].[63c]

[63a]Mitchell v. Davis, 205 S.W.2d 812 (Tex. App. 1947).
[63b]People in Interest of D.L.E., 645 P.2d 271 (Colo. 1982).
[63c]Colo. Rev. Stat. § 19-1-114.

§ G. Definition of "Religion" and "Religious"

p. 427, note 65 *Add*:

See generally Choper, *Defining "Religion" in the First Amendment*, 1982 U. ILL. LAW REV. 579; Note, 91 HARV. L. REV. 1056 (1978).